Lest We Forget

From Ardagh in County Limerick, BRENDAN FULLAM's banking career took him to many towns in Ireland. He now lives in New Ross, County Wexford. He has played Gaelic games in Killorglin, Kilrush, Clifden, Ballyshannon, Wexford and Tralee. The author of eight best-selling books on hurling, he is now retired and continues to visit former players and record their stories.

Lest We Forget

Gems of Gaelic Games and Those Who Made Them

Brendan Fullam

The Collins Press

FIRST PUBLISHED IN 2009 BY
The Collins Press
West Link Park
Doughcloyne
Wilton
Cork

British Library Cataloguing in Publication Data

Fullam, Brendan.
    Lest we forget : gems of Gaelic games and those who made them.
    1. Gaelic football–Ireland–History.
    2. Hurling (Game)–Ireland–History.
    3. Camogie (Game)–Ireland–History.

    I. Title
    796.3'3'09415–dc22
    ISBN-13: 9781848890152

Design and typesetting by designmatters

Typeset in Warnock Pro
Printed in Great Britain by MPG Books Limited

Photographs in prelims:
pp ii–iii: Jimmy 'Butler' Coffey, Tipperary v Limerick 1937 Munster final, about to whip
on a ground ball as Jackie Power attempts to hook. Paddy Scanlon in the Limerick goal is
on full alert; pp vi, xii and xiv: rural scenes in Ireland during the early years of the GAA.

Cover photographs:
Front (clockwise from top left): Mattie McDonagh, Meath; Leitrim win the 2006 Ladies
Connacht junior title; Paddy Cullen, Dublin; the 1951 All-Ireland hurling final, Tipperary
v Wexford; the 1937 Munster final, Tipperary v Limerick. *Spine*: Tim Landers, Kerry. *Back*
(clockwise from top left): Willie Hough, Limerick; Jack Rochford, Kilkenny; Tubberadora: All-
Ireland hurling champions in 1898 and 1899; Christy Ring, Cork; Roscommon's Dan O'Keeffe
in action against Mayo in the 1936 semi-final; Railway Shield won by Leinster in 1908.

To my brother Aodán,
in appreciation of his invaluable assistance
with all my books to date.

Fame is no plant that grows on mortal soil

   Milton

There is more, much more, in the life of a nation than politics and economics

   Thomas Davis

Ireland began to move towards her place among the nations of the world when her young men began to revive the athletic traditions of their forefathers

   William T. Cosgrave

Contents

Foreword

I am honoured to have been invited to write the foreword to *Lest We Forget*. In our 125th year we can expect many publications to acknowledge the achievements of our Association and while our history is immersed with wonderful occasions, at the heart of it all are the glorious feats of our players, be that at inter-county or club levels. The GAA is about many things. Our strong community ethos and sense of identity and immense pride in our own place is strongly felt by us all. Our games are at the core of our Association, activities that give immense satisfaction and fulfilment to players and spectators alike.

Most players during their lives only experience playing at club level. For them, the be all and end all is playing with their neighbour for the pride of the parish. Hoping to attain a coveted county title at some grade or other is their dearest target each year.

The inter-county scene today has a heightened profile, given the intense media coverage and analysis which our games receive daily. Such coverage has propelled our star players right into the public limelight. Down through the years, Ireland's national and local media have brought our star players right into our homes. Young children adopted these stars in their own back yards and played imaginary All-Ireland finals. I have no doubt that these stars, up to the present day, create a dream in the minds of these young children to help many of them to become the stars of tomorrow.

Lest We Forget is a snapshot of some great players and great games throughout our 125 years. The author could well have come up with a completely different series of players and games and still have left us enthralled at the end, such is the list of heroes in our Association who have graced our fields as hurlers, Gaelic footballers, camogie players and ladies' Gaelic footballers. The players featured in this book are just a representative sample of the thousands of inter-county players who gave their all in the cause of their county. Long may such players continue to thrill us! My wish is that inter-county players may realise that they have been given a wonderful talent and that they fully appreciate the honour of wearing their county jersey, just as thousands of their county men and women have done over the years since 1884.

Is mise
Nioclás Ó Braonáin
Iar-Uachtarán Cumann Lúthchleas Gael

Preface

This book is a companion to my earlier books, particularly *Giants of the Ash*, *Hurling Giants*, *Legends of the Ash* and *Captains of the Ash*. It will take its readers, decade by decade, on an epic journey of 125 years, as the GAA, 'one of the most successful and original mass movements of its day', celebrates a century and a quarter of glorious achievements.

In each decade, from 1884 to 2008, I have written about, as a minimum: a hurler; a footballer; a hurling game; a football game; a hurling team; a football team.

Between the various articles and team selections, several hundred of our Gaelic players have been called to mind.

The combination of famous names and thrilling games, linking the distant past with the present day, will bring to life for GAA enthusiasts many great and exciting moments. They will re-live memorable contests and feats of individual brilliance.

Players and games of the early days of the GAA will remind readers of the contribution made by, sadly, the oft forgotten giants of former times, who gave so much and thrilled so many, and sought so little.

To this end I have profiled, in pen pictures, ninety-eight greats of the early decades of the GAA.

This book, in its own way, is a celebration of 125 years of growth and progress.

Author's Note

Unless otherwise stated, all quotes by 'Carbery' (Paddy Mehigan) are taken from Seán Kilfeather (ed.), *Vintage Carbery* (Dublin, 1984)

All quotes by 'Sliabh Rua' (Phil O'Neill) are taken from Phil O'Neill, *Twenty Years of the GAA, 1910–1930* (Kilkenny, 1931)

1887–1900

Teams that participated in the
All-Ireland senior finals

COUNTY	FOOTBALL		HURLING	
	WON	LOST	WON	LOST
Clare				1
Cork	1	5	4	
Dublin	6	1	1	3
Galway				1
Kerry		1	1	
Kilkenny				4
Laois		1		
Limerick	2		1	
London		1		1
Louth		1		
Meath		1		
Tipperary	3		6	
Waterford		1		
Wexford	1	1		3

Fourteen counties participated in the senior finals.

The thirteen hurling finals involved ten counties, with five counties successful.

The thirteen football finals involved eleven counties, with five counties successful.

Tipperary set a record by appearing in nine senior finals and winning them all.

A HURLING GAME:

Kerry v Wexford, 1891 All-Ireland final

We toast you men of Ballyduff
You won it fair and square.
Like us to Dublin you did go
To venture and to dare.
* With Kingdom pride ranked side by side*
Without hindrance, let or fear
You won! Well done! But you'll hear again
Of the unbowed Shelmalier.

Kerry is football country. The county never contested a Munster minor hurling final, a Munster under-21 hurling final or a Munster intermediate hurling final.

However, their senior clubs, confined mainly to north Kerry, have often performed admirably against the hurling champions of the other Munster counties.

On occasions, individual players have been honoured by the Munster Railway Cup hurling selectors – Podd Nolan (Crotta), Pat Moriarty (Causeway), John Bunyan (Ballyduff), Christy Walsh (Kilmoyley) and Billy McCarthy.

Kerry has tasted success at junior level, winning All-Ireland titles in 1961 and 1972. In 1961 they were captained by Michael Hennessy of Ballyduff – also on the team were Niall Sheehy and Johnny Culloty of All-Ireland senior football fame. In 1972 they were captained by John Flanagan, a strapping athlete of 6 feet 4 inches, whom I saw in action a few times for his club Kilmoyley in Austin Stack Park, Tralee.

So even though Kerry has turned out to be the country's most successful footballing county, it wasn't until a dozen years after their All-Ireland senior hurling victory of 1891 that they won their first of many senior football crowns.

I have chosen the 1891 hurling final between Kerry and Wexford, played at Clonturk Park on 28 February 1892, because it was unique in many respects. It was:
- the last 21-a-side contest
- the last occasion that no number of points equalled a goal
- the first and only meeting of the counties in a hurling final

- to date, the only senior hurling title won by Kerry
- the first drawn hurling final
- the only final in the history of the game to go to extra time
- the last All-Ireland series where the county champions, without resorting to players from other clubs, were required to represent the county.

This was the fourth All-Ireland hurling final. There was none in 1888 because of what became known as the US 'invasion' of Irish athletes. Interestingly, in those four years seven counties contested the hurling finals: Tipperary v Galway in 1887, Dublin v Clare in 1889, Cork v Wexford in 1890 and Kerry v Wexford in 1891.

No hurling contests took place in either Connacht or Ulster in 1891.

In Leinster, only Wexford, Dublin, Kildare and Laois entered for the championship. However, the only game that took place was between Wexford and Dublin. This was won by Wexford, and following a walkover from Laois they became provincial title holders.

In Munster, Kerry had a great win over Cork, 2-7 to 0-3, at Killarney on 21 September. That victory earned them a place in the Munster final against Limerick, the only other county in Munster to take part in the hurling championship.

Because of the unexpected death of Charles Stewart Parnell on 6 October and the ongoing impact of the 'Parnell Split', it was feared for a while that the Kerry v Limerick game might not go ahead. Happily, it did.

The game took place at Newcastle West on 1 November with John Sheehy, secretary of the Limerick County Board, as referee. Kerry lost by 1-2 to 1-1. They lodged an objection which was upheld by the Central Council and a replay was ordered. The objection, it is believed, was based on a claim that time was up when Limerick scored the winning point. In the early days the solution to many an objection was to order a replay. This duly took place at Abbeyfeale on 31 January 1892.

On this occasion Michael Deering of Cork was in charge of the whistle. Michael, a native of Limerick, was chairman of Cork County Board for many years and in 1898 was elected president of the association.

Kerry won by 2-4 to 0-1 and, as in the game against Cork, gave evidence of their physical fitness, dexterity and hurling skills that included ground hurling and overhead striking.

The way was now clear for a Kerry v Wexford final. The programme of the day makes interesting reading:

First game: All-Ireland football semi-final – Dublin v Cavan

Second game: All-Ireland hurling final – Kerry v Wexford

Third game: All-Ireland football final – Cork v Winners of first game.

Kerry, represented by Ballyduff, were captained by John Mahony. Wexford, under the leadership of Nicholas Daly, were represented by Crossabeg.

Kerry lined out in their everyday long pants and wore a jersey of greyish colour with a gold band. They played in their bare feet. Wexford were described as being tastily dressed.

In those days, for the start of a game, hurling Rule 5 of the official guide stated:

> *The captains of the teams shall toss for choice of sides before commencing play, and the hurlers shall stand in two lines in the centre of the field opposite to each other, and catch hands or hurleys across, and then separate. The referee shall throw the ball along the ground between the players, not up high over their heads.*

By all accounts the game was a rousing contest – a physical encounter played with great dash, vigour and determination; yet at all times very sportingly. Reflecting on the game in later years, P. J. Devlin ('Celt'), a well-known GAA writer, had this to say: *It was such a contest as has never been seen before in a native arena. It may be youthful fancy or senile myopia, but I think there was more of the spirit of the ancient Fianna that day than ever since.*

Luck came to Kerry's rescue in the last seconds of the game. The score, according to the referee, stood at 1-1 each. A free was awarded to Wexford. As the sliotar was on its way to register a point, the referee, Patrick Tobin of Dublin and secretary of the Central Council, blew full time. In the controversy that followed, he stated that time was up when the ball was in flight and that he had no authority to extend the time beyond the hour. Patrick himself was a fine hurler, who in his time played with the Brian Boru club, of which he was a founder member. He also played with Faughs.

If Wexford felt aggrieved, Kerry too had cause for complaint. Their grievance centred around the goal that was awarded to Wexford in the twenty-second minute of the second half. As far as they were concerned the sliotar had crossed between the posts for a point. It appears to have rebounded off a spectator back into play and was then sent in for a goal.

Wexford felt that the final score should read 1-2 to 1-1 in their favour. Kerry, without disputing Wexford's last-second point, claimed the score at full time should have been 1-1 to 0-3 in their favour.

However, be that as it may, the final score as far as the referee was concerned was 1-1 each. Accordingly, as was within his discretion, he ordered an additional half hour of two moieties of fifteen minutes each.

Paddy O'Carroll

It took all the persuasive skills of Tom Slattery, chairman of the Kerry County Board, to get Tom Mahony, the Kerry captain, to agree to play the extra time. As the teams lined up for the additional half hour, they received wild applause from the spectators, who had witnessed a wonderful contest and were about to be treated to more of the same.

A historic occasion – though not, perhaps, perceived as such then – ended in victory for the Kingdom, 2-3 to 1-5.

The *Kerry Sentinel* summed it up well:

> *Difficult, indeed, would it be to find two teams of twenty-one men, each possessing the attributes which go to make the athlete perfect, as the representatives of Ballyduff and Crossabeg. In a word they were fast, wiry and long-winded, and strong and scientific, more even than the giants of old, of whom we read in fabled history.*

The spirit in which the game was played is reflected in the verse by a Wexford bard at the beginning of this article, which very sportingly saluted the victorious Kerrymen.

And this against a background of two All-Ireland defeats in a row. For in the 1890 final, Wexford were leading by 2-2 to 1-6 (a goal was better than any number of points) when Cork, with the permission of the referee, withdrew their team in the second half, alleging excessive rough play on the part of the Wexfordmen. On the recommendation of the referee, Central Council awarded the match and the All-Ireland title to Cork.

Kerry's victorious twenty-one in the 1891 final were:

> *John Mahony, Maurice Kelly, Michael McCarthy,*
> *Paddy O'Carroll, Pat Wynne, Michael J. O'Sullivan,*
> *Richard Kissane, James Crowley, Frank Crowley,*
> *Jack O'Sullivan, Tom Dunne, John Murphy,*
> *Maurice Fitzmaurice, Jim McDonnell, Thade D. McCarthy,*
> *Thade E. McCarthy, Michael Riordan, Pat Quane,*
> *Jackeen Quane, Pat Rourke, Michael Kirby.*

At Lixnaw railway station the team was afforded a hero's welcome. A dozen years passed before Kerry won another All-Ireland title – a football title, the first of many. From 1903 onwards, in every decade, Kerry would register unparalleled football success.

A HURLING PERSONALITY:

Mikey Maher (Tipperary)

*Many of them travelled there to help carry his giant frame to
its last resting place in Tipperary's St Michael's cemetery. To his
neighbours at Gleneffy (Galbally) he had been a big, soft-spoken,
kindly man who worked hard and was a well-liked neighbour. But
to the men of his native place who knew him in his prime, he was
Cúchulainn and Napoleon and Matt the Thresher. He was Big
Mikey and there would never be his like again.*

Séamus Leahy, from *The Tipperary Association Yearbook, 1982*

By 1900 Tipperary had annexed six All-Ireland hurling titles and
led the field ahead of Cork with four. Mikey Maher took part in five
of those Tipperary successes. He was captain on three occasions
– 1895, 1896 and 1898 – becoming the first player in hurling history
to achieve such an honour. Subsequently, only two other players had
the distinction – Dick Walsh of Kilkenny in 1907, 1909 and 1913
and Christy Ring of Cork in 1946, 1953 and 1954.

Mikey, one of hurling's great captains, led Tubberadora, a town-
land in the parish of Boherlahan, Tipperary, where they lived and
breathed hurling.

In 1895 the club supplied eleven of the victorious All-Ireland
team – thirteen in 1896 and fifteen in 1898. This was an era when
teams consisted of seventeen-a-side.

Mikey and his men made the colours of Tubberadora famous
– sashed jerseys of blue and gold and navy-blue knickerbockers.
They wanted to commemorate the centenary year of the 1798 in-
surrection with an All-Ireland victory. And they did, with wins
over Cork, Galway and Kilkenny.

Mikey was born in 1870. In his playing days he stood 6 feet 3
inches and weighed 15 stone. Mikey first came to prominence in
the Tipperary championship of 1895. Tubberadora defeated Rockwell Rovers and then Drombane before facing Suir View in the
county final. That game ended in a draw at 1-6 each. An extra half
hour was played and Tubberadora emerged as county champions
for the first time, 3-9 to 2-7. The game was played at Cashel before
a record attendance, who paid an entry fee of two old pence.

Tipperary had a big win over Limerick in the Munster final – 7-8 to 0-2. According to one press report (from *Tipperary's GAA Story* by Canon Philip Fogarty [Thurles, 1960]):

> *Ably led by the strong and fearless Mikey Maher, the style of the Tipperary hurlers was fast, free and open and their positional work perfect. In every unit there was sting and dash; in every line there was ability and method. With such a gallant combination, it looks as if Tipperary is going to make some history in the ancient pastime.*

Prophetic words indeed.

Mikey Maher was now on the road to stardom and a richly rewarding hurling career which brought him up to the 1904 Munster championship. His team, captained now by Tom Semple, beat Waterford in the opening round. The semi-final, against Limerick in Tipperary, has been described as '… a Homeric struggle, of red-hot intensity from beginning to end … with a minute to go, the figures were equal, but Mikey Maher whipped in the deciding score just in time to have it recorded. Tipperary 2-12, Limerick 3-8.'

The end came in the Munster final against Cork. It was a triumph for youth – Cork 3-10 Tipperary 3-4. Father Time had caught up with Mikey and a number of his colleagues.

Winners (Tubberadora) of the 1898 and 1899 hurling All-Ireland championship: *back row (l–r):* Watty Dunne, Will Devane, Ed Brennan, Mikey Maher (Capt.), E. D. Ryan, Jn. Ryan, Tim Condon; *centre row (l–r):* (Thomas Leahy, President), Phil Byrne, Jn. Connolly, Jack Maher, Denis Walsh, Jim O'Keeffe, Dick O'Keeffe, (Ml. Conlon, Sec.); *front row (l–r):* Tommy Ryan, Jack Maher ('Fields'), Ed Maher, Johnny Walsh.

Big Mikey, as he was affectionately known, was a born leader, revered and respected by those he captained. He never left any stone unturned to get the best out of his men.

Folklore has it that, with a view to improving the accuracy of his forwards, prior to the All-Ireland final of 1898, Mikey had them shooting at the band of a wheel in Walsh's kiln field in Tubbera-dora.

'Carbery' (Paddy D. Mehigan) once wrote of Mikey: 'Of the hundred All-Ireland captains I have seen, for inspired leadership and dynamic force in a crisis, I'll give the palm to Big Mikey of Tub-beradora.'

Big Mikey, who was ambidextrous, usually played at either mid-field or centre forward. Fearless and lion-hearted, rugged rather than stylish, he led tearaway assaults on opponents' goals and in so doing urged and inspired his colleagues to greater effort and deeds.

A press reporter portrayed Mikey as (from *Tipperary's GAA Story*):

> *... the most dangerous man on the 40 yards mark that a back was ever up against, and many of his shots sent terror into a goalkeeper's heart ... When things looked black for Tipperary, Maher would suddenly rise, tear up the field, sweep down all opposition and shoot ... Those Tipperary men's blood would boil; their virility would assert itself; they would drive into their men reckless of life and limb and actually walk over the stretched bodies of their opponents to victory.*

Mikey's character in private life contrasted with that on the playing pitch. 'Big, genial, stout-hearted, a huge man with a soft kindly countenance, he had a quiet, easy-speaking way with him that endeared him to all who knew him' (from *Tipperary's GAA Story*).

In 1918, at the age of forty-eight, Mikey moved to Galbally in County Limerick. Thereafter, in Boherlahan where it was said he 'carried more weight than a parish priest', he was perceived as a king in exile.

His hurling deeds were replicated, to some extent, by two of his nephews. Sonny Maher was full-forward on the three-in-a-row-winning Tipperary team of 1949 to 1951. His namesake, Michael Maher, matched Mikey's five All-Ireland successes, playing at full-back in the years 1958, 1961, 1962, 1964 and 1965. And in his displays in that position, the deeds and traits and strength of Uncle Mikey were brought to life again. For in those years with his flankers Mickey Byrne, Kieran Carey, Matt Hassett and John Doyle, the full-back line was fortress Tipperary, where no prisoners were taken.

Mikey died in Galbally in 1947 – 'one of the greatest Tipperary hurlers of all time, and one of its most revered personalities'. As the Irish adage says: '*Imíonn na daoine ach fanann na cnuic.*' But the memory of the deeds remains. For Mikey was, even before the concept was mooted, surely the first of the All-Time All-Stars.

A hurling selection

For convenience in selecting this seventeen-a-side, I have opted, positionally, for a second centre-half-back and a second centre-half-forward.

Pat 'Fox' Maher
(Kilkenny)

John Mahony   *Seán Óg Hanley*   *Dan Horgan*
(Kerry)   (Limerick)   (London)

Pat Coughlan   *Jim Stapleton*   *Dan Coughlan*
(Cork)   (Tipperary)   (Cork)

Nicholas O'Shea
(Dublin)

Nicholas Daly   *Ned Hayes*
(Wexford)   (Tipperary)

Paddy O'Riordan
(Tipperary)

Denis Walsh   *Mikey Maher*   *Stephen Hayes*
(Tipperary)   (Tipperary)   (Cork)

Jer Doheny   *William J. Spain*   *Denis Grimes*
(Kilkenny)   (Dublin)   (Limerick)

Mikey Maher – post-hurling days.

Pat 'Fox' Maher

One of the outstanding hurlers of the early days of the Association, Pat made his name not only as a goalkeeper but also as a full-back. Unfortunately, he was in the autumn of his career when he won his only All-Ireland medal in 1904 – when Kilkenny were on the edge of a glorious era. Pat excelled in the 1904 triumph. In the 1897 final against Limerick, he was outstanding in goal, despite defeat being Kilkenny's lot. Raymond Smith in *Decades of Glory* (Dublin, 1966) tells that he was 'awarded a silver-mounted hurley for his magnificent performance'.

John Mahony

A native of Ballyduff, John captained Kerry to the county's only hurling title to date. Born in 1863 to Jack and Bridget (née Doran), he remained a bachelor all his life and made his livelihood from fishing and thatching. On the hurling field he was a man of indomitable spirit, determined and fearless. John died in December 1943, aged eighty.

Seán Óg Hanley

Perceived by many as the outstanding hurler of his time, Seán Óg was vice-captain of the All-Ireland winning team of 1897. Playing at full-back, he stood apart in every game. He was the London full-back in the All-Ireland final of 1900 when the exiles came within a whisker of defeating mighty Tipperary, and in 1903 he once again filled that position. A man of quiet disposition, he cut an impressive figure on the playing pitch – broad-shouldered, 14 stone, 6 feet 2 inches tall and a *ciotóg*. He died in his fifties and was buried in Kensal Rise cemetery, London.

Dan Horgan

Dan was the Cork-born exile who captained the great London team in the 1900 All-Ireland final against Tipperary. To lose that day was a bitter disappointment. However, this brilliant hurler, 'a towering figure in defence', won a coveted All-Ireland medal in the 1901 final when London had a surprising win over Home champions Cork.

Pat and Dan Coughlan

Pat and Dan were two of five famous hurling Coughlan brothers from the famous Blackrock club – the others were Jerh, Denis and Tom. All five tasted All-Ireland success.

'Carbery' had this to say:

> Pat was five foot eleven and a master of strategy. A strong fearless man, he revelled in the close hard clashes of his period. Big Dan Coughlan was one of the finest wing full backs I have ever seen play. He was six foot and a half inch tall and carried a huge chest and shoulders. His strength was immense. I saw Dan lift a ball on his own line; the wind and fall were with him and he let fly – the ball hopped over the far line 140 yards away. Dan emigrated at the height of his hurling career.

Dan won his medals in 1892 and 1902. Pat won them in 1893 and 1894.

Jim Stapleton

Born in Thurles in May 1863, Jim was the first All-Ireland-winning hurling captain when he led Tipperary to victory in the 1887 final. An old timer described him as 'a powerful bullet of a man'. 'Carbery' described him as 'about five foot ten with powerfully muscled shoulders and arms, of endless pluck and stamina, weighing around twelve and a half stone in his hearty prime'. Jim was among the hurlers who travelled to America in 1888 with the 'invasion' party. He died in 1949. Willie Gaynor of Monadreen, Thurles, told me that when he was growing up in Thurles, Jim lived close to him and that he always wore a hat in public and had broad shoulders.

Nicholas O'Shea

Nicholas captained Dublin when they won the All-Ireland hurling title of 1889. As a native of Tipperary, it meant that the first two winning hurling captains were Tipperary men – Jim Stapleton being the other. Nicholas was born in 1862 of farming stock, at Tullohea, South-Lodge. Having worked for a while in Dublin, he bought a pub in Clonskeagh in 1893 – it is still in the O'Shea family. Nicholas was only forty-six when he died in 1908. His brother Pat was also a member of the successful 1889 team.

Nicholas Daly

Nicholas, who captained Wexford without success in the All-Ireland finals of 1890 and 1891, could be forgiven for believing that the gods were looking on him with disfavour. I say this because instead of losing both he might well have won them. Both were very close calls. Perhaps if he had exercised a little more discipline over his men, he might have won in 1890. They were ahead on the scoreboard when the game was abandoned and lost the decision in the council chambers. A punctilious referee could be said to have denied him in 1891.

Ned Hayes

Ned was captain of Two-Mile-Borris in 1900 when the club proved worthy successors to Tubberadora and Moycarkey in carrying the hurling flag for Tipperary. Ned also led successful Croke Cup and Railway Shield teams. In the 1900 campaign he captained his native Tipperary to victories over Cork, Clare, Kerry, Kilkenny, Galway and London. The final against London, at Jones' Road on 26 October 1902, was a great occasion for Tipperary. Their footballers also won the football title. Ned Hayes led the hurlers to Tipperary's sixth All-Ireland crown. The day ended with the lord mayor of Dublin, T. Harrington MP, entertaining the hurlers and footballers of London and Tipperary to dinner at the Mansion House.

Paddy O'Riordan

A native of Drombane, Thurles, Paddy was a deadly forward whose career in the Tipperary jersey began in 1894. Tradition has it that Paddy got all of Tipperary's scores, 6-8, in their 1895 All-Ireland win over neighbours Kilkenny, who managed only one goal. It is not official, and is in many ways hard to credit, given the calibre of many of the other players led by Big Mikey Maher. Raymond Smith, a writer well acquainted with Tipperary hurling lore, believes 'he had the distinction of getting most of Tipperary's tally', while Tom Barry of Cork was of the opinion that 'he was the best forward I ever saw'. Paddy emigrated to America in 1908 and no sooner had he put a foot on US soil than he was hustled away to play a championship final with Tipperary against Offaly. Later, we find him figuring as captain of a team of Irish-American hurling exiles from Chicago and New York that toured Ireland in 1911. Paddy died in Long Island, New York, in 1941.

Denis Walsh

Hailing from Tubberadora, Denis was one of the finest wing-forwards of the 1890s. He won All-Ireland medals in 1895, 1896, 1898 and 1899. He won his fifth All-Ireland medal with Tipperary, with a Boherlahan selection under the captaincy of Johnny Leahy in 1916 – twenty-one years after his first All-Ireland success.

Mikey Maher

Mikey is profiled in 'A hurling personality: Mikey Maher (Tipperary)'.

Stephen Hayes

Stephen Hayes was a member of the famed Blackrock hurling club. With a Blackrock selection, he captained his Cork team to the county's fourth All-Ireland hurling title in 1894 – the third of three in a row. According to Raymond Smith (in *Decades of Glory*): 'Names like Stephen Hayes live in the annals of Cork hurling'. A verse of a song called 'The Boys of Blackrock' goes like this:

Can you equal the Coughlans, the Ahernes, the Sheas,
Scannell, Cremin, Curtis and match Stephen Hayes
I can mention their names from the round of the clock
The men that won credit for Cork and Blackrock.

Stephen Hayes

Jer Doheny

Jer Doheny arrived on the county scene in 1893. There must have been many moments in his hurling life when he thought he would never win an All-Ireland title. He was on the losing sides in 1893 v Cork, 1895 v Tipperary, 1897 v Limerick, 1898 v Tipperary and 1903 v Cork in the Home final. But he finally found success in the 1904 final, when Jer led a Tullaroan selection to a great win over Cork (St Finbarr's), 1-9 to 1-8. Jer settled his team early on by scoring the opening point. It was Kilkenny's first All-Ireland crown. Great days lay ahead. Jer's son, also Jer, played with Waterford in 1943.

William J. Spain

The first of the dual medallists, William was a native of Nenagh, County Tipperary. In 1887 he won a football title with Limerick. Two years later he was a member of the Dublin hurling team, captained by Nicholas O'Shea, also a Tipperary man, that defeated Clare in the final, 5-1 to 1-6. Spain scored three of those goals. In April 1890 he emigrated to America.

Denis Grimes

Denis was born in 1864, and hurling soon became part of his daily activity. He captained a powerful Kilfinane selection when Limerick won their first All-Ireland hurling crown in 1897. The game was played at Tipperary on 20 November 1898. Their opponents were Kilkenny with a Tullaroan selection. The final score was Limerick 3-4 Kilkenny 2-4. In July 1899, Denis led what was basically the same lineout to victory in the Croke Cup competition of 1897. Kilkenny were again defeated 3-8 to 1-4. Shortly afterwards he emigrated to Wales, where he worked in the mines. He died in 1920 and was buried in Wales.

A FOOTBALL GAME:

Cork v Wexford, 1893 All-Ireland final

Phil Keating

Disappointment was Wexford's lot, under the captaincy of Phil Keating, in the football championship of 1890. A series of postponements saw the final delayed until 26 June 1892. By then the team representing the county, 'Blues and Whites', had been disbanded for over a year. In preparation for the final the team had only a few weeks' training. They proved no match for a fit and well-trained Midleton team representing Cork. The defeat was a double blow to Wexford, as Cork had already been awarded the hurling title at their expense.

Wexford looked forward to better things in the championship of 1893. By then teams consisted of seventeen-a-side and a goal was equal to five points.

The county was represented by a talented Young Irelands selection from Wexford town – one of the outstanding teams of their era. They could boast of having played 108 matches and losing only three – to Kilmore, the John Street Volunteers and Young Irelands from Dublin.

The Young Irelands club was founded by local men Joe Redmond, Joe Kingsbury and John Morris. The team was trained by Watty Hanrahan, who would later become secretary of the Leinster Council.

In the opening game of the championship, Wexford defeated the Westmeath title holders, Mullingar. They then faced Kilkenny in the Leinster final. At half time Kilkenny led by five points to one, and having complained of alleged rough play on the part of the Wexford men, refused to come back out. Wexford remained on the pitch for half an hour before being awarded the game and the Leinster title.

So, with one and a half games under their belt, Wexford prepared for a showdown with Dromtariffe from Cork, who, unopposed in Munster, had a place in the All-Ireland final without playing even one game. Their captain was Jack O'Keeffe.

The final was scheduled for 24 June 1894 at Ashtown Trotting Grounds. The condition of the pitch was disgraceful. So the goal posts were moved to the Phoenix Park, where the football final followed the hurling final between Cork and Kilkenny.

In Wexford two meetings were held to decide whether to strengthen the team by selecting some players from other clubs in the county. After much debate, it was decided it would not be fair to strengthen the team with several newcomers at the expense of loyal Young Ireland players, so outside inclusion was confined to just two – Frank Boggan from the Enniscorthy area and John Phelan from New Ross.

Like many a game of those times, this one ended in confusion. Indeed, what transpired is a good illustration of the type of controversy that plagued many a contest in the early days of the organisation.

According to Wexford's Comóradh an Chéid 1884–1984: *Things were rather even in a rough and tumble first quarter, but when Tommy O'Connor sent to the Cork net, the Wexford side found themselves with a comfortable lead at half time – 1-1 to 0-1.*

One account stated that Cork were heavier and faster than the Wexford men, but they did not possess the same footballing skills or combined movements.

Wexford started the second half in determined fashion, but both sides missed chances to score. Then the Wexford captain, Tom 'Skull' Hayes, gained possession. He evaded several opponents before being grounded on the 40-yard mark. No score resulted. *Comóradh an Chéid* takes up the story again: ... *with at least fifteen minutes to go ... the trouble – and there was plenty of it – started ... when Wexford's Curran was grounded unceremoniously. As he got up, he was kicked under the eye by a Cork player, with the ball 30 yards away. A general melee followed and the referee allowed a few minutes' cooling off period.*

At this stage the crowd had been cleared from the pitch and the threat of a serious assault on the offending Cork player was averted, as wiser counsel prevailed. The referee, T. Gilligan of Dublin, ordered that substitutes replace both the injured Wexford player and the Cork man who attacked him. Cork refused this arrangement and left the field. The referee waited for a further ten minutes before awarding the game to Wexford. Central Council upheld his decision.

Wexford supporters were delirious – their first All-Ireland crown.

Frank Boggan was the hero, fully justifying his selection as an outsider. Others to excel were John Phelan, Andy Furlong, John Bolger, Tom Hayes the captain and Tom 'Hoey' Redmond, one of the great footballers of that period, who in 1898 and 1899 won All-Ireland titles with Dublin. Tom later became a trustee of the association.

Tom 'Hoey' Redmond

The youngest member of the team was seventeen-year-old John Maginn (sometimes spelt McGuinn). He was the lightest too – just under 8 stone. And yet, neither youth nor weight was a handicap when it came to footballing ability. In 1897 John won a Croke Cup title.

John died aged twenty-seven on 1 August 1903. He was among the youngest ever to win an All-Ireland medal; you had Dick Fitzgerald of Kerry in the 1903 football final, played in 1905, aged seventeen and Brendan Considine of Clare hurling fame, aged seventeen in 1914. The youngest player to date to have taken part in an All-Ireland final was Patsy Lynch of Cavan, who was sixteen and a half when his county lost to Kildare 2-6 to 2-5 in the 1928 football final.

John Maginn

Five members of the Wexford team had played on the 1890 team that lost to Cork – Tom 'Skull' Hayes, Paddy Curran, Andy Furlong, John Doyle and Jack O'Connor.

Cork were unhappy with the decision to award the 1893 title to Wexford. At a meeting of the County Board, the secretary Michael Deering said they were not opposed to fair play, but Cork, he maintained, were winning hands down and that was why the row was created.

When the Young Irelands arrived back in Wexford town they were given a hero's welcome. They were met not only by their own fans and supporters but also by members of the other GAA clubs in the town, and carried shoulder high.

A special Mass was celebrated in the Church of the Immaculate Conception, Rowe Street. Later, four barrels of stout, supplied by Mr Norton, a local enthusiast, were consumed at the Young Irelands headquarters in Selskar Street – a premises with the unlikely title of the Temperance Hall.

The team that achieved a historic first for Wexford was:

Tom Redmond (goal), Tom 'Skull' Hayes (captain),
Jack Bolger, Paddy Curran, Mick Curran, Jack O'Connor,
Tommy O'Connor, John Maginn, Frank Boggan, John Phelan,
John Doyle, John O'Neill, Nick Lacey, William O'Leary,
Andy Furlong, James Maloney and Tom H. Redmond.

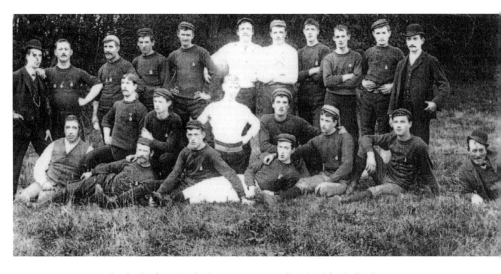

Young Irelands, the first Wexford team to win an All-Ireland football title – 1893. *Back row (l–r)*: A. Furlong, P. Curran, J. Doyle, J. O'Neill, F. Weafer, T. Hayes, T. Redmond, J. McGuinn, J. Morris; middle: J. Bolger, S. O'Rourke, W. Kenny, N. Lacey; *front (l–r)*: J. Kenny, J. Redmond, T. O'Connor, W. Leary, T. H. Redmond. Wexford 1-1, Cork 0-2 (match unfinished).

A FOOTBALL PERSONALITY:

James P. O'Sullivan (Kerry)

When the ball was set on play, O'Sullivan he did cry:
Rush on, rush on, bold Rangers, have victory or die.

James P. O'Sullivan, affectionately known and referred to as J. P. or 'The Champion', was an outstanding athlete who became All Round Champion of Ireland in 1891 at Ballsbridge, having been beaten into third place the previous year at the same venue.

He held a variety of official positions in the GAA, including vice-president, official handicapper, chairman and vice-chairman of Kerry County Board, Central Council executive and Central Council delegate.

He captained the famed Killorglin Laune Rangers, who in 1892 recaptured the Kerry title with a win over reigning champions Ballymacelligott. Victories over Cork (Clondrohid) and Waterford (Dungarvan), captained by Dan Fraher, brought the Kingdom its first provincial crown.

The Munster final against Waterford was played at Fermoy on 4 December 1892 on a pitch covered with snow.

Kerry, represented by Laune Rangers, lost the All-Ireland final to Dublin (Young Irelands) by 1-4 to 0-3. The game was played at Clonturk Park (the Meadow of the Boar) on 26 March 1893 under the whistle of Dan Fraher of Dungarvan.

P. P. Sutton reported on the game (from *Trail Blazers: A Century of Laune Ranges, 1888–1988* by Pat O'Shea [Killorglin, 1988]):

> *... the Kerrymen were equal in every respect to the Young Irelands, except in one – judgement and cleverness, and ... it was the grand discipline, combination and unsurpassed tactics of the Dubliners that enabled them to win. The Laune Rangers had the better of the play [but] ... could not score a major, whilst they lost a goal very softly.*

The *Freeman* had this to say about the final (from *Trail Blazers*):

> *Probably there has never been a more brilliant football match played in Dublin ... The fine kicking and determined dash of the Kerrymen ... could not be excelled, but the grand discipline,*

combination and unsurpassed tactics of the Young Irelanders enabled them to win.

J. P. and his men felt they were the better team. They were aggrieved that on a number of occasions, when they had worked themselves into a scoring position, the pitch was invaded and play halted. Pitch invasions were not at all uncommon in the early days. J. P. was also very critical of the unsporting behaviour of the Dublin supporters, described in the *Kerry Sentinel* as 'an irritating and annoying exhibition of metropolitan clannishness'. To prove a point, he offered a challenge to the Dublin team at a neutral venue. However, agreement on a venue was not reached and the challenge never materialised. In those days, hostility towards a visiting team was often par for the course, not only at inter-county level but also in local championships.

Seven members of the Killorglin rugby team played in the 1892 final – James P. O'Sullivan, who had played rugby with Killorglin at the tender age of seventeen, Jim J. O'Sullivan, the goalie and a cousin of J. P.'s, Tim Curran, Pat Teahan, Dan P. Murphy, Paddy O'Regan and Moss O'Brien.

The other team members were Jim Curran, John P. Murphy, Dr Bill O'Sullivan, John O'Reilly, Flor Doherty, Danny Clifford, and four who subsequently emigrated – Mick Hayes, Pat Sugrue, Mick Flynn and Bill Fleming.

Under J. P.'s captaincy, Laune Rangers dominated Kerry football from 1887 to 1890 and again in 1892 and 1893. In those years they travelled far afield to play games and their fame spread throughout Munster and even further. J. P. usually played at centre-half-back or centre-field, with his displays becoming the stuff of folklore.

His son, Dr Éamon, trained many a successful Kerry team in later years. The local GAA pitch in Killorglin – J. P. O'Sullivan Park – is named in his honour. It was originally a greyhound track and was purchased by the club in 1951 from John A. Foley, a local business-man, for £2,000. It had a fine surface. In my young years in Killorglin in the early 1950s, I played many a game on it with the local hurl-ing team, and spent countless, immensely enjoyable evenings with hurling colleagues belting sliotars in practice sessions. It had a sod that was ideal for hurling.

J. P. has been described as 'just over 6 feet 1 inch in height, weighing a little over 13 stone, light-limbed under huge shoulders'.

A contemporary, Dick Curtis, who played football with Dublin, said he was 'as fast as a deer and as strong as three men'.

P. J. Devlin, an old Fenian, who wrote under the pseudonym 'Celt', had this to say (from *Trail Blazers*): *Never had a team a finer captain than he who led Kerry that day against Dublin ... Were I to try and picture any of the Fenian champions of tradition I should evolve J. P. O'Sullivan of Killorglin, as I saw him that day.*

James Patrick O'Sullivan was born in 1867 in Brookhill, Kilgobnet in the parish of Tuogh. The eldest of four, he developed a keen interest in athletics, football and coursing.

He died suddenly on Wednesday 13 January 1909 at a coursing meeting at Castlemartyr. He was only forty-two.

'Carbery' knew J. P. well, and paid tribute following his untimely death (from *Trail Blazers*):

> *One must have lived in Kerry to appreciate how much the people therein – high and low, gentle and simple – loved their greatest of athletes and noblest of souls ... I fraternised freely with him, for J. P. was the best of companions, brimful of reminiscences on subjects dear to me ... his name was revered and his great performances rehearsed wherever Kerrymen gathered. The sad dignity and immensity of The Champion's funeral are spoken even today at Kerry turf fires. He was honoured in life for his upright, sterling character – outstanding member of an historic Gaelic clan.*

Yet though thy voice is hushed, the welcome stilled,
Thy spirit seems to live, pervade the air,
But can the void, the gap, be ever filled?
Can spirit fill an athlete's empty chair?
  Remembered, cherished, long shall be thy deeds!
At home and far across the roaring wave,
Around thy memory shall be twined the wreaths
That fame bids bloom on a hero's grave.
  And when a monument thy comrades raise
Upon thy grave, when Summer leaves have flown,
And winds of Autumn gently sound thy praise,
Be this the epitaph upon the stone –
  'Here lies a worthy son of Eoghan,
A Gael of Gaels, a master in the fight,
May his soul find rest before the eternal throne,
His spirit rest in God, his Lord his Christ.'
                'A visit to Brookhill', from Trail Blazers

J. P. O'Sullivan

A football selection

G. Charlemont
(Dublin)

Tim Curran   Con Fitzgerald   Matt Rea
(Kerry)   (Limerick)   (Dublin)

Paddy Finn   James P. O'Sullivan   John Kennedy
(Tipp)   (Kerry)   (Dublin)

Dick Curtis
(Dublin)

Willie Ryan   Malachi O'Brien
(Tipp)   (Limerick)

T. 'Darby' Errity
(Dublin)

Charlie McAllister   Jim Power   Wm. J. Spain
(Louth)   (Cork)   (Limerick)

Tommy O'Connor   Sam Maguire   Tom 'Skull' Hayes
(Wexford)   (London)   (Wexford)

G. Charlemont

Dublin won the first three All-Ireland finals they contested – 1891, 1892 and 1894. G. Charlemont manned the goal on each occasion and became the first Gaelic goalkeeper to win three All-Ireland medals. Efforts, on my part, to find his Christian name have failed. As regards the surname, it is the only time I have encountered it in the records of the GAA. I can't help wondering if he was a descendant of the earls of Charlemont who around the early 1700s acquired a 300-acre estate at Donnycarney. The 1894 final ended in controversy. The first game, at Clonturk Park, was a draw. The replay in Thurles came to an abrupt finish when Dublin walked off the field, trailing Cork by two points at the time. Central Council ordered a replay and when Cork refused, the game and the title were awarded to Dublin.

Tim Curran

He was a member of the famed Killorglin Laune Rangers team. He and his brother Jim played on the 1892 side beaten by Dublin in the final. A third brother, Tom, had emigrated to the US before the match. Tim, a national teacher by profession, was regarded as one of the best full-backs to have played the game. The three brothers used to play in the full-back line for Laune Rangers, a line known as 'Curran's Avenue – a one-way street – outwards only'.

Tim Curran

Con Fitzgerald

Con was a native of Glin in west Limerick. An outstanding athlete, he was once an Olympic nominee. Deeds of his awesome strength are legendary. He captained The Commercials to four successive county titles, 1895–8. When Limerick lost the Munster final of 1895 to Tipperary by five points to three at Kilmallock, their captain, Con Fitzgerald of the Commercials club, decided to embark on serious preparations for the following year. A strict training programme was put in place; the team was trained to the ounce.

It paid dividends, and saw them survive the close contests of 1896:

v Cork 1-2 to 1-1
v Tipperary 2-4 to 0-6
v Waterford 0-4 to 0-1
v Dublin 1-5 to 0-7.

In the final against Dublin, Con had a great game and was described as 'by far the swiftest man on the field'.

Matt Rea

Matt captained a Geraldines selection that brought successive titles to Dublin in 1898 and 1899 – their fifth and sixth All-Ireland crowns. A native of Glenroe in County Limerick, Matt was a sterling defender and could play in any position in the back division, including goal. He was a grand-uncle of Ned Rea, who won All-Ireland hurling honours with Limerick in 1973.

Paddy Finn

Paddy played a key role, as captain, in bringing Tipperary their second football title, when he led an Arravale Rovers selection to victory over Meath in 1895. In a letter I received from Willie Gaynor of Monadreen, Thurles, in January 2003 he told me: 'Paddy won an All-Ireland medal with Bohercrowe in 1889 and was captain of Arravale Rovers when they won the All-Ireland in 1895. His brothers Mick and Batt also played on that team. Tom O'Donoghue wrote a history of Arravale Rovers football teams but no photograph of Paddy and his brothers. The photographs of the 1889 and the 1895 teams do not show the Finns. Paddy Finn emigrated to New York and paid a visit to Tipperary after the Second World War. The *Tipperary Star* published an account of him, but no photograph was shown. Paddy had relations in Dublin, a man also called Finn who was in the faculty of Irish in UCD. Dublin Corporation employed his son as a sheriff. Thurles people now living in New York tell me they are unable to find out anything about Paddy Finn and his brothers.'

James P. O'Sullivan

James is profiled in 'A football personality: James P. O'Sullivan (Kerry)'.

The Dublin (Young Irelands) team, winners of the All-Ireland title in 1891, 1892 and 1894, captained on each occasion by John Kennedy.

John Kennedy

John made GAA history in 1894 when he became the first man to captain All-Ireland winning football teams on three occasions. He had previously done so in 1891 and 1892. He led a Young Irelands selection, one of the finest combinations of those days.

Quite a few of the players were on all three teams. As a result, they played and combined as a unit, which brought success in close contests. They also had the benefit, unlike their opponents, of not having to make the long trek to the capital to play the finals.

Dick Curtis

Dick played with Dublin in five All-Ireland finals – 1891, 1892, 1894, 1896 and 1897. He was on the victorious side on four occasions – losing only in 1896 to Limerick. He was one of the team's great footballers. As well as being an athlete and first-class footballer, he was also champion collar-and-elbow wrestler.

Willie Ryan

Willie Ryan of Bohercrow was probably Tipperary's greatest footballer of the early days. He was their key player in the county's second All-Ireland victory of 1895 when Meath were defeated, and was feted accordingly. Indeed, but for Willie, the Tipperary double of 1895 would not have been achieved on the afternoon of 15 March 1896 at Jones' Road. In 1891 Willie was imprisoned for his involvement in 'land war' activities. He wore the club and Tipperary football jerseys with honour and distinction for many years.

Malachi O'Brien

The outstanding footballer, not only of the Limerick Commercials team but of the All-Ireland campaign of 1887, Malachi was carried shoulder-high by his teammates when they alighted from the train in Limerick following their victory over Louth. According to a veteran who saw that final: 'The smallest man of the forty-two in that memorable first-timer of blue ribands was the best footballer I ever saw.'

T. 'Darby' Errity

Another of the great Dublin footballers of the 1890s, he played in five finals – 1892, 1894, 1896, 1898 and 1899. And as with his colleague Dick Curtis, the only loss was to Limerick in 1896.

Charlie McAllister

Louth might not have won their first game against Waterford in the 1887 championship but for the presence of Charlie McAllister in their lineout. He scored 1-1 in the second half – the goal proving to be the turning point in the contest. His brother Ned was also prominent in Louth's success, but both missed the final against Limerick because of a family bereavement. Ned and Charlie were active in the Gaelic League and were co-founders of the Northern brigade of the IRB.

Jim Power

Jim captained Cork to their first All-Ireland football title in 1890. His team, Midleton, met Laune Rangers of Kerry in the Munster final at Limerick With neither team having registered a single score, the game was abandoned after fifty-seven minutes when the ball burst. That, at any rate, is one account. Another states that with twelve minutes remaining the ball was kicked over the sideline and when it was brought back 'it was as dead as a flat tyre'. Sabotage! There was no replacement. The replay took place at Ballinteer. Jim Power had a brilliant game, and scored a particularly memorable point. With hands on hips, he met a clearance from the Kerry goal on the drop as it landed around the fifty-yard line and sent it back between the posts.

Tommy O'Connor

Sunday 24 June 1894 was a special day for the O'Connor family of the Wexford Young Ireland's team. Wexford defeated Cork in the 1893 All-Ireland final that day to become champions for the first time. Tommy O'Connor, who in his day was reputed to have scored more points than any other Gael in Ireland, played a key role. His goal in the second quarter of the game proved vital. Wexford won by 1-1 to 0-1. His brother, Jack, was also on the team, and his father, Edward, was a member of the team committee. Contrary to what some records suggest, a third brother, Peter, did not play in the 1893 final. Tommy was the longest-serving member of that historic winning team.

Sam Maguire

The name that has echoed down the decades, the Sam Maguire Cup was first presented in 1928 to Bill 'Squire' Gannon, the Kildare captain.

Sam was born near Dunmanway, County Cork, in 1879 – one of seven children of a Protestant west Cork family – farming stock, of modest means. He emigrated to England in 1897 and from the time of his arrival in London was associated with the exiles teams. He played with London (Hibernians) in three All-Ireland finals, all without success: 1900 v Tipperary, 1901 v Dublin, 1903 v Kerry. He was captain in 1901 and 1903. A postal official, Sam was for many years president of the London County Board. He was a friend of Michael Collins and, as Piaras Béaslaí recounted, 'did sterling work for him during the years of storm and struggle'.

Sam Maguire.

He was a major-general in the IRB and was chief intelligence officer in Britain. It cost him his job when he was eventually arrested and jailed. When released, he returned to Ireland and got a job in the newly established Irish civil service. Failing health saw him return to Dunmanway, where he died of TB, in relative obscurity, on 6 February 1927, aged forty-eight.

Dunmanway School, which Sam Maguire attended.

Peadar Kearney, who wrote our national anthem, knew Sam well and dedicated the following poem to him:

> *Proud to have hailed you friend,*
> *Long years ago!*
> *Amid the fogs and fumes of London Town,*
> *An Empire's mart –*
> *Astride the sluggish Thames,*
> *Building on plundered clans,*
> *Her dread renown!*
> * Strong in your deathless faith*
> *Oh heart of gold!*
> *Your kindly, generous smile*
> *Gave strength to all*
> *Who grasped your hand*
> *In that great brotherhood:*
> *Waiting throughout the years for Eire's call.*

Tom 'Skull' Hayes

Thomas Hayes

The grave of Wexford captain Thomas Hayes.

Wexford lost the hurling and football finals of 1890 to Cork under the captaincy of Nicholas Daly and Phillip Keating respectively. The following year, with Daly still captain, the hurlers lost to Kerry in the final. So in 1893, Tom 'Skull' Hayes, captain of the Young Irelands football selection that represented Wexford, set out to make amends. And he succeeded, as Wexford defeated Cork in the final by 1-1 to 0-1. Tom was known as a 'run about' man. He had no fixed position on the field, but instead followed the play and lent a hand as required. Liam Lahiff, writing in the *County Wexford Free Press*, recalled a visit to Crosstown cemetery in Wexford where he observed Tom's grave: *There is nothing there to say who or what the man achieved … I think it would be great if all the Gaelic clubs with the help of the County GAA Board could come up with some way of funding and erecting an appropriate monument over the grave.*

Surely a deserved honour for Wexford's first All-Ireland winning captain.

1901–1910

Teams that participated in the All-Ireland senior finals

COUNTY	FOOTBALL		HURLING	
	WON	LOST	WON	LOST
Cork		2	2	4
Dublin	5	1		2
Kerry	3	1		
Kildare	1			
Kilkenny			4	
Limerick				1
London		4	1	2
Louth	1	1		
Tipperary			2	1
Wexford			1	

Ten counties participated in the senior finals (including London).

It was the smallest representation of any decade.

The ten hurling finals involved seven counties, with five counties successful.

The ten football finals involved six counties, with four counties successful.

A HURLING GAME:

Cork v Kilkenny, 1907 All-Ireland final

It was 26 June 1908. The venue was Dan Fraher's field at Dungarvan. The occasion was the All-Ireland hurling final of 1907. It was Nore versus Lee. M. F. Crowe of Limerick was in charge of the whistle.

Cork's path to the final was:

v Limerick, 8-15 to 1-6

v Kerry, w/o

v Tipperary, 1-6 to 1-4

v Galway, 2-8 to 1-7 – game unfinished

v London, 1-14 to 0-5.

In the Munster final between Cork and Tipperary, both teams were in splendid form. Cork led at half time by 1-2 to 0-2. Well into the final quarter, the gap had narrowed to 1-5 to 1-4. Tipperary got a close-in free. The Cork citadel held. They then added a point.

This was Kilkenny's path to the final:

v Wexford, 2-17 to 1-3

v Offaly, 3-8 to 1-6

v Dublin, 4-14 to 1-9

When I met John T. Power, the Kilkenny goalkeeper, born in 1883, he recalled the game against Offaly for me with the following story:

> *Jack Rochford, full-back, said to me: 'I must have two drinks or I'll be no good at hurling.' 'Have the two drinks,' said I, 'and wait till the match is over and you can have as many as you like.' We won the match. I considered him a great full-back.*

He then mentioned some of the household names of that era – men like Jim Kelleher of Cork, Tom Semple of Tipperary, 'Tyler' Mackey of Limerick.

'How good was Tyler?' I queried. John T. looked at me and with firm and calm conviction said: 'He wasn't good enough for me – he couldn't score goals on me.'

Kilkenny, with a Mooncoin selection and wearing the Tullaroan jerseys, were captained by Dick 'Drug' Walsh of Mooncoin. Cork were represented by a Dungourney selection and captained by the redoubtable Jim Kelleher. The attendance exceeded 15,000. Fr James

B. Dollard, a Kilkenny man, whose mission was in Canada, threw in the ball and had to race for the line from the flying hurlers.

It was nip and tuck for the entire hour. Cork held a four-point advantage at the break – 4-2 to 2-4. The second half got under way with Kilkenny sending over three points without reply to narrow the gap to just one point. Cork replied with a point before Kilkenny made a vital switch, moving Paddy Lanigan to midfield. Points were exchanged, bringing the score to 4-4 to 2-8 – Cork two points to the good. The game was now a cliffhanger. The sliotar was moving at speed, on the ground and in the air.

Then Kilkenny struck with a Jimmy Kelly goal. There was a consultation between the umpires and the referee before the goal was allowed. For the first time in the game Kilkenny were ahead, and were never behind after that. Cork launched fierce attacks, and three times they almost scored goals. But on each occasion the combination of goalkeeper John T. Power and full-back Jack Rochford thwarted their efforts.

'Carbery' was at the game:

> ... that final of swaying fortunes and brilliant hurling ... Dan Fraher's fine field was a picture on that June day of 1908 ... The old Fenian himself had paid special personal attention to the pitch ... 'twas like a billiard table, and every man on the field was a master hurler ... From the opening sally, the pace was a cracker. Flying points at long range were a feature ... overhead hurling of rare beauty was enjoyed that day ... gloriously long hitters on ground and overhead.

Great names on both sides demonstrated all the skills that made the ancient game a treat to watch – the three Doyle brothers, Dan Kennedy, Jack Rochford, John T. Power, Sim Walton, Matt Gargan, Jimmy Kelly and Dan Grace, just some of the Kilkenny men. And from Cork: Jim Kelleher, John Roynane, Steva Riordan, Tom Mahony, Jerry Beckett and Tom Coughlan, to name but a few.

It was the greatest hurling exhibition witnessed up to then, and became the benchmark against which future contests would be measured.

If you include the Home final of 1903, this was the fifth final meeting of these counties. Two wins apiece, so this game would decide who would edge ahead. Just when it seemed that a draw was inevitable, Kilkenny snatched a dramatic winner. John Anthony of Piltown cleared his lines with a high delivery. Jimmy Kelly of Mooncoin judged the flight well as he raced to the falling sliotar. Without hesitating, he met it on the drop and watched triumphantly as it sailed between the posts. Game won, Kilkenny 3-12 Cork 4-8.

Fr Dollard recalled the great final in an article in the *Cork Examiner* in May 1921:

> *I do not think that either of these two teams ... were superior to the other ... It was a battle of giants, and clean and clever striking was the rule. There was such skill shown that no man was retired from injuries during the game and very few players were even scratched. There were alternate scores for either team, and only by sheer luck the Kilkenny men had their turn of scoring over, when the whistle blew.*

The barefoot ones – Kilmoyley, County Kerry champions 1907. Kerry, with a Kilmoyley selection, beat Clare by 1-12 to 2-5 in the first round of the Munster championship, following which they gave a walkover to Cork.

Jack Rochford and Mick Doyle, two
stalwarts of the 1907 Kilkenny team.

Rev. James Dollard.

A HURLING PERSONALITY:

John 'Tyler' Mackey (Limerick)

'Tyler' Mackey ended a seventeen-year span with Limerick when he retired from inter-county hurling in 1917 after losing the re-played Munster hurling final of that year against Tipperary at Cork Athletic Grounds. During all those years an All-Ireland medal eluded him. In 1910 controversy surrounded the 7-0 to 6-2 loss to Wexford owing to disallowed goals, while in 1911 a walkover was conceded to Kilkenny owing to a venue dispute. In 1912, with a now formidable team, Limerick led Cork by a point in the Munster semi-final when the following happened. Mick Byrne of Sarsfields pulled on a wing ball following a clearance by Andy Fitzgerald in the Cork goal. On it went to Paddy Mahony, lying loose on the other wing; another crisp stroke and the ball went to Dan Ken-nefick, who whipped it onto 'Major' Kennedy of Carrigtohill and the Limerick citadel fell. It was Cork's only score of the second half. Before the puck out hit the ground, the final whistle sounded: Cork 2-2 Limerick 1-3.

John 'Tyler' Mackey.

'Tyler' won two Munster titles when he captained Limerick in 1910 and 1911. He won many other honours, including county titles and tournaments, and played against the greats of Tipperary, Cork and Kilkenny. It is rather ironic that in 1918, the year after 'Tyler' retired, Limerick won the All-Ireland crown – something that had eluded 'Tyler' throughout his entire career.

'Tyler' was strong, fearless and impetuous; he had guts, stamina and willpower; he was full of heart, daring and courage – traits on the field of play that tended to conceal a gentle and generous nature. He played in an era when the exchanges were intensely physical. First-time hurling was the order of the day – overhead and on the ground. Delaying on the ball only invited physical punishment. 'Whip on the ball' was a phrase often heard.

'Tyler' lived for hurling. He would walk several miles to play a match, tog out by the side of a ditch, often play in his bare feet and then walk home.

The following interview with 'Tyler' from *The Mackey Story* by Séamus Ó Ceallaigh and Seán Murphy (Limerick, 1982) gives a feel for what the game was like in those days.

> *Jim ('Spud') Murphy of The 'Barrs was the toughest player I ever encountered ... 'Spud' was never one to bother overmuch with rules and to the end of his hurling days he remained a referee's pet problem ... A rash, reckless, devil-may-care centre field hurl-er and one of the hardest of hard men, he partnered at centre field Tim Nagle, the blacksmith of St Mary's, and not a pair in Ireland could boast that they mastered these two.*

In the Munster semi-final of 1915 Limerick and Cork renewed ri-valries, in a game that attracted heavy betting. With four minutes to go the game came to an abrupt end when Tim Nagle and 'Tyler' came to grips. The match was abandoned and the Munster Council decision to call a replay was overturned by Central Council by five votes to four following an appeal by Cork. The Munster Council suspended Tim and 'Tyler' for twelve months.

The rivalry between these tough-as-teak opponents started in a gold medal tournament at Killarney on 4 June 1911 in which Castleconnell defeated famed Dungourney by 6-4 to 3-2. Ever after, when they fielded against each other, word among the spectators was: 'Look out for the exchanges between Nagle and 'Tyler' – they are worth watching.'

So what kind of stuff was 'Tyler' made of? We get an idea from this excerpt from *The Mackey Story*.

> *There was no ban in my early days. We had a rugby team in Castleconnell ... I kept fit during the winter by playing with this team. One memorable weekend I played a Transfield Cup rugby match with Richmond on the Saturday, participated in a strenuous Munster hurling championship game on Sunday and was at Killaloe regatta the following day, August Monday, and rowed in four boat races.*

Man of bronze! He was the son of Michael, who also played and was active in GAA affairs in the early days of the Association, and father of Mick and John who for over a decade and a half would grace the hurling scene in the 1930s and 1940s.

Even before Tyler retired, his immense contribution to hurling was recognised. On 2 February 1913 he was presented with a cheque for £100 by the Gaels of Limerick in recognition of his services to native games. Despite the passage of time, the name John 'Tyler' Mackey lives on in hurling lore.

A hurling selection

Jim 'Hawk' O'Brien
(Tipperary)

Seán O'Kennedy   Jack Rochford   Dan Kennedy
(Wexford)   (Kilkenny)   (Kilkenny)

Dick 'Drug' Walsh   Jim Kelleher   Tim Doody
(Kilkenny)   (Cork)   (London)

James Roynane
(Cork)

Matt Gargan   Dick Doyle
(Kilkenny)   (Kilkenny)

John 'Tyler' Mackey
(Limerick)

Paddy Brolan   Paddy Maher 'Best'   Tom Semple
(Tipperary)   (Tipperary)   (Tipperary)

Paddy D. Mehigan   Dick Doyle   Hugh Shelly
(Cork)   (Wexford)   (Tipperary)

Upon his native sward the hurler stands
To play the ancient pastime of the Gael,
And all the heroes famed of Innisfail
Are typified in him – I see the bands
Of the Craobh Ruadh applauding with their hands,
The Fianna shouting over Clui-Mail,
Oisin and Finn with eager faces pale,
Caoilte and goll are there from fairy lands.

And fierce Cúchulain comes, his Godlike face,
With yearning wild to grip in hand once more
The lithe camán and drive the hurtling ball.
In Walsh's, Kelleher's, and Semple's grace
He sees again his glorious youth of yore,
And mourns his dead compeers and Ferdia's fall.

'The Hurler' by Rev. James B. Dollard, dedicated to
'Drug' Walsh of Kilkenny, Tom Semple of Thurles
and James Kelleher of Dungourney

Jim O'Brien

Jim was known affectionately as 'The Hawk' O'Brien because of his speed of action, unerring eye and lynx-eyed performances between the posts. Though fragile of frame, he was among the outstanding net minders of his time. In his early days he hurled in Dublin and took part in many Leinster championships. He was a member of the 'Old Thurles Blues' selections, captained by Tom Semple, that won All-Ireland honours in 1906 and 1908 for Tipperary. Under the same leadership Munster honours followed in 1909 but they had to give way to Kilkenny in the final. Jim died in 1951.

Seán O'Kennedy

Seán is profiled in 'A football personality: Seán O'Kennedy (Wexford)'.

Jack Rochford

The name Jack Rochford and great full-back play are synonymous. Jack, of Tullaroan fame, was born in 1882 and died in 1953. He won seven All-Ireland hurling medals in a golden Kilkenny era from 1904 to 1913. Only once in seven All-Ireland finals did Jack's immediate opponent succeed in scoring a goal.

Dan Kennedy

Dan was another great Kilkenny player in the early years of the twentieth century. He won six All-Ireland titles between 1905 and 1913. In his last final in 1916 Tipperary denied him a seventh medal. Paddy Mehigan of Cork told how he was outplayed in the replay of the 1905 hurling final by the brilliant defensive hurling of Dan Kennedy.

Dick 'Drug' Walsh

A native of Mooncoin, Dick was born in 1878 and lived to be eighty. Always superbly fit and possessing a great sense of position, he was among the leading exponents of defensive play. He won seven Leinster titles, all of which paved the way to All-Ireland success. On three of those occasions he was captain – 1907, 1909 and 1913 – and so followed in the footsteps of Mikey Maher of Tipperary to become the second man to lead his county to three All-Ireland wins. He has, however, another honour that is his alone and will always remain so. He is the only hurler to have captained sides of seventeen-a-side (1907 and 1909) and a side of fifteen-a-side (1913) to All-Ireland glory. In 1915 he trained the Laois team that defeated Cork in the final. Benefit matches were played for 'Drug' Walsh at Waterford on Sunday 17 September 1911. In the football game Kilkenny and Waterford drew 1-3 to 0-6. In hurling, Erin's Own (Waterford) played a draw with Mooncoin, 0-3 to 1-0.

Jim Kelleher

A hurler and a horseman, Jim excelled at both. His was a household name in hurling circles long after he played his last All-Ireland final in 1912. From Dungourney in east Cork, 'Carbery' described him as 'perhaps the noblest Roman of them all' and added that in the twenty-six major matches he saw him play, he always emerged as the outstanding man of the hour. His All-Ireland titles came in 1902 as captain, and the following year under the captaincy of Steva Riordan. John T. Power, the Kilkenny goalkeeper of that era, said: 'The outstanding man of my time was Jim Kelleher.' John 'Tyler' Mackey of Limerick said that 'never as good a man came out of Cork.'

Tim Doody

Tim's inclusion is a reminder of the presence of London teams of exiles in the hurling and football finals of the early years of the twentieth century. Tim was a dual player and a native of Tournafulla, County Limerick. He was on that stalwart team of hurling exiles who, against all the odds, came within a whisker of causing a hurling sensation in the All-Ireland final of 1900 against Tipperary. In 1901, led by Jack Coughlan of Clare, he was on the team of Munster exiles that took the All-Ireland hurling crown overseas for the first and only time with a 1-5 to 0-4 win over Cork. He featured on the losing sides of 1902 and 1903, suffering a double defeat in the 1903 finals. These games took place on 12 November 1905 at Jones' Road. London hurlers lost to Cork; London footballers lost to Kerry. It may well be that Tim is the only man to have played in two All-Ireland senior finals on the same day.

James Roynane

From Dungourney and known as 'The Tall Sweeping Menace', James was a contemporary of the renowned Jim Kelleher. He played in his first All-Ireland final in 1901, when Cork went under to London.

All through the decade 1901–1910 he was a regular on the Cork teams, when the county won six provincial titles that included five in a row from 1901–1905. He won his only All-Ireland title in 1902. For some reason his name does not feature on the Cork winning team of 1903. Kilkenny came between him and All-Ireland success in 1904 and 1907. Again in 1905, a Kilkenny objection to Cork's initial All-Ireland victory resulted in a replay, which Cork lost. So having played in five of the six All-Irelands that Cork contested, his reward was one title. His last major game in the Cork jersey was the Munster final of 1910 when the Limerick team led by 'Tyler' Mackey caused one of the surprises of the year with a sensational 5-1 to 4-2 win.

Matt Gargan

Matt was a fine midfielder and a star among a galaxy of hurling stars during a golden Kilkenny era. 'Carbery' often saw him in action:

> Of good medium stature, square and very bony, with powerful shoulders and sturdy legs ... No spare flesh here – bone and sinew alone contribute to his 12 stone and a half ... he is the personification of concentrated vitality – always moving, always watchful as a cat.

Matt won six All-Ireland titles. Mick Neville of Wexford, a contemporary, singled Matt out for special mention.

Dick Doyle

Dick was one of three brothers that made the Doyles of Mooncoin famous in hurling circles. The other two were Eddie and Mick. Between them they won eighteen All-Ireland medals – Dick seven, Eddie six, Mick five (Eddie won a seventh as a sub in 1913). Dick is remembered as a great forward who always sought out a better-placed colleague. When he raced for possession he created an air of expectancy among supporters.

Tyler Mackey

'Tyler' is profiled in 'A hurling personality: 'Tyler' Mackey (Limerick).'

Paddy Brolan

A hurler of determination and indomitable spirit, Paddy was known as a gifted first-time striker of a ball. This was the style of game he played in a Tipperary forward line under the inspired leadership of their captain, Tom Semple. An Old Thurles Blues hurler, Paddy was on the All-Ireland winning teams of 1906 and 1908 that defeated Dublin – in 1908 after a draw. He was on the losing sides in 1909 and 1913, when their neighbours Kilkenny proved superior. In 1910 he played in the hurling game against Cork at Fontenoy. In an epic Munster final victory over Cork in 1906, 3-4 to 0-9, Paddy was among the stars. He was missing from Tipperary's selections of 1916 to 1918, but was back in 1919 for the Munster semi-final with Cork. It was a typical Tipperary/Cork clash – close marking, first-time pulling, hard knocks and an attitude of 'get on with the game'. Tipperary led by a goal at the three-quarter stage. 'Carbery' tells us that 'excitement grew with the rush of events, and Ballintemple Woods re-echoed Leeside cheering as the Southerners pulled up and pulled out on the whistle'. Cork won by 2-4 to 2-3. At county level Paddy called it a day after that game. He died in 1956.

Paddy Maher 'Best'

A son of Two-Mile-Borris, Paddy was a hurler and a long-distance runner. We learn the following in *Tipperary's GAA Story*:

> *... he could literally run without tiring all day and go out to beat the best with a disregard of diet and training that would appal present-day athletes ... He was a star amongst the many stars of Borris ... He was of an iron constitution and could run and did run, to many a venue many miles away – and afterwards compete there.*

For the 1908 hurling final at Athy, the Tipperary team set forth from Thurles, but to their consternation Paddy was missing. They would need him. In the Railway Shield game against Leinster he had scored eleven points in fifteen minutes. When they arrived in Athy there was Paddy finishing a hearty meal. He had cycled the whole journey. His greeting to them was simple: 'What kept ye?'

Tom Semple

A native of Thurles, Tom led by example and inspired colleagues. 'What is your fear boys while Semple is with you?' From his county debut in 1900 until he called it a day in 1912 he played in every champion-ship match. He won three All-Ireland titles – 1900, 1906 and 1908, captaining the team on the last two occasions. He was also captain in 1909 when a Dick Walsh-led Kilkenny outfit held them goalless at Cork in the All-Ireland final: Kilkenny 4-6 Tipperary 0-12. Standing 6 feet 3 inches, he was a master of ground hurling, grounders of up to 90 yards, we are told. He would lift and strike in preference to handling. 'A deer of a man and a glorious striker of a ball,' wrote 'Carbery'. Tom Semple died in April 1943. His name lives on in Semple Stadium in Thurles.

Paddy Mehigan

Paddy's overall contribution to the GAA was immense. Many of us know him as 'Carbery' – who wrote vivid accounts of hurling and football games – accounts that often left you feeling you were witnessing the action, the clash of the ash, the whirr of the sliotar, the thud of body on body. Paddy was born on St Patrick's Day 1884 in Ardfield, County Cork. He played with London in the All-Ireland final of 1902, when the exiles fell victim to his native county. On re-turn from London he joined the famous Blackrock club with whom he won hurling honours. Paddy was a member of the Cork team beaten by Kilkenny in the All-Ireland final of 1905. As a sportsman he was an all-rounder – hurler, footballer, bowl player and a first-class athlete. He died in 1965.

Dick Doyle

A potent forward and a prolific scorer, Dick captained Wexford in 1910 to All-Ireland success – their first title. They defeated Lim-erick, led by 'Tyler' Mackey, by 7-0 to 6-2. In the Leinster final against Dublin Dick accounted for 3-1 of Wexford's 3-3 total. He did even better in the final game against Limerick, scoring four of their seven goals. It is reasonable to speculate that without Dick Doyle Wexford might not have won the 1910 crown. Born in 1879, in his playing days Dick stood 5 feet 10 inches and weighed 13 stone. He died in 1946.

Hugh Shelly

An Old Thurles Blues player, Hugh took part in six All-Ireland finals with Tipperary, with a success rate of 50 per cent. Dublin were beaten in 1906 and 1908 and Kilkenny were overcome in 1916. The losses were to Kilkenny in 1909 and 1913 and Dublin in 1917. He captained Tipperary in 1911 when a substitute game was played in lieu of the All-Ireland final after Limerick conceded a walkover to Kilkenny. Hugh was also captain against Cork in the Munster final of 1912. He has been described as a skilful and talented forward who possessed a great turn of speed. All through his playing days he was a leading Tipperary forward. Hugh's hopes of further glory were dashed by Limerick in the Munster semi-final of 1918. It took two titanic contests to decide the issue. The first game finished 5-2 apiece. 'In a hectic ending to which no description could do justice, Paddy Leahy handballed the equalising goal into the net just as the referee's whistle was ready for blowing' (from *Tipperary's GAA Story*). The following scores in the replay allow the imagination to conjure up what the contest was like: half time: Limerick 2-1 Tipperary 0-1; full time: Limerick 3-2 Tipperary 2-2.

And so ended the county hurling career of a great player.

A FOOTBALL GAME:

Kerry v Kildare, 1903 All-Ireland final

It was the All-Ireland Home final of 1903. The contestants were Kerry and Kildare. It was the first time these counties had clashed at this stage of the championship. In preparation for the contest both teams underwent a most thorough training schedule – believed to have been the first such step since the championships began.

Teams were still seventeen-a-side. And the sideposts formed part of the scoring area. Kerry were represented by a Tralee Mitchels selection and Kildare by a Clane selection.

On the road to the final Kerry had the following results:

v Waterford	4-8 to 1-3	
v Clare	2-7 to 2-0	
v Cork	1-7 to 0-3	
v Mayo	2-7 to 0-4	

In the Leinster final, Kildare had a close call from Kilkenny. A drawn game led to a replay. In that second meeting, a point that gave Kildare victory was disputed and a second replay was ordered. The Kildare path from the Leinster final onwards was:

v Kilkenny   1-2 to 0-5 (a draw)
v Kilkenny   1-6 to 1-5 (point disputed)
v Kilkenny   0-9 to 0-1
v Cavan   0-8 to 0-0

It also took Cavan three games to dispose of Armagh in the Ulster final – two draws that yielded five points to both teams on each occasion and at the third attempt it was victory for Cavan by eight points to four – a victory that gave the men of Breffni a second Ulster title.

In those days the championships were running almost two years in arrears, so the final of 1903 did not take place until 23 July 1905. The venue was Tipperary, with Patrick McGrath in charge. A close contest of excellent football provided much exciting fare.

Kildare, captained by Joe Rafferty, lined out all in white. Kerry, in red jerseys with green cuffs and collars, were led by Tim O'Gorman, whose twin brother Jim was also on the team. Both counties had huge followings. A Kerry train broke down on the way and had to be replaced. Its supporters arrived when the game was in progress and added further congestion to an already capacity crowd – now estimated at between 12,000 and 15,000.

It is hard to believe that for this All-Ireland contest a rope served as a paling between spectators and the pitch. The rope, from time to time, bulged inwards as the crowd surged forward to view exciting passages of play.

There was a contrast in styles – Kerry, high fielding, firm hands, kicking and punting; Kildare, hand passing and combined movements, mixed with an accurate kicking game. Both teams played an open style. At half time the score stood Kildare 0-2 Kerry 0-1. The start of the second half was delayed as the crowd was moved back off the playing area.

With about ten minutes remaining and the score reading three points to two in Kerry's favour, Kildare launched an attack along the wing. It took them behind a line of spectators who had encroached. A movement finished with Paddy Dillon in the Kerry goal being beaten. Kildare supporters went wild. Kerry protested the goal, but to no avail. The referee allowed it, and Kildare were two points up. They quickly added another: Kildare 1-3 Kerry 0-3. The entire arena was agog. Defeat was facing Kerry but the Kingdom, through John Fitzgerald, pulled a point back. With two minutes to go, Dick Fitzgerald took a Kerry free.

The dying seconds are described by Paddy Foley in *Kerry's Football Story* (Tralee, 1945).

> *Leinster's greatest goalman Jack Fitzgerald ... held it safely, but in so doing pulled the second leg behind the line! He caught the ball and kicked clear to the wing. But the goal umpire raised the fatal green flag. Kildare disputed the score. The referee abided by the umpire's decision and allowed the goal ... Kerrymen, in the wildest abandon, rushed in over the pitch, throwing up hats and coats and hugging the players. Pandemonium ruled. The referee blew and blew the whistle unavailingly to get the ground cleared with the Kildare players and followers protesting against the score. As the referee could not get the game restarted he awarded the match to Kerry declaring the score – Kerry 1-4 Kildare 1-3.*

Central Council ordered a replay, at Cork on 27 August, with M. F. Crowe as referee. The capacity crowd of over 12,000 saw a game played at a level that matched the high standard of the previous contest. 'Carbery' takes up the story:

> *Kildare won the toss and opened brilliantly. The perfect fielding and long, accurate kicking of Cribben, Merriman and Rafferty in defence surprised spectators, whilst the artistic footwork of Losty, Conlon, Bracken and Scott in front was a revelation to those who thought Gaelic football a game of strength and force alone.*
>
> *Kerry were not to be outdone in skill, however. The O'Gorman pair were nimble wingers with great hands. Stack was a tireless ranger and director of operations. McCarthy, Kirwan and Myers kicked that new yellow ball half a field's length and in front of all was the tall, rangy scoring brain with craft and art – Dick Fitzgerald – the peerless goal getter and deadly drop-kicker, who revolutionised football attack.*

With four minutes to go, Kerry, who were having the better of the exchanges, led 0-7 to 0-4. 'Carbery' again:

The All White men, from a sweeping ball by Rafferty, tore down-
field at lightning pace. Losty on the right raced clean away, and
reached the 21 yards mark before swinging a perfect centre in.
Conlon and Kennedy pounced on it, and before Dillon realised
it, the ball was in the net for the only goal of the hour.

So they were to meet again. Kildare, it was felt, had got a lucky draw. The following day the newspapers described it as 'a sensational game' and 'as exciting a football match as ever was seen'.

The second replay was fixed for 15 October at the same venue, with the same referee. The quality of the football and the excitement of the contests had gripped the imagination. Gate receipts of £270 broke all previous records for a championship contest. The game was another thriller, despite the standard falling somewhat short of the drawn match. Heavy rain fell on the morning of the game. At half time Kerry led by three points to two and in the second half began to exert a tighter grip. They had learned more from the earlier meetings than the Lilywhites. When the Kingdom went six points to two ahead, Kildare lost their rhythm and spent the closing moments on the defensive. Kerry won by 0-8 to 0-2. Gaelic football had taken on a new meaning.

T. F. O'Sullivan in *The Story of the GAA* (Dublin, 1916) wrote:

Prominent rugby and soccer men helped to swell the receipts
and the magnificent spirit in which the match was played won
unstinted admiration ... The matches were the most sensational
played since the inception of the association and did more to
increase the funds of the Central Council and to develop Gaelic
football than any previous contests for championship honours ...
the spirit in which the games were played won the admiration
even of those who were hostile to Gaelic pastimes.

The last hurdle of the championship was cleared by Kerry at Jones' Road, Dublin on 12 November when they defeated London (Hibernians) by eleven points to three. It was Kerry's first All-Ireland football crown – sixteen years after the championships had begun. In the years ahead they would win titles in every decade and would permanently lead the field from 1946 onwards.

At a Central Council meeting on 12 November 1905 it was proposed, seconded and unanimously adopted that 'the Kildare team be presented with a set of gold medals as a souvenir of the great Home final, and in recognition of their services to the association.'

Reflecting, in later years, on those memorable encounters, Dick Fitzgerald wrote (from *Kerry's Football Story*):

> *In my long career I never remember to have seen more deter-*
> *mined games ... Football took a turn for the better about this*
> *period. I must be pardoned for claiming that this was mainly*
> *due to the memorable meetings of Kerry and Kildare. Certain it*
> *is that both counties gave football a fillip that marked, as it were,*
> *the starting point of the game as we know it today.*

A FOOTBALL PERSONALITY:

Dick Fitzgerald (Kerry)

Dick Fitzgerald from Killarney, popularly known as 'Dickeen', was a prince of footballers and a footballing strategist. One of the most colourful personalities the game has ever known, he was a player whose skills and craft were unsurpassed – a footballing genius who often screwed frees between the posts from the corner flag.

In the 1903 final against Kildare – played in 1905 – Dick, then just seventeen, tall and lanky, led the Kerry attack. With perfect feet and hands, combined with deadly marksmanship, he was destined for greatness. It was, I believe, 'Carbery' who described him as 'the tall, rangy scoring brain with craft and art – the peerless goal getter and deadly drop-kicker, who revolutionised football attack'.

Dick's next two All-Ireland medals were won in the finals of 1904 and 1909 at the expense of Dublin and Louth. Then came his turn to be a successful captain, starting in 1913 with the drawn final and replay of the Croke Memorial tournament against Louth – two games of magnificent football that attracted huge crowds and further enhanced the image of Gaelic football. For three successive years, 1913 to 1915, Dick captained Kerry in All-Ireland finals – all, remarkably, against Wexford, at that time a rising power in football.

Kerry won in 1913 by 2-2 to 0-3 and again in 1914 after a replay, 1-3 to 2-0 and then 2-3 to 0-6. Ninety-three years would pass before

Kerry were again led to successive All-Ireland victories by the same captain – Declan O'Sullivan in 2006 and 2007. It was Wexford's turn in 1915 when they won by 2-4 to 2-1 – a victory that heralded a golden era for the Model county.

Dick was now in the autumn of his footballing career and other matters took over. Owing to a dispute, Kerry withdrew from the championship of 1916. Dick became involved in the Volunteer movement and was interned in Frongoch after the Easter Rising. There, Kerry, captained by Dick, played a football game against Louth, captained by Alderman Tom Burke, Kerry winning by a point.

During a long and brilliant career Dick won five All-Ireland titles, and won Munster medals on a regular basis. Time and again he saved Kerry from defeat with his accurate shooting and expert free taking, often in pressure situations and from what appeared to be impossible angles.

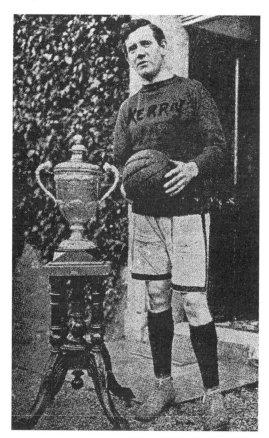

The late Dick Fitzgerald.

Dick wrote a book in 1914 titled *How to Play Gaelic Football*, which proved to be a popular production. He trained the Clare team that lost by nine points to five to Wexford in the football final of 1917.

Let us now fast forward to 1930. On Friday 26 September the Kerry footballers had completed their training and were fully fit for Sunday's All-Ireland final against Ulster champions Monaghan, who had surprisingly beaten Kildare – All-Ireland champions of 1927, 1928 and finalists in 1929 – by two points in the semi-final.

Then came the saddest of news: Dick Fitzgerald had died unexpectedly – aged forty-two. Shock and sorrow spread throughout the Kingdom. While Croke Park contemplated arrangements to honour his memory on Sunday, there were many in the Kingdom who felt the game should be called off. With time now of the essence there was frenzied activity. Eventually it was agreed the game should go ahead and that a display of sympathy and appreciation in Dublin would be a most fitting tribute.

On Monday 29 September, the day after the final in which Kerry trounced Monaghan by 3-11 to 0-2, Dick Fitzgerald was laid to rest in Killarney. The huge funeral was attended by representatives from all levels of the GAA and from the four provinces of Ireland.

Dick was educated at St Brendan's, Killarney and later at Mungret College, Limerick. There, a friendship blossomed with Phil O'Neill ('Sliabh Ruadh'), a brilliant writer. After Dick's death, Phil wrote the following poem in tribute.

Over Loch Lein, where the sad moon pales,
Rises a caoine for a Chief of the Gaels,
A leader gone from the fighting line –
A scion true of the Geraldine!
  Through the mist of years his name will gleam,
When he blazed the trail with his Kerry team,
And brought to the 'Kingdom' name and fame
In the greatest tests of the Gaelic game:
Kildare and Wexford and Louth can tell
Of his deeds, and now his requiem swell,
And tribute pay to a gallant foe,
Who played the game as we Gaels know.
  And when Ireland called when the fight was thick,
She called not in vain on our old friend Dick,

For he came with the boys who were never slack,
Who were led by Ashe and Austin Stack,
And he did his time on the cold plank bed,
When all thought Ireland's cause was dead.
  And now he's gone from the field of fame,
But thousands still shall speak his name,
And tell of his deeds on the Gaelic field
For the Irish crown and the Railway Shield.
  And whilst the Gaels the old games play,
And Kerry still may hold the sway,
We'll speak of him as a pioneer
Of the cause and the games we all hold dear,
And many a prayer will arise, I ween,
From the Gaels who knew and loved 'Dickeen'.

Killarney's GAA pitch – the magnificent Fitzgerald Stadium – is dedicated to Dick's memory.

Phil O'Neill ('Sliabh Ruadh').

A football selection

For the convenience of selecting a seventeen-a-side team, I have opted, positionally, for a second centre-half-back and a second centre-half-forward.

Paddy Dillon
(Kerry)

William Merriman   *Larry Cribben*   *Jim Brennan*
(Kildare)   (Kildare)   (Dublin)

Pierce Grace   *David Kelleher*   *Jack Grace*
(Dublin)   (Dublin)   (Dublin)

Joe *Rafferty*
(Kildare)

Austin Stack   *Mick Mehigan*
(Kerry)   (Cork)

Tim 'Thady' O'Gorman
(Kerry)

Willie Losty   *Dick Fitzgerald*   *Frank 'Joyce' Conlon*
(Kildare)   (Kerry)   (Kildare)

Willie Mackessy   *Jack Dempsey*   *Bob Quane*
(Cork)   (Dublin)   (Tipperary)

Paddy Dillon

Paddy Dillon of Killarney was the Kerry custodian at the dawn of the Kingdom's days of Gaelic football glory. He was rivalled only at the time by Kildare's Jack Fitzgerald. Paddy kept goal at a time when the scoring area from sidepost to sidepost stretched a distance of 45 feet. He was fearless and daring. He didn't go in much for fielding and catching, instead tending to either fly-kick or punch clear the incoming ball. Paddy qualified for six All-Ireland finals with the Kingdom. He was victorious in 1903 v Kildare in the Home final and London in the final; 1904 v Dublin; and 1909 v Louth. Kerry lost in 1905 to Kildare and in 1908 to Dublin in the Home final, and in 1910 they conceded a walkover to Louth. In later life Paddy lost an arm in a railway accident. A benefit match was played for him on 26 October 1919 at Croke Park between Kerry and old rivals Kildare. Victory went to the Leinster men, 1-2 to 0-3.

William Merriman

William Merriman was a teammate of Larry Cribben's. He, like Larry, was a brilliant defender – perfect fielding and long accurate kicking. He excelled in the three games of the 1903 All-Ireland final against Kerry (played in 1905). Kildare lost that final but made amends when they defeated the Kingdom in the final of 1905 (played in 1907). William played his club football with Clane.

Larry Cribben

I first heard the name Larry Cribben during my school days with the Patrician Brothers in Ballyfin, County Laois. There was a particular student, who would on occasions let out a mighty yelp – 'up for the ball Larry Cribben', with tremendous emphasis on 'up'. Larry was a member of the great Kildare team of the early years of the first decade of the last century. He hailed from the Clane club and won his first All-Ireland medal in 1905 when the Lilywhites defeated the Kingdom. He was still playing for Kildare when, under the captaincy of Larry Stanley in 1919, the county won its second All-Ireland football crown. Larry was a masterful defender, skilled at long, accurate kicking out of defence. He was born in 1880 and died in 1962 of a heart attack. He won fourteen county senior titles between hurling and football – his first in 1900 in football and his last in 1916 when he won both. Larry played with Kildare for twenty years. In the 1919 final, playing in goal against Galway, he said to his full-back: 'If "Knacker" Walsh is causing you any problems I'll go out and mark him for you.' 'Knacker' was a potent Galway forward.

Jim Brennan

Between 1901 and 1910 Dublin won five of the ten football finals. Jim Brennan played in four of those: 1902 when Tipperary in the Home final and London in the final were defeated; and the three-in-a-row of 1906, 1907 and 1908, Cork being overcome in the first two and then in 1908, Kerry in the Home final and London in the final. He played in the 1904 final when they lost to Kerry by five points to two. Dublin were beaten by Louth in the Leinster final of 1910 in a game in which Jim Brennan was outstanding. He was a member of the Keatings club. I have failed to establish if he was

Dublin born. Years later, Jim Brennan, then Séamus Ó Braonáin, became director of broadcasting in Radio Éireann. He occupied that position at the time of the broadcast by Micheál O'Hehir of the All-Ireland football final of 1947 from the Polo Grounds, New York.

David Kelleher

A native of Charleville, County Cork, David was an athlete of wonderful endurance and skill. He excelled as a hurler, footballer, oarsman and golfer and loved to attend coursing meetings. He won three football titles in a row – 1906, 1907 and 1908 – with his adopted Dublin, captaining the team in 1908. David also played in the hurling final of 1908 which was lost to Tipperary after a replay. He usually played at centre-half-back and was a member of Geraldines club.

Pierce Grace

A medical doctor by profession, Pierce Grace hailed from Tullaroan in County Kilkenny. Like his brothers Dick and Jack he excelled at Gaelic games. During his student days in Dublin he played for Dublin in the hurling final of 1908 which was lost to Tipperary after a replay. He won football titles with Dublin in 1906 and 1907. On his return to his native Kilkenny he had the honour of being a member of the county's three-in-a-row-winning hurling teams of 1911, 1912 and 1913. Pierce won four county hurling titles with Tullaroan. I believe Pierce and Frank Burke, a Kildare man who played with Dublin, to be the only two players to win more than one All-Ireland medal in both hurling and football. Pierce's brother Dick came on as a sub in the All-Ireland hurling final of 1909 and went on to win four more All-Ireland titles with Kilkenny. He played with Kilkenny until 1926. Dick was a powerful defender – in the words of Carbery, 'a master hurler and as hard as nails'.

Jack Grace

Jack Grace of Tullaroan, a brother of Pierce and Dick, went to Dublin as a young man, where he worked in the drapery business. He was an outstanding dual player and played with the Kickhams club. Fate was unkind to him on the hurling field. He lost three finals with Dublin: the 1902 Home final to Cork after a replay, in 1906 to Tipperary and 1908 again to Tipperary after a replay. He was much luckier on the football field. Dublin contested six of the ten football finals between 1901 and 1910. Jack played in them all and won five, and was captain in the years 1906 and 1907. So in total Jack played in nine All-Ireland finals. 'Carbery' played with and against Jack and rated him and Bill Mackessy of Cork as the two greatest dual players he had seen. He described Jack as 'no more than 5 foot 9 in height but he was beautifully built, twelve and a half stone of solid bone and muscle; he had the heart of a lion. He was an outstanding hurler and had few equals as wing back in his period – his ground drives off right and left were of surpassing length and his stamina seemed endless. In football he showed rare judgement, was a sound fielder and an accurate kicker.' Jack died in the prime of life in 1915.

Joe Rafferty

Joe Rafferty was the Kildare captain in the 1903 All-Ireland football final against Kerry. He led a team resplendent in their all-white kit – the Lilywhites. Joe was a great leader – he would emerge from defence with the ball and foray up the pitch to launch an attack on the opposition posts. He played with the Naas club and won his first and only All-Ireland in 1905. He was still playing with Kildare in 1915 when he captained his county in the semi-final of a Wolfe Tone Memorial game against Wexford, played at Waterford. He used to practise his skills with the staff members of Clongowes College in the evening.

Austin Stack

One of a family of eight children, Austin Stack was born at Ballymullen, Tralee on 7 December 1879. He was a law clerk by profession. Two interests dominated his life – football and politics. Austin was deeply committed to the ideals of the GAA and Fenianism; in both fields he possessed remarkable organisational ability.

He was very much to the fore in promoting football in Tralee in the early years of the twentieth century. A fine footballer, he usually playing at half-back, and won All-Ireland titles with Kerry in 1903 and 1904. In 1903 he was perceived as the organiser of the whole Kerry team, and their success was attributed to his untiring efforts. He was captain in 1904.

With his club Tralee Mitchels he won eight successive county titles and was its first secretary. He held positions at all levels in the GAA, inlcuding secretary and chairman of Kerry County Board. He was a member of the Munster Council and the Central Council and was Kerry's delegate to Congress. He was president of Kerry County Board from 1918 until his death.

As a member of the Irish Republican Brotherhood he led the movement in Kerry. He was involved in the struggle for independence and was chosen as Minister for Home Affairs in the First Dáil.

He was secretary of Sinn Fein from 1917 until his death on 27 April 1929, when he was not yet fifty. On 1 May 1932, the Tralee sports field was officially named Austin Stack Park as a tribute to his memory.

Mick Mehigan

Mick Mehigan, a brother of Paddy Mehigan ('Carbery') had a long career in the Cork football jersey. His won his only All-Ireland medal in 1911 when captaining Cork to victory over Antrim, 6-6 to 1-2. Two other great players on that Cork team were Billy Mackessy and Jerry Beckett – all three described by 'Carbery' as 'three thundering footballers'. Munster titles were won in 1906 and 1907, but on each occasion defeat to Dublin was Cork's lot in the All-Ireland final. Mick won another Munster title in 1916, following which they lost to Mayo in the All-Ireland semi-final. He must have felt a little hard done by in 1909. That year, in the Munster final in Limerick, Cork beat Kerry by 2-8 to 1-7 in a game where Kerry walked off the pitch at one stage but were persuaded to return. Following a Kerry objection, a replay took place in Cork – 'a splendid exhibition of football, fought at dazzling pace'. Two points separated two fine teams in the end. Victory went to Kerry. Mick Mehigan was left to ponder what might have been as he saw Kerry progress to victories over Mayo and Louth and All-Ireland glory.

Tim O'Gorman

More popularly known as Thady, Tim O'Gorman was born in Tralee in the late 1870s. He captained Kerry to All-Ireland honours when the county won its first football title. It was the 1903 crown, won in 1905 after three epic meetings with Kildare. Tim won a second medal in 1904 when, under the captaincy of Austin Stack, Kerry

defeated Dublin in the final. He was there again for the 1905 campaign, when Maurice McCarthy was captain. But Kildare won the day to take their first crown. Tim's twin brother, Jim, played with Kerry in the three years 1903–1905. Both were members of Tralee Mitchels club, and won several county titles, the first in 1902. Tim had a lifelong association with his club and with football.

Tim's son, Jimmy, won a minor All-Ireland in 1931 and senior titles in 1939, 1940 and 1941.

Jim's son, Michael, won a minor All-Ireland in 1933. Their nephew, Bill, won an All-Ireland medal in 1926 when Kerry beat Kildare after a replay. Bill got the equalising goal – the only goal of the game – in the drawn game.

Willie Losty and Frank 'Joyce' Conlon

Willie Losty and Frank 'Joyce' Conlon from the Clane and Roseberry clubs respectively were two of Kildare's most dangerous forwards. Losty was a prince of sharpshooters, while Conlon played a major role in the Kildare goal that took the final of 1903 to a third game. Their artistic footwork and, indeed, that of their forward colleagues was a revelation to those who thought Gaelic football a game of strength and force alone. In the 1919 final, Frank was as deadly as ever. Kildare defeated Galway by 2-5 to 0-1. Frank scored 1-2 of Kildare's total.

Dick Fitzgerald

Dick is profiled in 'A football personality: Dick Fitzgerald (Kerry)'.

Willie Mackessy

Willie Mackessy of famed Blackrock was a gifted dual player. In a career that lasted from 1901 to 1912, he played in seven All-Ireland finals – three in hurling and four in football, including the Home final of 1901 which Cork lost to Dublin. In the era 1901–1910 Dublin won five of the ten football titles and defeated Cork in the successive years of 1906 and 1907. Willie was captain in 1907. In a brilliant career, he was rewarded with only one All-Ireland medal in each code – 1903 in hurling, 1911 in football. And so he became the first player in Gaelic games to win dual honours with his native county.

Jack Dempsey

A member of successful Dublin football teams in the first decade of the twentieth century, Jack Dempsey was a Wexford man and one of the outstanding midfielders of those days. He won four Leinster titles – 1902, 1904, 1906 and 1907. All except 1904 were converted into All-Ireland titles. In 1902 Tipperary were defeated in the Home final and London in the final. Successive victories over Cork followed in 1906 and 1907. Jack was captain in 1902. He was a member of the Emmets club.

Bob Quane

Bob Quane of Aravale Rovers, a man of great footballing ability, was captain of the Tipperary football team when they set forth in quest of All-Ireland honours in 1902. So widespread was his fame that on one occasion he went to the US to assist Tipperary exiles in a match against Kerry. He also refereed a number of games. He was on the All-Ireland winning team of 1895 captained by Paddy Finn, and won a second football title in 1900 under the leadership of Jack Tobin. In that year, in the Munster championship against Limerick, Tipperary had one of their toughest games. A superb display by Bob was a major factor in Tipperary's hard-earned 2-4 to 2-1 win. And so to 1902 and high hopes – Tipperary's fourth appearance in a football final and no defeat so far. But victory was not to be. They came through in Munster with wins over Limerick and Kerry, the latter by a point in a replay. Galway fell at the semi-final hurdle. In the final – the Home final – they came up against a Dublin team represented by a Bray Emmets selection. They lost by six points to five. That defeat was avenged in 1904 when Bob led Tipperary to victory over Emmets in the Croke Cup by 2-4 to 0-4 and then clinched matters with a five points to two win over London Irish. Bob died on 5 October 1909. He was in the prime of life, in his thirties. A huge crowd came to say farewell to a footballing hero – one of the county's best – when he was laid to rest in Tipperary town.

Bob's death had an unexpected sequel. In the Munster football final of 1909 Cork beat Kerry. However, the Kingdom found reason to object. It was heard and upheld by the Munster Council, which awarded the match to Kerry. But Kerry did not want a bloodless victory. They agreed to a replay at Cork Athletic Grounds and it was decided to give the gate receipts to Bob Quane's widow.

1911–1920

Teams that participated in the
All-Ireland senior finals

COUNTY	FOOTBALL		HURLING	
	WON	LOST	WON	LOST
Antrim		2		
Clare		1	1	
Cork	1		1	3
Dublin		1	2	1
Galway		1		
Kerry	2	1		
Kildare	1			
Kilkenny			3	1
Laois			1	1
Limerick			1	
Louth	1			
Mayo		1		
Tipperary	1	1	1	2
Wexford	4	2		1

Fourteen counties participated in the senior finals.

For the first time all four provinces were represented.

The ten hurling finals involved eight counties, with seven counties successful.

The ten football finals involved eleven counties, with six counties successful.

A HURLING GAME:

Dublin v Tipperary, 1917 All-Ireland final

The hurling final of 1917 brought Dublin and Tipperary into opposition. Tipperary were represented by a Boherlahan selection, captained by the indomitable Johnny Leahy, and it included his brothers Paddy and Mick and other famous hurling names like Hugh Shelly, Stephen Hackett and their goal man, 'Skinny' O'Meara.

A Collegians selection represented Dublin. Collegians had affiliated as a club in 1914 and drew their players from UCD, the Veterinary College, St Patrick's Training College and St Enda's.

The counties had already met on three occasions in the final – 1896, 1906 and 1908. Each time victory went to the Premier county, the 1908 final going to a replay.

The Collegians selection of 1917 did not contain one Dublin-born player. There were four from Tipperary, three from Cork, three from Limerick and two from Clare – a total of twelve from Munster with Kilkenny, Laois and Kildare supplying one each.

The lineout was:

Tommy Daly
(Clare)

John Ryan (captain)   *Seán Hyde*   *P. Kennefick*
(Limerick)   (Cork)   (Cork)

Charlie Stuart   *Martin Hayes*   *Martin Hackett*
(Clare)   (Limerick)   (Tipperary)

Bob Mockler   *Seán O'Donovan*
(Tipperary)   (Cork)

Jim Cleary   *Hugh Burke*   *Tommy Moore*
(Tipperary)   (Tipperary)   (Kilkenny)

Joe Phelan   *Mick Neville*   *Frank Burke*
(Laois)   (Limerick)   (Kildare)

The paths to the final – there were no semi-finals in 1917 – were:

Tipperary:
v Kerry: a walkover
v Clare: 3-6 to 1-2 unfinished at Limerick
v Limerick: 3-4 to 3-4 (a draw)
v Limerick: 6-4 to 3-1 (replay)

The Munster final replay was 'Tyler' Mackey's last game for Limerick – who had earlier beaten Cork by 5-8 to 7-1 in 'one of the fastest and most scientific expositions of hurling witnessed in Limerick for a long time' (from *The Mackey Story* by Séamus Ó Ceallaigh and Seán Murphy [Limerick, 1982]). And yet, despite such praise for the standard of hurling in evidence in the province, John Ryan, the Dublin captain and a native of Caherline in east Limerick, came away from the Munster final replay convinced that his team would succeed against Tipperary. Proof, perhaps, that victory is often governed as much by a state of mind as anything else.

Dublin's path to the final:
v Meath: a draw in the first round but I cannot find any reference
             to the game
v Offaly: 3-6 to 3-1
v Kilkenny: 5-1 to 4-0

Writing on the Leinster final, 'Vigilant' said:

> *Dublin from the very start showed superior tactics in passing the ball and in every movement and motion that makes for combined play, and in speed they were also the superior side.*

The All-Ireland final was played at Croke Park on 28 October before an attendance of 12,000. Weather conditions were good. Dublin were in search of a second title and their first since 1889, when they were captained by a Tipperary man, Nicholas O'Shea. Tipperary were seeking a tenth All-Ireland hurling crown. They were the reigning All-Ireland champions and favourites to retain their title. They had in their lineout eleven of the winning team of 1916.

Four Tipperary men lined out with the Metropolitans against

their native county – Bob Mockler, a prince of midfielders, Jim
Cleary, Hugh Burke and Martin Hackett.

The Hackett brothers would figure on opposite sides – Stephen
with his native Tipperary, Martin with his adopted Dublin. So no
matter what happened, the Hackett family was assured of a medal.

Full-forward on the Dublin team was Mick Neville, a native of
Kilfinny, County Limerick, who features in *A hurling personality:
Mick Neville* (Limerick and Dublin). I met his son, Fr Ronnie, a
short while before he celebrated the golden jubilee of his ordination
on 31 May 2008. Fr Ronnie was one of a family of four boys – three
of whom became priests. There was one girl, Eithne, a prominent
camogie player at UCD. Little wonder – her father's daughter, who
learned to hurl with her brothers in the field at home.

By way of preparation for the 1917 final, Dublin had undertaken
some special training – scientific one might say, when measured
against the traditional approach of the times. The game opened
at lightning pace, Dublin taking a point lead. They then lost their
centre-forward, Hugh Burke, with a broken collarbone. He was
replaced by Brendan Considine, who had been omitted from the
original selection because of training sessions missed. He was
a very experienced and talented young player who had won an
All-Ireland title with Clare in 1914. Dublin continued to attack,
found the net twice in quick succession, and a bewildered Tipperary found themselves 2-2 in arrears before they raised a flag. But
they did rally and by half time had narrowed the gap: Dublin 2-2
Tipperary 2-0.

In the second half Dublin defended the railway goal and faced the
sun. Tipperary cut the lead to one point. Inspired by their captain,
John Ryan, a powerfully built man of 6 feet 3 inches, Seán Hyde,
who had played for Cork in the 1915 final against Laois, and Tommy
Daly in magnificent form in goal, who had won a junior All-Ireland
medal with Clare in 1914, the Dublin defence stood firm.

Then suddenly, as in the first half, Dublin enjoyed a purple patch.
Not once, nor twice, but three times they found the net. Their supporters were ecstatic. Tipperary were reeling. But not for long. Back
they fought. It was now do or die. They banged in two goals and
sent over a point. But it wasn't enough. Willie Walsh of Waterford
blew full time. The scoreboard read Dublin 5-4 Tipperary 4-2. As
'Sliabh Ruadh' noted: 'Tipperary, last year's champions (1916), suffered a sensational defeat after a sensational game.'

After the 1916 final, Sim Walton, the Kilkenny captain, congratulating Johnny Leahy on Tipperary's victory, said: 'We were the better hurlers', to which Johnny replied: 'We were the better men.'

After the loss to Dublin, and for many days hence, Johnny Leahy was left to ponder how Tipperary lost the game. Even in his final days as he drifted in and out of consciousness, he was heard to mutter about the 1917 All-Ireland hurling final that they had let slip from their grasp.

A HURLING PERSONALITY:

Mick Neville (Limerick and Dublin)

The contents of this article were made known to me when I met Mick's son, Fr Ronnie.

Mick Neville was born in the parish of Croagh-Kilfinny on 14 February 1891. It was a hurling stronghold and during Mick's infant years a love of hurling and GAA affairs were fostered within him.

Mick was one of a family of eleven – six girls (four of whom became Little Sisters of the Poor) and five boys. He was in his early teens when he went to Dublin to serve his time in the pub business and learn the trade. He took with him his love of hurling. Initially, he played with the Commercials club and when that club disbanded he joined Faughs.

For boys like Mick, accommodation was provided over the bar, with a housekeeper coming in to make their meals. The first bar Mick worked in was in Baggot Street, and he often recalled his first Christmas Day there. The housekeeper came and prepared the dinner, left it on the fire and then went home. The owner, it seems, must have lived elsewhere. Mick never felt so lonely. He walked the streets alone, and crying. Fr Ronnie reckons that would have been Christmas 1906 or 1907.

In 1910 at the age of nineteen he won his first county title with Faughs; he won his seventh in 1922. From the day Mick joined the Faughs club he grew in stature as a hurler and it was not long until his talents were noted by the county selectors. By 1913 he was an automatic choice on the Dublin team, having played his first senior inter-county game a few years earlier against an American touring team.

Getting time off for training was next to impossible. Indeed, in those days players were not allowed to take their hurleys or togs into their place of employment. If you got an injury that required stitching or medical attention you dropped into the Mater on the way home after the game and went back to your job in the bar that night. On one occasion, following a hard game at Croke Park, Mick returned to his place of work in Parliament Street with a plaster over one eye. He was told to get from behind the counter until the plaster was off. He was so offended he never went back. He went and stayed with Tommy Moore, a Kilkenny man who was a colleague on the Dublin hurling team, and probably worked for Tommy for the rest of his time in Dublin.

Mick encountered many of the greats of those days and friendships blossomed. There was Bob Mockler of Tipperary, a brilliant midfielder – a bread-van driver with Bolands Bakery. Fr Ronnie said that Bob sent them a Christmas cake every year and used to visit them for a few days in Kilfinny.

There was Brendan Considine of Clare, a talented hurler and footballer. Fr Ronnie remembers going with his father to meet Brendan in Harcourt Street when he was chairman of the ACC to get a loan for a silage barn and feeder – which they did.

'Builder' Walsh from Kilkenny, an outstanding wing-back, worked for the Customs. When he was in charge, in later years, of custom affairs at Foynes at the time of the clippers, he visited Mick at Kilfinny and invited the entire family to Foynes to view a clipper.

Another colleague was Harry Boland, who hurled with Faughs and was secretary of Dublin County Board. He also played many games with Dublin. Harry won fame, not only in the GAA world but also in the field of political activity.

Mick had tremendous admiration for that great Kilkenny fullback Jack Rochford – one of the cleverest he met. Two other defenders he held in very high regard were Connie Sheehan of Cork and Seán O'Kennedy of Wexford.

Johnny Ryan of Tipperary – not to be confused with John Ryan of east Limerick, the Dublin captain of 1917, or Johnny Ryan of Moycarkey of Tipperary fame in the 1930s and early 1940s – was Mick's closest friend during his days in Dublin. Johnny set up his own pub in Cathedral Street near the Pro-Cathedral, off O'Connell Street. He was a brilliant hurler and played a major role in Dublin's All-Ireland victory over Cork in 1920.

Mick met many times with that sterling Cork defender, Seán Óg Murphy. The duels between them were as famous as those that followed between Seán Óg and Martin Kennedy of Tipperary. Mick was a strong, sturdy full-forward, who indulged in first-time ground hurling and overhead striking to great effect.

He played in five All-Ireland finals:

1917 when Dublin beat Tipperary

1919 when Dublin lost to Cork

1920 when Dublin avenged the 1919 defeat

1921 when Dublin lost to his native Limerick

1923, of which more anon.

By 1923 Mick had returned to Limerick and purchased a pub in Kilfinny. Now for the first time he was eligible to play for his own county. It was an era before the 'declaration rule' came into being. Mick looked forward to the championship and the prospect of proudly wearing the green and white jersey of Limerick.

Kerry were well beaten in the first round of the Munster championship in July at Tralee. Cork were overcome at Thurles in October in the semi-final and Tipperary were defeated in the provincial final at Cork Athletic Grounds in March 1924. Mick had won a coveted Munster medal.

Donegal fell at the All-Ireland semi-final stage in late April. It was in this game that players wore numbers on their jerseys for the first time. In the other semi-final Galway accounted for Kilkenny, reigning All-Ireland champions. Of all the All-Ireland finals that Mick played in, this was the one that meant most to him. It would be a dream come true – victory with his native Limerick. The 1923 final with Galway was not played until 14 September 1924. Limerick were firm favourites. Absent from the Limerick lineout, however, was star goalkeeper Mick Murphy. His loss proved too much. A fine Galway team won by 7-3 to 4-5.

Mick won four Leinster titles and two All-Ireland medals with Dublin and one Munster title with Limerick, together with Thomond Feis and other tournament successes. Following retirement, Mick became treasurer of the West Limerick GAA Board in 1924 – a position he held until 1948. He was a county senior selector in the 1930s and 1940s, and was the Limerick delegate to the annual GAA Congress at Easter. Mick also found time to referee many county championship matches.

Mick died on 12 September 1973, ten days after Limerick won their seventh and, so far, last All-Ireland senior hurling crown.

Mick Neville.

HURLING PERSONALITIES:

The Doyles of Mooncoin (Kilkenny)

Where the thrush and the robin their sweet notes entwine,
On the banks of the Suir that flows down by Mooncoin.

In Dournane, in the parish of Mooncoin on the River Suir in south Kilkenny, lived a Doyle family in the border years of the nineteenth and twentieth centuries. By present-day standards Ellen (nee Dunphy) and William had quite a large family – six boys and three girls.

There were Tom, Andy and Jim. Andy studied in the US for the priesthood, was ordained there and served in the ministry in Minnesota. Jim was ordained in St Kieran's, Kilkenny, on 10 June 1923 for the American mission. He died in Los Angeles, California, on 25 October 1950, aged fifty-three. His family brought him home for burial.

There were Katie, Johanna and Ellen. Katie joined her brother Fr Andy in Minnesota in 1921 and became his housekeeper. In her young days she was a talented singer and step dancer. During her time in Minnesota she helped organise the St Patrick's Day parade. She returned home in 1950.

There were Dick, Eddie and Mick – a hurling trinity, hardy sons of the soil, who between them captured nineteen All-Ireland hurling medals – the largest collection of All-Ireland senior hurling medals won by any household. It is worth noting, however, that the Graces of Tullaroan were not far behind with a collection of fifteen that included football and hurling medals; Jack, five in football; Pierce, two in football and three in hurling; Dick, five in hurling.

The Doyle brothers of Mooncoin collectively made the Doyle name famous. Despite the passage of time, 'The Doyles of Mooncoin' remain synonymous with hurling greatness.

I spent a few very enjoyable hours in the company of Seán Hogan (son of Ellen and nephew of the Doyles) and his sister-in-law Mary and learned much about the Doyles of Mooncoin.

The Doyles were born into a hurling atmosphere that permeated the very soil and air of their native parish. The Mooncoin club was established in 1886. A Master O'Neill, who taught in the local national school, was a driving force and inspirational figure in promoting hurling among his pupils.

Hard work on the home farm, and other physical labour – under a tendering system the Doyles maintained the road between Dournane and Mooncoin and preparatory work for this involved quarrying stone: hard, physical sinew-building work – moulded the Doyle brothers into fit, durable athletes who could readily cope with the rigours of an hour's exchanges and exertions on the hurling field.

They made their own hurleys from black sally which they cut on the Waterford side of the river. One of those hurleys – used in 1913 – survives. I had the honour of holding it.

Dick, who showed exceptional promise from an early age, played for his province at the age of seventeen in a Railway Shield game at Carrick-on-Suir, before donning the Kilkenny jersey. He had travelled to the match as a spectator and was pressed into action when a number of the Leinster players failed to turn up. Dick was a courageous attacker and a player who believed firmly in combined effort. He generated an air of expectancy in supporters, because whenever he moved to the ball he usually succeeded in gaining possession and turning that possession to team advantage. In the

The Doyle family of Dournane. *Standing (l–r)*: Cathy, Tom, Neddy, Dick, Mike; *seated*: Johanna, Fr Andy, Ellen (mother), Fr Jim, Ellie.

physical exchanges of those days Dick was rarely tumbled. Indeed, he is credited by John T. Power of Piltown, himself a fine specimen of manhood, of being the only player to have taken him off his feet. Dick played his last game for Kilkenny in the Leinster final of 1919 – lost to Dublin by 1-5 to 1-2.

While Dick usually played on the right-wing of attack, his brother Mick played on the left. Mick was of lighter build. He was very skilful, classy, stylish and possessed many delicate and deft touches. His forte was doubling on the overhead ball – something he would have practised time and again in the local playing field.

Eddie's talents lay in defensive play – mainly in the half-back line. He played a more robust game than his brothers and always marked his man tightly – a trim, fit, solidly built athlete weighing 11½ stone.

Dick, generally regarded as the best of the three, won his seven All-Ireland medals in 1904, 1905, 1907, 1909, 1911, 1912 and 1913. Eddie won his medals in the same years except that in 1913 he came on as a sub. In 1913 teams were reduced from seventeen to fifteen-a-side and the position in defence normally occupied by Eddie no longer existed. Eddie loved to proclaim that he never played in a losing All-Ireland final team. In saying this, he chose to discount the Home final of 1903 when he was on the Kilkenny side trounced 8-9 to 0-8 by Cork. Mick won five medals – the same years as Dick and Eddie, apart from 1904 and 1905.

The 1904 All-Ireland final was played at Deerpark, Carrick-on-Suir, on 24 June 1906. It was Kilkenny's first title – a sweet one-point victory over Cork. A plaque at the entrance to the field in Carrick-on-Suir commemorates the occasion. The story is told that the train driver and fireman who were in charge of the train that brought the Kilkenny supporters to the game detached the engine, drove it along the track and stopped at the pitch in Deerpark. On each occasion that Kilkenny scored, they let off a loud whistle. When Cork scored they let off steam.

In 2004, the centenary of that All-Ireland victory, a special award was issued in appreciation of the feats of Eddie, at the Lory Meagher Heritage Centre.

In the 1905 All-Ireland final replay against Cork – played on 30 June 1907 at Dungarvan, before 10,000 spectators – in which Dick and Eddie played, their brother Fr Andy, who had arrived home that morning on holiday from Minnesota, travelled direct to the game and threw in the ball. A neighbour of the Doyle family was on the way home after the pubs had closed in Mooncoin. He knocked on the window and said: 'Doyle, are you there? The boys won – and Andy is home from America, he threw in the ball.'

Their collection of medals also included tournament successes, county titles and Leinster championships. They might well have won more All-Ireland titles. In 1910, a dispute within the county saw the Doyles refusing to line out for the county team and Kilkenny failed to advance. The Tullaroan players were absent in 1906. Kilkenny were ruled out of the championship in 1908 because of a dispute over the Railway Shield trophy. In 1916, further friction resulted in the Doyles and the great Jack Rochford not lining out in the final against Tipperary.

Hurley used in the 1913 All-Ireland final.

Another cherished success was the winning of the Railway Shield. Shields for hurling and football were put up by the Great Southern and Western Railway company in 1905. It was an inter-provincial competition, and the first to win it twice in succession or three times in all retained it. When Leinster and Munster met at Kilkenny on 19 July 1908 both had already won it twice, so the winner would retain the shield. The game attracted a crowd of 15,000. Leinster were represented by fifteen Kilkenny men, including the three Doyles, Mick Cummins from Wexford and Bob O'Keeffe from Laois. The game, refereed by Tom Irwin of Cork, was won by Leinster by 0-14 to 2-5, with Dick and Mick Doyle contributing to the Leinster tally.

Inter-Provincial Contests 1905 – 1908

The Railway Shields

The Railway Shield won by Leinster in 1908

Because Kilkenny players made up the bulk of the team, the Noresiders were given possession of the shield. Today, it is proudly displayed in Kilkenny City Hall. 'Drug' Walsh of Kilkenny captained the team. Fr James Dollard, home from Canada, threw in the ball. It was presented to him at the end, and he took it back to Canada as a souvenir.

The Doyles always played well. They were shining stars in a golden Kilkenny era that produced several immensely talented hurlers. But if one were to select one particular occasion when all three played superbly, it would have to be the 1909 hurling final against Tipperary, played on 12 December at the Cork Athletic Grounds. Kilkenny led at half time by ten points – 3-4 to 0-3. At the final whistle, in a famous victory, Kilkenny were six points to the good – 4-6 to 0-12.

Ten of that victorious team hailed from Mooncoin. They are worth remembering: Dick Walsh, Jim Dunphy, the three Doyles, Joe Delahunty, Jim Ryan, Dick Doherty, Jimmy Kelly and Bill Henebery, who got three of the four goals.

By the end of the decade the careers of the Doyles at all levels had ended. They left behind them an indelible imprint. The Doyles of Mooncoin – the hurling brothers, Dick, Eddie and Mick – will forever rank with the immortals of the great and ancient game.

A hurling selection

Andy Fitzgerald
(Cork)

'Wedger' Meagher   Connie Sheehan   Paddy McInerney
(Tipperary)   (Cork)   (Limerick)

Amby Power   Willie Hough   Tom Finlay
(Clare)   (Limerick)   (Laois)

Tim Nagle   Bob Mockler
(Cork)   (Tipperary and Dublin)

Mick Doyle   Jimmy Murphy   Ned McEvoy
(Kilkenny)   (Tipperary)   (Laois)

Brendan Considine Sim Walton Jimmy 'Major' Kennedy
(Clare)   (Kilkenny)   (Cork)

Andy Fitzgerald

The mighty Andy of the famed Blackrock club, among the best goal men of his time, was much admired by 'Tyler' Mackey of Limerick who, no doubt, sent him a few testing shots from time to time. Andy was quick and confident. But even Homer was known to nod; and so did Andy. He must have had occasional nightmares about the easily stoppable ball he nonchalantly pulled on in the All-Ireland final of 1912 against Kilkenny. It hit a rut and hopped just over his goal line. Cork lost an All-Ireland they might well have won 2-1 to 1-3. Nine years had elapsed since their previous win. It would be seven more before their next title.

Patrick Meagher

Known to all hurling followers as 'Wedger', Patrick Meagher will always be associated with the Toomevara 'Greyhounds' – a team of hurlers from the little village in north Tipperary. Fleet of foot, this team in 1913 seemed destined for the highest honours. 'Wedger', playing at right corner back, captained Tipperary with a Toomevara selection that year. They defeated the might of Boherlahan in the Tipperary championship and swept through Kilkenny in the Croke Memorial final. After disposing of Waterford, Clare and

Cork in the Munster campaign, an All-Ireland title beckoned, a first since 1908. However, a row broke out between the Tipperary County Board and the GAA authorities concerning the distribution of Croke Memorial funds, and Toomevara were asked not to play Kilkenny in the All-Ireland final. Having initially gone along with the County Board request, they later changed their mind and travelled; but perhaps not in the best state of mind. They lost a brilliant final, 'the fastest hurling final that we have ever witnessed', according to the *Freeman's Journal*. 'Wedger' was 'on the run' for a period during the struggle for independence. He was caught and imprisoned, and his health suffered. When he retired from hurling he became the Tipperary county secretary. He emigrated to America in 1927 having accompanied the Tipperary hurlers on their tour of the US the previous year.

Connie Sheehan

Connie Sheehan of the Redmonds club was one of the finest full-backs of his day. His first game for Cork was in 1910 against Limerick at Tralee in the Munster championship. He played for his county for a dozen years after that. 'With muscles brown, although you are growing old and frail, it is seldom you let Cork go down.' Connie was captain in 1915 when Cork lost the All-Ireland final to Laois.

Paddy McInerney

Paddy McInerney was born in County Clare in 1895. It was, however, in the Young Ireland (County Limerick) and Limerick jerseys that he achieved hurling fame. He won All-Ireland titles in 1918 and 1921 and was captain in 1923 when Galway defeated Limerick in the final. He ranked with the finest defenders of his day and was a great believer in ground hurling – getting to the ball first and despatching it outfield 50 or 60 yards or even more. He took the emigrant ship to America on 19 September 1925 and settled in New Mexico where he died in 1983 without ever losing his love for hurling or homeland.

Amby Power

Amby Power was twenty-seven when he was appointed captain of the Clare team in 1914. It was a team of strong, well-built men, many of them over 6 feet, including Amby, a native of Quin, who

stood at 6 feet 2 inches and weighed around 13 stone. Clare's performances in Munster finals up to then were:
1888 v Cork – game never played
1889 v Kerry – a walkover
1899 v Tipperary – lost by 5-16 to 0-8.
1901 v Cork – lost by 3-10 to 2-6.

For the Munster semi-final of 1914 against Limerick at Mallow, Clare did special training at Lahinch and Quin under the guidance of Jim Hehir, father of Micheál of magical broadcasting voice. It paid dividends. They disposed of the Limerick challenge, a team of considerable talent at the time; they had already defeated Kerry. Clare now faced Cork at Thurles before an attendance of about 12,000 in the Munster final. Tom Semple, of Tipperary hurling fame, was in charge of the whistle. Clare lasted the pace better in a keen, close contest that ended in a welter of excitement and a one point win – Clare 3-2 Cork 3-1. On 18 October at Croke Park, Amby made hurling history when he led Clare to All-Ireland victory over Laois by 5-1 to 1-0. His brother Joe shared in that triumph. Amby died on 23 February 1960.

Willie Hough

Willie Hough came from the parish of Monagea in west Limerick. In the GAA world he was in many respects a man apart – hurler, footballer, referee, delegate, administrator and office holder. His contribution to the association was immense. His county hurling career began in 1913 when he played with Waterford while a student at De La Salle College in Waterford. From 1915 he wore the Limerick jersey with distinction for a dozen years. 'Carbery' described him as 'a regular Hercules of a man'. He was a great centre-half-back and a master of the ground stroke – a neat, clean, crisp striker of perfect timing, a product of regular practice. With his wing men, Jack Keane and Dinny Lanigan, he formed a half-back line of such defensive prowess that it became known as the Hindenburg Line. Willie won All-Ireland titles in 1918 when he was captain and again in 1921. He lost in 1923 when Galway defeated Limerick. *Rugadh é i 1892 agus d'éag sé i 1976.*

Tom Finlay

Tom Finlay was only seventeen when he played in the All-Ireland final of 1914 against Clare. That year in the Leinster final against Kilkenny Tom was given an inter-county hurling 'baptism of fire', marking the highly talented Matt Gargan. It was Tom who got the last-minute goal that dethroned the Noresiders. A year later at wing-back he played one of his finest games in the Laois colours in a career that lasted over fifteen years. Victory over Cork in 1915 was special – the Rebel men had household names in Connie Sheehan, Seán Hyde, Mick Byrne, 'Major' Kennedy, Tim Nagle and Seán Óg Murphy. Earlier in the Leinster championship, Laois had for the second year in a row defeated Kilkenny, Laois playing 'a masterful game right through the hour' ('Sliabh Rua'). Kilkenny too had household names – Sim Walton, Dick Grace, Pat Clohosey, Dan Kennedy, Jack Rochford and John T. Power. Tom was a native of Clough, Ballygeehan, and a product of St Kieran's College in Kilkenny, where his hurling skills were perfected. He won his second All-Ireland with Dublin in 1924 and was chosen at right-corner-back on the Laois Team of the Millennium. As well as being a first-class hurler, Tom was also a great horseman. He was a member of the army jumping team that represented Ireland in the years 1928 to 1935.

Bob Mockler

Bob Mockler was a native of Horse and Jockey. In a career that lasted seventeen years, Bob was among the outstanding midfielders of his time. He was strong and unerring under the falling ball and this, coupled with a drive of great length, made him a masterful performer at midfield. Bob played with his native Tipperary in the 1909 hurling final which was lost to Kilkenny. He was on the losing side again in 1913 when Kilkenny again proved superior. By 1915 Bob was residing in Dublin and playing with the Faughs club and the Dublin team. Laois defeated them in the Leinster final of 1915. Bob won his first All-Ireland medal when Dublin defeated Tipperary in the 1917 final. He played in four more All-Ireland finals. He was on the losing sides of 1919 and 1921 (when he was captain) to

Cork and Limerick respectively. He also captained the 1920 Dublin team and avenged the loss of the previous year to Cork. Bob won his third All-Ireland title in 1924 when the Metropolitans defeated reigning All-Ireland champions Galway. That victory brought the curtain down on Bob's inter-county hurling career.

Tim Nagle

Tim Nagle hurled with the St Mary's club. A blacksmith by profession, he was, it is fair to say, as strong as a horse. A powerful midfielder, he had some hectic exchanges with 'Tyler' Mackey of Limerick. Egan Clancy of the Limerick team of those days recalled a June day in 1911 when Dungourney and Castleconnell were invited by the Killarney Feis Committee to play for a set of gold medals. Before the game, the great Jim Kelleher of Dungourney turned to Egan and said: 'I want to introduce you to Timmy Nagle, the lad that's going to spike Tyler's guns today. Watch his style. He is very fast and snappy. This is his first inter-county game'. Ever afterwards when the two lined out on opposite sides, spectators would say: 'Look out for the exchanges between Nagle and Tyler'. The day the Croke Memorial foundation stone was laid in Thurles on 17 March 1920, Cork and Tipperary played a hurling game and Tim was honoured with the Cork captaincy. It was one of Tim's last games with Cork.

Mick Doyle

Mick is profiled in 'Hurling Personalities: The Doyles of Mooncoin'.

Jimmy Murphy

Jimmy Murphy was a forward on the Tipperary team of 1913 that lost the All-Ireland final to Kilkenny. In the 1916 final he won his only All-Ireland medal, when the same counties contested the final. That game was played on 21 January 1917. It was around that time that Jimmy went to Dublin to take up employment. Dublin hurling in those days was backboned by players from the country and working in the city. Jimmy played with the Faughs club and was on the Dublin team that beat Kilkenny for the provincial crown of 1917. There were no All-Ireland semi-finals that year and the finalists were Leinster champions Dublin and Munster champions Tipperary. Jimmy could not bring himself to play against his native Tipperary, and it cost him an All-Ireland medal. And in Tipperary it was generally felt that his absence from their forward line may have cost the county the hurling title. Dublin won by 5-4 to 4-2. Two of his contemporaries, Dinny Lanigan of Limerick and Tommy Moore of Kilkenny, regarded Jimmy as one of the best forwards at the time. Dinny said Jimmy was 'a centre-forward who would cut through an iron gate'. Jimmy Murphy – 'the demon from Horse and Jockey'.

Ned McEvoy

Ned McEvoy played in the All-Ireland finals of 1914 and 1915 – losing to a fine Clare outfit in 1914 and springing a major surprise by mastering a legendary Cork team in 1915. Ned played at centre-field with the Laois captain Jack Finlay in the 1915 success. But he was also a fine forward. This was confirmed to me by one of the great men of hurling, Pa 'Fowler' McInerney, who was adorned by the jerseys of Clare, Dublin, Munster and Leinster. 'Fowler' remembered Ned as one of the great players he hurled against – one of the many.

Brendan Considine

Brendan Considine – hurler, footballer, rugby player and boxer – came from a great Clare sporting family. He was also involved in the War of Independence. In 1914, aged just seventeen, he won

Brendan Considine (right) and a professor at St Flannan's College (left) with Tull Considine (behind). This picture was taken while Brendan was 'on the run'.

an All-Ireland hurling title with Clare when Laois were defeated. Brendan played at right-full-forward in that game. The same year he also played with the Clare senior football team against Kerry. As a banker, he found himself stationed in different counties. He was on the Dublin hurling team of 1919, beaten by Cork in the final. He gave an outstanding display of football for Dublin in the Leinster final of 1919 when going under by a solitary point to Kildare, 1-3 to 1-2. Brendan gave further evidence of his footballing prowess in the replayed Leinster final of 1921 at Croke Park on 18 September when he excelled with Dublin in their 3-3 to 1-2 win over Kildare. He lined out for Cork in the Munster hurling final of 1920, a game played at Cork Athletic Grounds on 2 April 1922 when Limerick were defeated. He wore the Waterford colours in 1925. At the Cork Athletic Grounds in 1930, he played his last game for Clare in the Munster final defeat to Tipperary. Brendan died suddenly in December 1983 aged eighty-seven.

Sim Walton

Sim Walton of Tullaroan had two sporting loves – hurling and greyhounds – and had success in both. Known as 'Little Sim' on the hurling field, he was a supreme performer, operating at either centre-half or full-forward. He gained vast experience and skill by playing on veteran defender Pat 'Fox' Maher in training sessions at the local pitch. Sim was a man of medium build and weighed around 11 stone. He was one of four Kilkenny men who, in the space of ten years, won seven All-Ireland hurling medals – a feat that still stands and may never again be equalled. He was captain in 1911 when Kilkenny got a walkover from Limerick, in 1912 when Cork had to give second best, and again in 1916 when he came within ten minutes of winning an eighth All-Ireland medal. However, a great Tipperary rally dashed his hopes. He was eighty-six when he died in 1966.

Jimmy Kennedy

Better known to hurling folk as 'Major' Kennedy, Jimmy was a potent hurling forward with Carrigtohill and Cork, in a hurling career that lasted sixteen years. In 1912 he scored a famous goal for Cork – their only score of the second half and the last puck of the game – in a Munster championship match with Limerick at Waterford. This is how 'Sliabh Ruadh' described the goal: 'Leading by a point coming on to time, Limerick fought like demons. Then Byrne (Mick) of Sarsfields pulled at a wing ball, up to Kennefick (Dan). The latter crossed to Kennedy of Carrigtwohill and the Limerick citadel fell.' Jimmy won Munster medals in 1912, 1915, 1919 and 1920, and also went on to contest the All-Ireland finals of those years. He won his only All-Ireland title in 1919, when he was captain and Dublin were defeated. In the other finals, Cork were beaten by Kilkenny (1912), Laois (1915) and Dublin (1920). We read of Jimmy lining out with Cork teams in 1926 and 1927, but he did not play in the Munster or All-Ireland finals of those years – he did, however, play in the first game of the 1926 Munster final.

A FOOTBALL GAME:

Kerry v Louth, 1913 Croke Memorial Fund final

The Croke Memorial football final – the culmination of a series of hurling and football tournament games first mooted in early 1910 with a view to erecting a suitable memorial to Archbishop Croke, first patron of the GAA – which took place between Kerry and Louth on 4 May 1913, ended in a draw and was replayed on 29 June. Both games were played at Jones' Road, in ideal weather conditions, and both were epic contests. They further enhanced the image of Gaelic football and gave impetus to its potential as a thrilling spectacle. Not since the days of the memorable Kerry/Kildare games had such exhibitions of Gaelic football been seen.

A brief glance at the background will set the scene. Kerry and Louth contested the All-Ireland final of 1909, which Kerry won by 1-9 to 0-6. Louth became All-Ireland champions in 1910 as a result of a walkover from Kerry. Louth, again, won the title in 1912 with a win over Antrim. So when both teams met in the Croke Memorial final there was a lot of honour at stake. And Louth were still reigning All-Ireland champions.

Letters and comments in the media prior to the game, by supporters of the rival camps, gave an added attraction and spice to the coming contest. There was huge interest. Excursion trains ran from all over the country and for the first time trains ran from Dingle and Cahersiveen. Many could not gain admission and gates were locked well before the throw-in. The attendance was estimated at about 26,000, for the first football match with the numbers on each team reduced from seventeen to fifteen. In the re-arranged lineout, Louth played with two full-backs and an extra forward. Kerry lined out as per the modern game.

There was a contrast in styles too. Louth played a short game of ground passes, while Kerry played high fielding and long kicking. The play dazzled; spectators marvelled. A rousing first half saw scores level at half time: Louth 1-0 Kerry 0-3. Thrills continued throughout the second half, and with time running out Louth got an equalising point. The game ended Louth 1-1 Kerry 0-4. Gate receipts yielded a record £750.

Now to the replay, with Jack McCarthy of Cork again in charge. The date was 29 June; the venue Jones' Road, despite the Munster counties wanting a southern venue so as to facilitate their follow-ers. The 'paper talk' started again and gained momentum when word reached the Kingdom that the Belfast Celtic association club had granted leave of duty to George Blessington, an old Scottish international soccer player, and James Booth to coach and train the Louth team. Kerry took to training at Tralee and Killarney. Subscriptions poured in from home and abroad.

On the day of the game, Dublin never saw such an 'invasion'. The ground was packed with an estimated 50,000 people; thousands were refused admission. Gates receipts hit a new high at £1,183. Louth played 'soccer' style – short, snappy ground passes. Kerry played the aerial game – reach for the sky, field high, followed by a long delivery. A thrilling first half saw the teams level: Kerry 1-0 Louth 0-3.

On resumption, Louth won a free – the first of the game – and pointed for the lead. Kerry responded to tie matters again. Then there followed a spell of 'superb, thrilling football, scrupulously clean, that roused the spectators to a frenzy. The cheers were deaf-ening ... A great match, singularly free from fouls and providing what was probably the finest game of Gaelic football ever played'.

Kerry launched an attack down the wing; the ball was sent diagonally across the posts. John Skinner, sprinting in, met the ball in his stride and a grounder rattled the net. Pandemonium ensued among the Kerry supporters. Louth showed signs of tiring, but added another point. Kerry, however, stayed the pace better and added the remaining scores. A memorable struggle ended Kerry 2-4 to 0-5.

Comments on the game are interesting:

A classic exhibition of Gaelic football in which the finer features of the game were displayed to advantage in spite of the sweltering heat ('Sliabh Ruadh')

The crowd was simply enormous ... The 'wee county' were done with in the final ten minutes and Kerry won the greatest encounter ever witnessed at the headquarters of the Gael (*Irish Independent*)

The game was a great triumph for Kerry football methods. They have evolved an effective and often attractive style of catch and swing and kick ... It was a triumph for the GAA, but more than all a triumph on account of the exemplary behaviour of all the contributing units – officials, spectators and players ('Carbery').

In Kerry bonfires blazed throughout the county. Bands paraded. Messages of congratulations poured in from overseas and from home – *ó cian agus ó comhgar*. And many Kerry poets and bards sat down and composed poems and songs to celebrate a famous, and never to be forgotten, victory.

A FOOTBALL PERSONALITY:

Seán O'Kennedy (Wexford)

Seán O'Kennedy was a native of the Barrow-side town of New Ross, County Wexford. He excelled as an oarsman, a hurler and a footballer. He was a fine referee too and held many official positions in the GAA. He was one of the county's finest ever athletes. Standing 6 feet tall and turning the scales at around 14 stone, he was more than a handful for any opponent.

As early as 1907 and 1908 he was picked for Leinster in the Railway Shield competition in both hurling and football. His first great moment of national glory came in 1910 when he was a member of the Wexford hurling team, captained by Dick Doyle, that defeated Limerick by one point at Jones' Road, on 20 November.

Seán played a great game at full-back. In the closing stages, Limerick swept in on the Wexford goal, time after time, in search of a winning score. The *People* reported that 'O'Kennedy did Herculean work' and added that 'Wexford began to tire but Seán O'Kennedy, Dick Fortune and Sim Donohoe can run for two hours as well as one.' It was this stamina and staying power that saved the day for Wexford in those hectic closing stages, when Seán O'Kennedy, in particular, played like a man inspired.

In a few short years Wexford entered a golden era in Gaelic football, and Seán O'Kennedy was destined to play a major role. It began in 1913 and ended in 1918.

There was nothing to suggest that Wexford were on the road to record-breaking football performances when an indifferent display, supported by a freak goal, gave them an unexpected win over Laois in the first round of the Leinster championship of 1913 by 1-4 to 1-3. Next came Dublin. At half time the game was scoreless. A Dublin goal early in the second half spread a feeling of unease, but a quick point by Seán O'Kennedy steadied the Slaneymen and they went on to win well, 2-3 to 1-0.

Now for the big test – the Leinster final against the All-Ireland title holders, Louth. Six minutes remained; the score, Louth 2-2 Wexford 1-3. Wexford swarmed upfield; only the goalkeeper and one back remained in defence. It was now or never. Seán O'Kennedy headed towards the 21-yard line and let fly a fierce shot. It rebounded off the goalkeeper, and the in-rushing Wexford forwards sent it to the net. Soon it was all over. A sensational result. Wexford were Leinster champions for the first time since 1893.

Antrim fell in the semi-final and Wexford now faced as good a Kerry team as ever represented the Kingdom in the final on 14 December before an attendance of 20,000. 'It was a battle of giants,' reported the *Kerryman* – a game the Kingdom won by 2-2 to 0-3. Two of those Wexford points were scored by Seán O'Kennedy. In Kerry, Wexford were perceived as 'dashing, crafty, fearless, a cluster of great players destined to make football history'.

In 1914 Seán was appointed captain. Victories over Meath, Kilkenny, Dublin, Louth and Monaghan brought Wexford face to face, again, with Kerry in the All-Ireland final on 1 November. It was a game of magnificent football. Early in the game Seán O'Kennedy scored a goal with a cannon shot. He followed with a second to leave Wexford ahead at half time by 2-0 to 0-1. Wind-assisted in the second half, Kerry forced a draw with a pointed free in the closing moments. Final score: Wexford 2-0 Kerry 0-6.

In the replay on 29 November, Wexford, having led by 0-6 to 0-0 at half time, lost by 2-3 to 0-6. Their hour had not yet come. But great days lay ahead.

For the next three years Seán was captain. He led Wexford to three All-Ireland crowns, displaying high levels of enthusiasm, energy, dedication and at all times inspiring leadership. He was like a general in the field, spotting weaknesses and making switches. Kerry were beaten in the final of 1915, following which Seán said:

> *Our victory was a deserved one and I felt confident that with the team we were lining out against Kerry, we would defeat them. Throughout our training, we met with no mishap and consequently were spared an amount of worry that we had to contend with in the 1913 and 1914 preparations ... The manner in which the team stood the desperately hot pace is the best tribute that could be paid to our trainers who spared no effort in having us as fit as could be.*

Mayo fell in the final of 1916, as Wexford recorded two in a row. Now, picture the scene in the Leinster final of 1917 against Dublin. Three minutes remained. The score Dublin 1-1 Wexford 0-3. It looked like the end of the road and then it happened.

Jim Byrne sent in a free from midfield; Seán O'Kennedy fisted the ball, extending its flight by some 20 yards. There to grasp it at the edge of the square was Aidan Doyle. The New Ross-based Ballyhogue man took a few steps towards goal and sent a mighty kick to the back of the Dublin net.

Onward Seán led his men to an easy win over Monaghan and then a final showdown with Clare, who had accounted for Waterford, Tipperary, Cork and Galway under trainer Dick Fitzgerald of Kerry fame.

It was a tough, rough game. Tackling was severe. Seán was singled out for some very harsh treatment. But Wexford prevailed, 0-9 to 0-5. The unseemly behaviour continued after the game. As the referee was presenting Seán with the match ball, a Clare player nipped in, grabbed it and made off, only to be quickly apprehended.

On 2 June 1918, at New Ross, Seán led Wexford to victory over Kilkenny in the opening round of the championship. Four weeks later Wexford faced Kerry in a tournament final at Croke Park. Seán was due to go to hospital for major surgery, but he postponed that and led his team to victory over a dumbfounded Kerry fifteen. After that Wexford had to line out without their captain's inspired leadership. Carlow and Louth were overcome. In the final, Wexford were fortunate to survive a Tipperary challenge. It was a close call – 0-5 to 0-4.

On 31 August 1919 Wexford faced Dublin in the Leinster semi-final – a game that saw the return of Seán O'Kennedy, now fully recovered from his operation. Wexford lost by 0-11 to 1-1. 'Sliabh Ruadh' said it was 'a powerful game' and that 'splendid football was served up from start to stop'. It was Wexford's first Leinster championship defeat since 1912. It was all over. *Ní bhíonn in aon rud ach seal.*

That golden era set all kinds of records and rare achievements. Let's briefly examine them. Wexford won six provincial titles in a row, 1913–1918, and contested the All-Ireland final in each of those years. Seán was captain on four consecutive occasions, 1914–1917. The Slaneymen won four All-Ireland titles in a row, 1915–1918. It is a record that still stands, though subsequently equalled by Kerry. Seán was captain on three of those occasions, 1915 –1917, a record that remains unequalled. The four-in-a-row successes of 1915–1918 were all refereed by Pat Dunphy of Laois, whom Wexford must surely have looked upon as a lucky mascot.

Nine players figured in all four All-Ireland winning teams: Jim Byrne, Gus O'Kennedy (a brother of Seán), Martin Howlett, Rich Reynolds, Aidan Doyle, Tom Doyle, Tom Murphy, Tom McGrath and Paddy Mackey.

Paddy Mackey is the only Wexford player with seven Leinster medals – six in football, one in hurling; and five All-Ireland medals – four in football, one in hurling. Interestingly, Paddy is a native of Kylemore, The Rower, County Kilkenny. To make him eligible for Wexford at the time, Seán O'Kennedy provided him with a bed at his home in Quay Street, New Ross.

Barney Roice, a team sub, was said to have won six Leinster medals and four All-Ireland medals without playing a game. However, Mervyn Moore, in an article in *Comóradh an Chéid*, noted that he played in the All-Ireland semi-final of 1915 against Cavan.

In his student days, Seán hurled in Dublin. 'Carbery', who knew him, was particularly taken by his 'wonderful strength, skill and endurance, his cool scheming brain to see a scoring opportunity, his unselfish feeding of men better placed'.

The lure of the playing field had a magnetic effect on Seán. He must surely have been in the autumn of his playing days when named in goal for the Wexford hurling team in the Leinster semi-final against Kilkenny at Croke Park on Sunday 15 October 1922. Kilkenny won.

Co. Wexford Football Team
Established Records, All Ireland Champions 1915, '16, '17, '18. Leinster Champions, 1913, '14, '15, '16, '17, '18.

Wexford's four-in-a-row heroes. *Back row (l–r)*: John Wall (Bunclody), Frank Furlong (Wexford), Rich Reynolds (Wexford), Tom Mernagh (New Ross), Val Connolly, sub (Enniscorthy), Jack Crowley, sub (Wexford); *centre row (l–r)*: Denis Asple, selector (Ballyhogue), Tom Doyle (Ballyhogue), Martin Howlett (Campile), Father E. Wheeler (Wexford), P. J. Mackey (New Ross), P. D. Breen, selector (Castlebridge); *front row (l–r)*: Tom Murphy (Enniscorthy), T. McGrath, goal (Wexford), Jim Byrne, Captain 1918 (Wexford), Sean O'Kennedy, Captain 1915–16 and 1917 (New Ross), Aidan Doyle (New Ross), Barney Roice, sub (Wexford), Gus O'Kennedy (New Ross). *Inset*, Ned Black (Enniscorthy).

A FOOTBALL PERSONALITY:

Frank Furlong (Wexford)

Born in 1891, Frank was a native of Wexford town, a butcher by trade and a footballer of no mean ability. He was also a fine athlete who played handball and did some running. Frank was immensely strong with a powerful pair of shoulders, and stood about 5 feet 8 inches and at peak fitness weighed 11½ stone.

I recently met two of his sons, Tom and Nick, both now in their eighties, and learned much about their father and his footballing days. Frank belonged to Wexford's greatest footballing era, when the county won six Leinster titles in a row, 1913–1918, and four All-Ireland titles in a row, 1915–1918.

Frank, who usually played in the forwards, was on the Wexford team that beat Louth, reigning All-Ireland champions, in the Leinster final of 1913 by 2-3 to 2-2 – his first provincial crown. He was recalled to the first fifteen for the Leinster final against Dublin in 1915 – won following a replay. The real days of glory lay ahead as he won three All-Ireland titles in a row, 1915–1917. He was injured for the successful campaign of 1918.

Training in those days, long before the arrival of managers, masseurs, dieticians, warming up and cooling down sessions, was very much up to each player himself. You went to the field every evening and training consisted of exchanges involving high fielding, long kicking, physical tussles and maybe a round or two of the field. It was an era when players left the field of play due to injury as a last resort. They wouldn't give it a say to spectators, opponents or colleagues that they couldn't take what was being dished out. Tom and Nick remember hearing of the time that 'Tearin' Tom Doyle got his toes broken – did not, indeed would not, go off – and when the game was over the boot had to be cut from his foot. Similarly with Frank: he broke four fingers and played on. There was no question of going off.

And what kind of player was Frank? Certainly not stylish or classical. Tom and Nick remember talking to their father's best friend and team colleague Rich Reynolds. Rich used say that Frank was a great footballer, very strong, full of fire and energy – but rough, very rough.

As Wexford, with a Blues and Whites selection, prepared to take the field on 7 November 1915 for their third successive All-Ireland final against the Kingdom, their captain Seán O'Kennedy had a few words to say: 'If we are to beat Kerry today each one of us must do the job we have to do in our position and master our opponent.'

Walking onto the pitch Seán said to Frank: 'Remember what I said', to which Frank replied: 'You'll have your work cut out for you. Dickeen Fitzgerald is no mean man – you master him and I'll master my man.'

Early in the game as Dick and Seán O'Kennedy challenged for a ball, Frank arrived to give Dick a hefty shoulder and momentarily rattled him. He then turned to his captain and said: 'There's your problem solved, I'll look after my man now.' I looked at Tom and Nick after that little episode was related. They both smiled. 'You wouldn't call him stylish,' I suggested. Both heads shook gently. 'A no-nonsense player, maybe?' There were nods of approval.

In previews, the match was billed as 'the game of the century'. It turned out to be a thriller for the 30,000 attendance that paid £1,004. Glory for Wexford by 2-4 to 2-1.

Frank never liked the idea of outsiders on the county team. 'There are enough good men in Wexford,' was his opinion. The selectors, however, thought otherwise as Jim Byrne, a Carlow man, and Paddy Mackey, a Kilkenny man, were regular choices during those golden years. In a later era Frank used to say that Paddy Kehoe of Gusserane was one of the finest footballers he ever saw.

There comes a time when every player realises it is time to retire. And so it was with Frank. He had a half-brother called Andy – many years his junior. One day in a practice session Frank went to field a high ball only to see Andy fly past him to field and clear. 'Do that again,' said Frank 'and I'll forget that you are my brother.' Well, it happened again, whereupon Frank put his hands on his hips and called Andy over. Frank extended his hand. They both shook hands as Frank said: 'You have made me realise I'm past my best.' And with that Frank walked off the pitch into retirement.

Andy emigrated to America. His footballing ability opened doors for him in 'the land of the free'. He played full-back on the New York team that defeated Kerry before an attendance of 40,000 – the largest gathering up to then to witness a Gaelic contest in America at the Polo Grounds, New York on 29 May 1927.

A year later New York were in Ireland for the Tailteann Games with Andy at full-back and in brilliant form. He returned to America after the games, where he spent the rest of his days.

After 1918 no more All-Ireland football glory came Wexford's way. Frank Furlong, one of the greats of the glory days of 1913 to 1918, died in 1956 at the relatively young age of sixty-five.

A football selection

Dan Mullins
(Kerry)

Paddy Mackey	*Maurice McCarthy*	*Jim Byrne*
(Wexford)	(Kerry)	(Wexford)

Tom Rice	*Jim Smith*	*Tom Doyle*
(Kerry)	(Louth)	(Wexford)

Frank Courell	*Pat O'Shea*
(Mayo)	(Kerry)

O. Markey	*Seán O'Kennedy*	*Rich Reynolds*
(Louth)	(Wexford)	(Wexford)

Jack Skinner	*Aidan Doyle*	*Gus O'Kennedy*
(Kerry)	(Wexford)	(Wexford)

Dan Mullins

Dan was set a testing task when he succeeded Paddy Dillon in the Kerry goal. However, he rose to the occasion in brilliant fashion. Small of stature and agile as a cat, he possessed all the key qualities of a good goalkeeper. He had a cool temperament and wonderful judgement. He was rarely beaten by the ground ball – often diving full length to bring off a save. A native of Tralee, he arrived on the county scene in 1913 and was the number one Kerry custodian for the remainder of the decade. He played in the memorable Croke Memorial games of 1913 against Louth, won Munster titles in 1913, 1914, 1915 and 1919 and won All-Ireland medals in 1913 and 1914.

Paddy Mackey

A Kilkenny man who came from The Rower, Paddy was an outstanding dual performer for his adopted Wexford. As a hurler, he was rewarded with provincial and All-Ireland medals in 1910, when Wexford scored victories over Dublin and Limerick respectively. He had a most rewarding football career, which included six successive Leinster titles from 1913 to 1918 and four successive All-Ireland titles from 1915 to 1918. With five All-Ireland senior medals to his credit, he tops the list in Wexford.

Maurice McCarthy

Maurice, from Castleisland, played his football with Tralee John Mitchels, usually at right-corner-back. No greater Kerry player ever pulled on a football jersey. He was a masterful defender, stylish and possessing the safest of hands. He was a mighty kicker of the ball – on the ground or in the air – and skilful too with the drop-kick, which he could despatch over 50 yards. He was once credited with a point from 80 yards. Maurice won five All-Ireland titles – 1903, 1904, 1909, 1913 and 1914. He was captain in 1905 when Kerry failed to Kildare. He retired on a number of occasions, only to be recalled by the selectors. He finally called it a day after defeat by Wexford in 1915.

Jim Byrne

A native of Ballymurphy in County Carlow, Jim qualified as a national teacher and taught in Poulfur in south Wexford. He won six successive Leinster titles with Wexford between 1913 and 1918 and four successive All-Ireland crowns between 1915 and 1918, captaining the team in the last of these. He was a rock-solid defender and usually took all the frees.

One occasion of key importance was the 1915 All-Ireland final against Kerry, reigning All-Ireland champions of the two previous years at the expense of Wexford. Picture the scene: about ten minutes remain and the scores are level at 1-3 to 2-0. Wexford win a free about 30 yards out. It is entrusted to Jim Byrne. He sends a mighty kick that passes through outstretched hands and dips under the crossbar for a goal. Wexford supporters go wild. Wexford then force a fifty. Another mighty kick from Jim and the ball sails above the crossbar and 10 yards beyond. Pandemonium! Kerry pull back a point. Referee Pat Dunphy blows the final whistle. Wexford are All-Ireland senior football champions.

After his playing days, Jim held many positions at County Board level and represented Wexford on the Leinster Council in 1924 and 1925. He refereed many matches, including the football finals of 1923 (Dublin v Kerry) and 1930 (Kerry v Monaghan).

Tom Rice

Tom was a student at Rockwell College, where he played rugby. Back in the Kingdom, this native of O'Dorney excelled at Gaelic football with Tralee Mitchels and the Kerry team. He won three All-Ireland titles – 1909, 1913 and 1914 – and five Munster titles – 1910, 1912, 1913, 1914 and 1915. Tom played at right-half-back. A Canon Breen who often saw him in action declared he was the greatest back he had seen in twenty years. Tom's brother, Jack, also played with Kerry.

Jim Smith

One of the finest defenders of his day, Jim was a member of the Louth team that beat Dublin by 0-3 to 0-0 in the Leinster final of 1910. Louth subsequently got a walkover from Kerry in the All-Ireland final. Jim was captain in 1912 when Louth defeated Antrim in the All-Ireland final to take their second title.

He was still captain in 1913 for the great Croke Memorial final against Kerry – a draw, with the Kingdom winning the replay. A measure of the quality of Louth football teams of that era can be gleaned from their 2-3 to 2-2 victory over All-Ireland champions Wexford, then at the height of their glory, in the Wolfe Tone Memorial semi-final of 1916. Jim played his football with the Fredaghs Club.

Jim was a well-known cattle dealer, and according to a story told by Raymond Smith in his fine book *Decades of Glory*, Jim was present when a deal was being struck with Frank Dineen for the purchase of Croke Park. Whether or not his bargaining talents were required isn't clear.

Tom Doyle

Known to followers as 'Tearin' Tom' because of his style of play, Tom, from Ballyhogue, would thunder up the field out of defence and launch an attack, inspiring his colleagues. He was full of heart and energy.

Frank Courell

Frank was a member of a great Mayo footballing family from the town of Ballina. He gave many outstanding performances for his club and county in the early decades of the last century. A versatile performer, Frank captained Mayo in 1916, and for the second year in a row they beat Roscommon in the Connacht final. Victory over Cork in the All-Ireland semi-final at Athlone by 1-2 to 0-2 was followed by an objection. A replay was ordered at Croke Park, Mayo winning by 1-2 to 1-1. The All-Ireland final was played at Croke Park on 17 December. A brilliant Wexford team captained by Seán O'Kennedy won their third of a famous four-in-a-row sequence. Final score: Wexford 3-4 Mayo 1-2.

Pat O'Shea

A native of Castlegregory, Pat is regarded as one of the greatest Kerry midfielders of all time. He would soar into the air to grasp with perfect timing the dropping ball – no wonder he was known as 'Aeroplane' O'Shea. He retired from the game in his football prime, but not before he had annexed All-Ireland titles in 1913 and 1914 and Munster titles in 1910, 1912, 1913 and 1914.

O. Markey

An outstanding member of a great Louth team in the early years of the last century, this Ardee club man was on the team beaten by Kerry in the All-Ireland final of 1909. He won his first All-Ireland medal in 1910 when Louth received a walkover from Kerry, and in 1912, a 1-7 to 1-2 win over Antrim gave him a second All-Ireland victory. In 1913 he took part in one of the most memorable contests in Gaelic football – the Croke Memorial final – a draw and replay against old rivals Kerry. Kerry won the replay by 2-4 to 0-5. Later that year, Louth lost their provincial and All-Ireland crown when going under to Wexford in the Leinster final. A goal four minutes from time clinched it for the Model county by 2-3 to 2-2. A year later, the fortunes of this fine footballer and his native Louth were on the wane when they were beaten by a now rampant Wexford in the provincial final.

Seán O'Kennedy

Seán is featured in 'A football personality: Seán O'Kennedy'.

Rich Reynolds

Rich, from Wexford town, was a player of great consistency. He won four successive All-Ireland titles and six successive Leinster titles with his native Wexford. His combined play with Gus O'Kennedy was a feature of the Wexford attack. Rich weighed only 8 stone in his playing days. Years after he had retired someone who had read about him said to him: 'You must have been some bit of stuff', to which Rich replied: 'Ah, look at the men I had around me. They never passed me a ball that would put me in trouble.'

Jack Skinner

Jack was a Cork man, a native of Mitchelstown, who played rugby in his school days. When he took up Gaelic football he became one of the best forwards of his day. Little wonder: he was coached by Dick Fitzgerald from whom he learned all the tricks of forward play. Jack was a great opportunist and deadly accurate. He got many telling scores for Kerry during his six years with the county, 1909 to 1914. He won All-Ireland medals in 1913 and 1914. He played with Tipperary in 1915, having taken up an appointment in Clonmel. Kerry and Tipperary met in the Munster semi-final. Kerry fears of Jack Skinner proved unfounded, with Tom Costelloe mastering him. A local bard honoured Tom:

> But who can equal Costelloe,
> The hero of the game?
> He held the mighty Skinner up
> Of Louth and Kerry fame.

Aidan Doyle

Aidan, the big Ballyhogue man, was a potent figure in the full line of attack. He got many a telling score for the Model county. In 1913 Wexford faced Dublin, then formidable opponents, in the Leinster semi-final at Wexford Park. It was scoreless at half time. Twice in the second half, in the space of five minutes, Aidan crashed the ball to the Dublin net. The game ended 2-3 to 1-0. In the Leinster final against Louth, Aidan played from the early stages of the game with a broken jaw. In the 1915 All-Ireland final against Kerry, with the Kingdom holding a slender one-point lead approaching half time, a movement involving Gus O'Kennedy and Rich Reynolds saw the ball despatched to Aidan, who promptly shook the rigging with a mighty drive. It was a key score at a vital stage. Half time, Wexford 1-2 Kerry 1-0. Full time, Wexford 2-4 Kerry 2-1. Wexford All-Ireland champions – the county's second title and first of a great four-in-a-row. In the Leinster final of 1917 against Dublin three minutes remained and the Slaneymen trailed by 1-1 to 0-3. Then a Jim Byrne free from midfield was fisted onwards by Seán O'Kennedy to the grasping hands of Aidan Doyle, who swerved, took a step and sent the ball crashing to the net.

Gus O'Kennedy

Gus, from New Ross, was a brother of Seán. He sacrificed individual glory in favour of combined efforts, for the benefit of the team. It helped bring him and his native Wexford four successive All-Ireland titles and six successive provincial titles.

1921–1930

Teams that participated in the
All-Ireland senior finals

COUNTY	FOOTBALL		HURLING	
	WON	LOST	WON	LOST
Cavan		1		
Cork			3	1
Dublin	3	1	2	2
Galway	1	1	1	4
Kerry	4	2		
Kildare	2	2		
Kilkenny			1	1
Limerick			1	1
Mayo		1		
Monaghan		1		
Tipperary			2	1

Eleven counties participated in the senior finals.

The ten hurling finals involved six counties, with all six successful.

The ten football finals involved seven counties, with four of those successful.

This was the only decade when every county that contested the hurling final won the title.

A HURLING GAME:

Leinster v Munster, 1927 Railway Cup final

Let us first of all look back briefly at a previous inter-provincial competition.

The first Railway Shield competition was played in 1905, when Leinster won in both hurling and football. The following year Munster won both. So when the southern province won the football shield again in 1907, the Kerry County Board was presented with the shield (the first team to win it twice was to retain it) because Kerry had supplied the largest number of players.

The hurling was not decided until 1908; in the spring of that year Munster defeated Leinster. Each province had now two wins. So when they met in the final of the next series at Kilkenny on 19 July 1908 a winner had to emerge. As a consequence, the game attracted a huge crowd of 15,000. A great save by John T. Power of Piltown in the closing minutes deprived Munster of a draw – final score, Leinster 0-14 Munster 2-5.

The seventeen-man Leinster team was captained by 'Drug' Walsh: Eddie Doyle, Mick Doyle, Dick Doyle, Dick Doherty, Jimmy Kelly, Tom Kenny, Dan Kennedy, Dan Stapleton, Matt Gargan (who in 1905, representing Waterford, had starred with Munster), Sim Walton, Jack Keoghan, John T. Power, Jack Anthony, Jack Rochford – all from Kilkenny; Bob O'Keeffe of Laois and Mike Cummins of Wexford.

The Railway Hurling Shield, proudly won by Leinster, was presented, after some controversy, to the Kilkenny County Board because they had supplied the bulk of the team. Today the Shield occupies a prominent place in Kilkenny City Hall.

Let us now fast-forward two decades. At the Congress of 1926, the then secretary of the Cork County Board, Pádraig Ó Caoimh, proposed that the inter-provincial championships be revived. His suggestion was accepted and it was agreed that the finals would be played on St Patrick's Day at Croke Park.

Munster, with an all-Kerry selection, won the football with a 2-3 to 0-5 win over Connacht. It was a close call. With a draw looking likely, Frank Sheehy put Munster ahead with a point, and then, just before the final whistle, Éamon Fitzgerald of Caherdaniel found the net. In the semi-final against Ulster at Cavan, Munster, backboned by Kerry players with two from Tipperary and one from Cork, were fortunate to survive. In a very exciting encounter, Ulster, with a brilliant goalkeeper from Belfast, led by five points at half time. However, at the call of time Munster had a point to spare, 1-8 to 3-1.

The hurling game proved a thriller, regarded by keen judges of the game as one of the best exhibitions of the game up to that time.

In the semi-final, Leinster defeated Connacht at Portlaoise on 21 November 1926 by 7-6 to 3-5. With no team from Ulster, Munster had a bye into the final. Both teams featured legendary names. Leinster were captained by Wattie Dunphy of Mooncoin, who had led Kilkenny to All-Ireland glory in 1922. The Munster captain was Seán Óg Murphy of Blackrock, who had been playing with Cork since 1915 and was their captain when they won the All-Ireland title in 1926.

From the throw-in, the game was bewilderingly fast; marking was close; the ball was being despatched at pace. Approaching half time Leinster led by three points to one. Then 'Gah' Ahern struck with a bullet-like shot that beat Tommy Daly in the Leinster goal. Level at the break, 1-1 to 0-4.

The second half surpassed the first in brilliance and excitement.

Michael 'Gah' Ahern.

Points by Lory Meagher, Mattie Power and Dinny O'Neill put Leinster ahead. Big Jim Hurley at midfield for Munster sent in a long ball and in a flash Martin Kennedy had it in the net. Level again, 2-1 to 0-7. There followed a rapid exchange of points, two to either side – Willie Gleeson (Munster), Lory Meagher (Leinster), John Roberts (Leinster), and Eudi Coughlan (Munster). Still level. It was all action now and excitement mounted. Suddenly Leinster were four points ahead – a goal from Mattie Power followed by a point from Henry Meagher. Eudi Coughlan and the Ahern brothers 'Gah' and 'Balty' sent over points to reduce the gap to one point. Two raspers from Martin Kennedy were dealt with by Tommy Daly in the Leinster goal.

The seconds ticked away as the Leinster defence stood solid. Dinny O'Neill gained possession – he found Lory Meagher and the ball sailed over the bar. Soon it was all over: Leinster 1-11 Munster 2-6.

And as the crowd streamed away from Croke Park they reflected on a blossoming hero of the future – Lory Meagher of Tullaroan and Kilkenny.

Four Munster men and one from Connacht played on the Leinster team – Tommy Daly, Pa 'Fowler' McInerney and Ned Daly from Clare, Garrett Howard from Limerick and Mick Gill from Galway – all members of the Dublin hurling team.

I remember asking Garrett Howard what was his most memorable inter-provincial game. He answered without hesitation:

> *Definitely the inaugural Railway Cup game in 1927 ... The midfield duet – Lory Meagher and Mick Gill against Tull Considine and Jim Hurley – was worth travelling to see. Phil Cahill, Eudi Coughlan, Martin Kennedy and 'Gah' Ahern were terrific forwards opposing Leinster backs ... It was considered by many to be one of the best games ever in the Railway Cup series.*

The 1924 Dublin team. Mick D'Arcy (2nd last row, 1st on left) played for Munster in Inaugural Railway cup final 1927 (he features on p. 100)

The lineout for games in those days is rarely available. Such is the case with the winning Railway Cup team. However, from various different observations, I have deduced that the following is the likely lineout of the first hurling team to win the Railway Cup.

Tommy Daly
(Clare and Dublin)

Eddie Doyle   *Pa 'Fowler' McInerney*   *Jim Byrne*
(Kilkenny)   (Clare & Dublin)   (Laois)

Ned Tobin   *Wattie Dunphy*   *Jim 'Builder' Walsh*
(Laois and Dublin)   (Kilkenny)   (Kilkenny and Dublin)

Mick Gill   *Lory Meagher*
(Galway and Dublin)   (Kilkenny)

John Roberts   *Dinny O'Neill*   *Henry Meagher*
(Kilkenny)   (Laois and Dublin)   (Kilkenny)

Garrett Howard   *Ned Fahy*   *Mattie Power*
(Limerick and Dublin) (Clare and Dublin) (Kilkenny and Dublin)

None of the Dublin players was a Dublin native – hence the second county given in each case.

As he was in 1932: the legendary Dr Tommy Daly being carried from the field following Clare's dramatic victory over Galway in the 1932 All-Ireland senior hurling semi-final at Limerick. He was then in his nineteenth year of senior inter-county competition.

Those nine Dublin players further enhanced their hurling status the following September when they featured on a Dublin team that comprehensively defeated Cork by 4-8 to 1-3 in the All-Ireland final. And that Cork team contained ten of the Munster panel.

The Munster team was chosen from the following players: John Joe Sheehy (Kerry) (more famed as a footballer but a class hurler too), Tull Considine (Clare), Johnny Leahy, Mick D'Arcy, Phil Cahill, Martin Kennedy (Tipperary), Michael Murphy, John Joe Kinnane, Willie Gleeson, Mickey Cross, Bob McConkey, Mickey Gibbons (Limerick), Seán Óg Murphy, 'Marie' O'Connell, Michael Murphy, Jim O'Regan, Jim Hurley, 'Gah' Ahern, 'Balty' Ahern, Moss Murphy, Dinny Barry-Murphy, Eudi Coughlan (Cork).

The Railway Cup contests blossomed and flourished. They were even played during the war years, when other competitions were suspended. Their glory days peaked in the mid-1950s when attendances exceeded 50,000. After that, unfortunately, the glamour of the competition gradually waned and in the border years of the twentieth and twenty-first centuries attendances dropped to a mere handful.

Unfortunately, no written account of the hurling and football games of that very fine and most entertaining competition exists.

In writing about the Railway Cup, it is worth recording that it was this competition that first introduced us to the distinctive broadcasting style of Micheál Ó Muircheartaigh from Dún Síon in the Dingle Peninsula. On St Patrick's Day, 1949 Munster faced Leinster in the Railway Cup football final. To Micheál, not yet nineteen, fell the task of telling the story of the game in our native tongue. The contest ended all-sqaure, 2-7 each. Some fifty years later, Micheál is still going strong in his profession.

A HURLING PERSONALITY:

Mick D'Arcy (Tipperary)

We'll chant their praises loud and strong,
O'er mountain, moorland, hill and glen;
And keep their memory green in song,
Tipperary's fearless hurling men

Tom Keating

Born in Grange, Nenagh in 1901, Mick was educated at the local convent national school and at Nenagh CBS. He then went to that hurling nursery across the Shannon, St Flannan's College, Ennis. The inaugural competition of the Harty Cup – a trophy presented by Dr Harty, the then archbishop of Cashel, for a hurling competition between the secondary schools and colleges of Munster – took place in 1918. Mick D'Arcy was a member of the St Flannan's Harty Cup team. The trophy was won by Rockwell College, and it took until 1944 for St Flannan's to taste success.

Mick continued his studies at UCD, where he was immediately drawn to hurling, winning Fitzgibbon Cup medals in 1923, 1924 and 1927. Also on the team on each occasion was that outstanding goalkeeper, Clare man Tommy Daly, who at the time was playing his county hurling with Dublin.

Mick's talents were spotted by the Dublin hurling selectors and he formed part of the county panel in 1923 and 1924. It brought him an All-Ireland medal in 1924 when Dublin, with a team consisting of all non-residents, defeated Galway in the final by 5-3 to 2-6.

The Tipperary team that toured the USA in 1926: *back row (l–r)*: Paddy Power (Boherlahan), Jim O'Meara (Toomevara), Phil Purcell (Moycarkey Borris), Arthur O'Donnell (Boherlahan), Martin Mockler (Moycarkey Borris), William Ryan (Moycarkey Borris), Wedger Meagher (county board secretary), person unknown; *centre row (l–r)*: T. J. Kenny (Portroe), Frank McGrath (manager), Johnny Power (Boherlahan), Michael Leahy (Boherlahan), Stephen Kenny (Cloughjordan), Johnny Leahy, Captain (Boherlahan), Phil Cahill (Holycross), William O'Brien (Moycarkey Borris), Patrick O'Dwyer (Boherlahan), J. J. Hayes (Moycarkey Borris); *front row (l–r)*: Martin Kennedy (Toomevara), Paddy Leahy (Boherlahan), Thomas Duffy (Lorrha).

The following year, 1925, a new rule allowed a player residing outside his native county to declare for his county, and Mick declared for his native Tipperary. The decision bore fruit. In Munster, Kerry, Cork and Waterford fell, Antrim were heavily defeated in the semi-final and Galway were overcome in the All-Ireland final by 5-6 to 1-5. Mick D'Arcy's All-Ireland medal with Tipperary, under the captaincy of Johnny Leahy, became a cherished possession.

In 1926 plans were made for the Tipperary hurlers to set forth on a hurling tour of the US. It would last from 11 May to 24 July. However, where Mick D'Arcy and his brother Jack were concerned, there was a snag. Some members of the government had reservations about the trip. As well as involving hurling, they believed the trip also included the gathering of funds for the republican movement.

Mick and Jack were refused permission to travel. Being in 'government jobs', they were told that if they went they would have no jobs to come back to. As it turned out, the decision was taken out of their hands. Their mother reminded them that jobs were a scarce commodity at the time and that what they had was permanent and pensionable. She said 'No' and that was that.

Mick and Jack joined the Tipperary panel on the team's return from the US tour and made preparation for the Munster championship.

Jack was born in 1898. He went to UCG and qualified as an engineer, before taking up an appointment with Cork Corporation. Jack hurled with Tipperary from 1919 to 1927; he was on the team that lost to Kilkenny in the classic All-Ireland final of 1922. He won his only All-Ireland medal in the 1925 defeat of Galway. Jack died in Cork in 1972.

Limerick were defeated in the Munster semi-final of 1926 and Tipperary then faced Cork in the Munster final. It took three meetings to decide the issue. The sending off of Tipperary's Martin Mockler is believed to have cost Tipperary the game in the third encounter.

Writing about the second game, the late Raymond Smith (in *Decades of Glory*) said:

> *At midfield, Jim Hurley of the 'Rockies and Bill ['Love'] Higgins of Cobh were opposed by Mick D'Arcy and Pat Collison ... And if Mick D'Arcy was a sportsman to his fingertips and a hurler without peer in the midfield sector, so also was Jim Hurley of Cork ... now Mick was showing all his flowing power at midfield.*

From 60 yards he sent all the way to the net – a golden goal that levelled scores.

Tipperary had found their rhythm in attack. Twice Seán Óg and his fellow backs had to concede seventies; from the second of these Mick D'Arcy placed the ball beautifully in the square and with a flash of Martin Kennedy's stick it was rattling the net.

Mick won a League title with Tipperary in 1927, and the same year was chosen on Munster's inaugural Railway Cup team, defeated by Leinster in a thriller on St Patrick's Day at Croke Park. As far as I can trace, Mick played his last championship game at Cork Athletic Grounds on 3 July 1927 in the Munster championship against Limerick. Tipperary lost by 3-4 to 3-1. Writing on the game 'Carbery' said: 'It was rain, rain, and more rain! The teams defeated the elements.'

When his playing days were over, Mick D'Arcy maintained his links with the GAA and hurling in his capacity as trainer and selector of UCD teams. He was also chairman of the UCD hurling and football club. His love of Gaelic games was immense. He encouraged everyone to play them.

Mick was one of countless idealists who were cornerstones of the GAA down through its history – men who, on and off the field, gave so much and sought nothing in return.

Mick revelled in the Fitzgibbon Cup triumphs of UCD over their arch-rivals UCC. The competition between the two colleges was intense and the games were often ferociously contested.

All who met Mick loved him for his integrity, dedication and gentlemanliness. Proof of this came one day in the 1960s when the students decided to draft a motion for the removal of the 'ban' on so-called foreign games. It was a move that disturbed Mick, as he recalled the humiliation of being spat on by Crown forces as he entered Croke Park. The wound was deep; the scar remained. He told his students of his past experience and explained quietly, but with a sense of sadness, that if they went ahead with the motion he would have to resign as chairman. They withdrew the motion and in so doing reflected the level of esteem and affection in which they held Mick D'Arcy. Mick died in Dublin in 1964.

A HURLING PERSONALITY:

Phil Cahill (Tipperary)

Many who saw Phil Cahill of Holycross in action and who later witnessed the deeds of Mick Mackey and Christy Ring on the hurling field used say that for pure hurling skill Phil was in their class.

He had a tremendous burst of speed and, as he careered along the wing, could lift the sliotar at full speed and – without handling – send it over the bar, often from the most acute of angles. Phil, however, did not possess the physical power or strength of Mackey and Ring. As a stylist and speedster, he was often the target of unwarranted and unsporting attention. He took severe punishment and suffered many bad injuries. And yet he always returned after injury to perform as brilliantly as ever.

Phil played in an era when there was no such thing as All-Stars, Hurler of the Year or Man of the Match awards. And if there were he would certainly have been a contender.

He wore the blue and gold of Tipperary for the first time in 1923 when the Premier county defeated Clare in the first round of the Munster championship. It was a year of big wins in the first round in Munster: Limerick 8-5 Kerry 2-2; Cork 13-4 Waterford 0-1; Tipperary 11-2 Clare 1-4.

Tipperary lost the Munster final to Limerick by 2-3 to 1-0 and surprisingly Phil Cahill was omitted. Having regained his place in 1924, he played in all championship games until the end of 1931. He won all the honours – All-Ireland titles in 1925 and 1930 and Munster titles in 1924, 1925 and 1930. He played for six successive years for Munster in the Railway Cup (1927–1932) – 1927 being the inaugural year. He won four successive titles (1928–1931) at a time when selection for your province was a much envied honour, and a medal a prized possession. A National League medal was won in 1928 under the captaincy of Johnny Leahy of Boherlahan – won on a points system – fourteen from eight games, following draws with Dublin and Laois. Also that year he was chosen on the Tailteann Games hurling team. Phil won four county titles: 1922 mid-Tipperary (Boherlahan) selection, 1924 south Tipperary (Boherlahan) selection, and two with Moycarkey, 1932 and 1933.

Phil was a member of the Tipperary team that toured the US in 1926. The driving force behind the tour was Phil's brother, Patrick, president of the Chicago GAA and a prominent attorney. It was the first team to cross the Atlantic since the US 'invasion' of 1888. They travelled from coast to coast and played games in Boston, Chicago, San Francisco, Buffalo and finally at the Polo Grounds, New York. All games were won handsomely and Martin Kennedy, doyen of full-forwards, was credited with twenty-seven goals.

Phil played his last game in the county colours on 25 June 1933 at Davin Park, Carrick-on-Suir, when Tipperary lost to Waterford in the Munster championship by 5-5 to 5-2. Later that year Phil pulled on a hurling jersey for the last time at Thurles when he helped Moycarkey defeat Borrisokane by 1-7 to 1-0 in the county final.

In *Tipperary's GAA Story* by Canon Philip Fogarty, Phil is described as 'Ireland's best wing-forward', while 'Green Flag' in the *Irish Press* called him 'one of the greatest stylists hurling has every produced'.

Phil Cahill was only in his forties when he died in 1945.

I remember a reader of the *Irish Independent* submitting in 1949 a rugby team of the Five Nations for that year and a hurling team of players he had seen in action in his lifetime. The paper made one or two changes in both, following which the hurling team read:

Paddy Scanlon
(Limerick)

Charlie McMahon   *Seán Óg Murphy*   *John Joe Doyle*
(Dublin)   (Cork)   (Clare)

Jackie Power   *Paddy Clohessy*   *Paddy Phelan*
(Limerick)   (Limerick)   (Kilkenny)

Timmy Ryan   *Lory Meagher*
(Limerick)   (Kilkenny)

Phil Cahill   *Mick Mackey*   *Christy Ring*
(Tipperary)   (Limerick)   (Cork)

Jimmy Langton   *Martin Kennedy*   *Mattie Power*
(Kilkenny)   (Tipperary)   (Kilkenny)

Fifteen great men, each a master hurler. Collectively they span half a century, from Seán Óg in 1915 to Christy in 1963.

A hurling selection

Tommy Daly
(Dublin)

Pa 'Fowler' McInerney   Seán Óg Murphy   Dave Murnane
(Dublin)   (Cork)   (Limerick)

Mick D'Arcy   Jim Regan   Dick Grace
(Tipperary)   (Cork)   (Kilkenny)

Jim Hurley   Mick Gill
(Cork)   (Galway)

Phil Cahill   Mick King   Eudi Coughlan
(Tipperary)   (Galway)   (Cork)

Bob McConkey   Martin Kennedy   Michael 'Gah' Ahern
(Limerick)   (Tipperary)   (Cork)

Tommy Daly and Pa 'Fowler' McInerney also played with their native Clare during their hurling careers.

Mick D'Arcy, a Tipperary native, also hurled with Dublin.

Mick Gill won an All-Ireland with Galway in 1923 and with Dublin in 1924 and 1927.

A FOOTBALL GAME:

Kerry v Kildare, 1926 All-Ireland final

There's joy tonight in Kerry hearts
From Doon to Farranfore,
From Scartaglin to Beauty's Home,
From Dingle to Rathmore.
From sweet Listowel to dear Tralee,
From Headfort to Kenmare,
The very hills ring out with glee
Since Kerry beat Kildare.

P. C. O'Connor

Kerry and Kildare both experienced a golden era in Gaelic football around the same time. However, Kerry's lasted longer and bore more fruit.

Between 1923 and 1934 Kerry won eleven Munster crowns, losing only in 1928. Six of those titles led to All-Ireland glory – 1924, 1926 and a four-in-a-row from 1929 to 1932 that equalled Wexford's record-breaking feat of 1915 to 1918.

Kildare won every Leinster title – six in all – between 1926 and 1931 and contested every All-Ireland final in that period except 1930. Two successive All-Ireland titles in 1927 and 1928 seems meagre reward for a great team. The 1926 final was lost after a replay. So let us now look at those two games.

Kerry and Kildare had not met since the finals of 1903 and 1905. And what memories those epic contests evoked, especially the days of the 1903 final – three absorbing contests, the first in Tipperary town and the next two in Cork.

The 1926 final between Kerry and Kildare was played at Croke Park on 5 September. Thirty-four special trains conveyed supporters to Dublin. An estimated 37,500 packed Croke Park on a glorious autumn day. It was a record crowd, surpassing for the first time the rugby international attendance.

There was a contrast in football styles – Kildare with combined passing movements, Kerry with high fielding and accurate kicking. It all added to the glamour of the occasion. For more than three-quarters of the game Kildare dominated. Larry Stanley was superb, while at centre-half-back Jack Higgins drove his low kicks an extraordinary distance.

Jack Higgins was one of football's immortals – a master centre-back. He played with Cavan in the 1923 All-Ireland semi-final against Kerry, as did his fellow county man Paul Doyle. Both were stationed in the Northern province at the time. Kerry won by 1-3 to 1-2.

Jack was chosen on the Tailteann Games teams of 1928 and 1932. He was member of the Kildare team that won six successive Leinster titles from 1926 to 1931 and was still there in 1935 to win a seventh provincial medal. He played in seven successive Railway Cup finals from 1928 to 1934, losing on only two occasions, 1931 and 1934.

Jack played in six All-Ireland football finals. He won two – 1927 v Kerry and 1928 v Cavan. The 1926 final was lost to Kerry after a

replay. Jack was captain in 1929 when Kildare failed to the Kingdom by 1-8 to 1-5. Again in 1931 Kerry proved too good. And in
1935 Cavan avenged their 1928 defeat.

But Kerry had a hero too – Johnny Murphy of Cahersiveen, not
yet twenty-two. At corner-back he proved unbeatable. With five
minutes to go Kildare led by six points to three – the score no in-
dicator of their superiority. Kerry launched attack after attack. All
were beaten back by a solid Kildare defence. With less than three
minutes to go Con Brosnan was in possession near the Hogan
Stand. He kicked across in front of goal – Bill Gorman rose high,
grasped firmly, side-stepped Matt Goff and the ball was in the net.
Kerry 1-3 Kildare 0-6 and the referee blew the final whistle.

The replay took place on 17 October. Fifty special trains ran and
again Croke Park was packed. The weather was once more glorious and the game one of the greatest yet played.

Kerry's stalwart of the drawn game, Johnny Murphy, was absent
– he lay on his deathbed in Tralee. Kildare were by a short margin favourites and led by 0-3 to 0-2 at the break, having played
with slight wind advantage and twice hit the Kerry posts. Midway
through the second half the scoreline remained unchanged. Kerry
forced a fifty and Kildare, in attempting to clear, conceded another.
It was taken by Jerh Moriarty. John Joe Sheehy kept it from going
wide by boxing it across the posts. It was met by Tom Mahony,
who fisted to the net. Kildare hit the Kerry crossbar, but at the call
of time it was Kerry 1-4 Kildare 0-4, a seventh title for Kerry. And
even though at one stage they looked like being outclassed, their
superior stamina showed in the end.

'Sliabh Ruadh' said the game would 'go down to history as the
greatest yet played':

> *Kerry's triumph ... was superior only in victory to the defiant
> defence of the Short Grass county that, with victory within sight,
> tasted defeat with a dignity worthy of the best traditions of the
> Gael.*

'Mac Lir', writing in the *Voice of Labour*, said:

> *Kerry was undoubtedly the superior fifteen and if Kildare was un-
> lucky in not winning the drawn game, the 'Kingdom' would have
> been much more than unlucky not to have won on Sunday.*

'Mac Lir' listed four factors as contributing to Kerry's win – superior grit and the will to victory; better fielding; a stronger mid-field; and Larry Stanley rendered ineffective.

Jubilation in Kerry was tempered somewhat by the death of Johnny Murphy a few days after the replay. The Killarney Pipers' Band, playing appropriate airs, led the funeral to Kilavarnogue near Cahersiveen where Johnny was laid to rest.

A FOOTBALL PERSONALITY:

Larry Stanley (Kildare)

I often heard my father talking about the brilliance of Larry Stanley as an exponent of Gaelic football. And I knew by the way he spoke that the name Larry Stanley and football greatness were synonymous. His catching, his flair as a jumper and holder of the ball were traits that set him apart. He cut a fine athletic figure – a six footer, who turned the scales over 12 stone. One of a family of ten children – seven boys and three girls – Larry was captain of the 1919 Kildare team that brought the county its second football title. Larry played his club football with Caragh and the 1919 team – a really splendid combination – was selected from Caragh, Clane, Kilcock, St Conleth's, Maddenstown and Two Mile House.

Kildare were appearing in their first final since 1905 when they defeated Kerry. On their way to the 1919 final they beat Laois at Newbridge College Grounds by 3-5 to 2-5 before a huge crowd. After that Westmeath fell in the Leinster semi-final by 4-3 to 1-5. On Sunday 7 September they faced Dublin, who had dethroned Wexford – six-in-a-row Leinster title holders 1913–1918; four-in-a-row All-Ireland winners 1915–1918 – in the Leinster final. It was a hard and brilliant game. Kildare came through with a point to spare, 1-3 to 1-2. Larry Stanley was outstanding.

'The finest player that ever appeared in Gaelic football ... his performance from beginning to end was brilliant. Not once did he fail to capture the leather with that extraordinary spring and one handed grasp for which he has become noted,' said one report.

His practice sessions were painstaking. He trained himself to kick accurately by chipping a football into a bucket hung from the rafters of a barn at home. He described the hours of practice on the pitch: 'I started by taking shots close in, and getting them over the bar; then I would move out slightly until I had mastered every distance and angle.'

Kildare's All-Ireland semi-final meeting was with Cavan. Played at Navan on 14 September, the Leinster men had a good win, 3-2 to 1-3.

Their opponents in the final were Galway, who had two close calls in Connacht: v Mayo, 1-3 to 1-2, and v Roscommon, 1-6 to 0-5

Galway's semi-final opponents were Kerry. It was a draw the first day, 2-6 to 3-3, with Galway winning the replay, 4-2 to 2-2. They entered the final on 28 September, therefore, with good credentials.

About 30,000 thronged Croke Park. Trained by John McDermott of Naas, Kildare's superiority was evident from early on and increased as the game progressed. Larry Stanley stood out on a team that appeared to have no weak link. Much was expected of Galway, but in Kildare they met a really first class team – splendid and spectacular in their game of fielding, tackling and kicking, a performance to compare with the best up to then.

Kildare led at half time, 1-2 to 0-0; at the final whistle it was 2-5 to 0-1. Larry Stanley got two of those points and Frank Conlon, who was on their 1905 winning team (played on 16 June 1907), contributed 1-2. Larry's brother Jim was a member of the 1919 winning team. He played under the name Jim Reilly. Being a priest, he could not in those times play as Jim Stanley.

Larry Stanley played in two more All-Ireland finals. For the 1923 campaign he was based in Dublin and playing his club football with Garda. The non-resident declaration rule was not in operation at the time, so Larry found himself wearing the Dublin jersey.

Provincial honours were won when Meath were defeated 3-5 to 0-0 and the All-Ireland final was reached when Mayo were overcome by 1-6 to 1-2. Awaiting them now were the men from the Kingdom.

Dublin, All-Ireland champions of 1921 and 1922, had a fine team and several wonderful footballers – among them their superb midfielder John Murphy and classy forward Frank Burke, a Kildare man. Here is what Tom Humphries of *The Irish Times* said of the Dublin team of that era:

Frank Burke, a Kildare man who excelled as a dual player with Dublin, winning
hurling titles in 1917 and 1920 and football titles in 1921, 1922 and 1923.

My grandfather ... wore the green and white of the O'Tooles club in Dublin ... His time was the period from 1919 onwards, when Dublin and Kildare won sixteen of seventeen Leinster titles. A residual fondness for the Lilywhites and the deeds of Larry Stanley stayed with him all his life.

Dublin and Kerry faced each other at Croke Park on 28 September 1924 for the 1923 All-Ireland final. Long before the throw-in, the ground was packed. Twenty-nine special trains had conveyed supporters to the capital. It was Kerry's first appearance in a final since 1915 when they lost to Wexford. A thrilling contest saw Kerry putting in a finish of characteristic dash. But it wasn't enough – Dublin were victors by 1-5 to 1-3, their third title in a row and their fourteenth in all.

The men of that historic win came from all four provinces – Tipperary, Mayo, Cavan, Carlow, Dublin, Meath and Kildare. They may have lined out as:

Johnny McDonnell
(Carlow)

John Synott	*Paddy Carey*	*John Reilly*
(Dublin)	(Dublin)	?

John Murphy	*Joe 'Stonewall' Norris*	*Paddy Kirwan*
(Dublin)	(Meath)	(Cavan)

Paddy McDonnell	*Joe Synott*
(Carlow)	(Dublin)

Larry Stanley	*Martin Shanahan*	*Joe Stynes*
(Kildare)	(Tipperary)	(Kildare)

Paddy O'Beirne	*Joe Sherlock*	*Frank Burke*
(Mayo)	?	(Kildare)

Larry Stanley was back in the Kildare jersey for the 1926 final against Kerry.

> *The Leinster hopes soared mountain high*
> *When Stanley got the ball,*
> *For many thought that from his try*
> *The Kingdom's fort would fall.*
>
> P. C. O'Connor, from *In Praise of*
> *Heroes: Ballads and Poems of the GAA*
> by Jimmy Smyth (Dublin, 2007)

The game went to a replay. Kerry won. Referring to the drawn game one journalist wrote: 'The Kildare men played perfect football, Stanley was their outstanding performer. He brought down balls with one hand from prodigious heights and sent them goalwards with deadly accuracy.'

Larry Stanley was not on the Kildare teams of 1927 and 1928 that won successive All-Ireland crowns at the expense of Kerry and Cavan respectively. It is said that he was the subject of some 'special attention' in the 1926 All-Ireland final replay against Kerry, following which he decided to concentrate on athletics. It is of interest to note that Kildare won those two All-Ireland titles with the same fifteen players.

Larry returned for the Leinster final against Meath in 1930, which was won after a replay. However, he did not play against Monaghan in the All-Ireland semi-final which was surprisingly lost by 1-6 to 1-4. In the All-Ireland semi-final of the previous year, 1929, Kildare easily beat Monaghan 0-9 to 0-1. It is said that for the All-Ireland semi-final of 1930 against Monaghan, the Kildare players were told to take things easy and make a game of it. If this is true, they paid the penalty.

Larry's county career ended following a second and final comeback in 1933. In a footballing career that began in 1916 he played only seventeen times for his native Kildare, due mainly to his commitment to athletics.

As well as a magnificent Gaelic footballer, Larry was also a talented athlete and a high jumper of international standard. In 1924 he competed at the Olympic Games in Paris. In the same year, in the inaugural Tailteann Games at Croke Park, Larry fought a terrific duel with the newly crowned Olympic high jump champion, Harold M. Osborn of the USA.

In 1970 Larry was the second to be enrolled in the Hall of Fame – an honour first bestowed on John Joe Sheehy of Kerry in 1963. Ten years later, Larry was the first recipient of the All-Time All-Star award. I met him at the same reception in 1983 (when Jim McCullagh of Armagh was similarly honoured) and told him how much my father admired him. I got his autograph, which is reproduced here (see page 109). He was proud to identify with his native Kildare.

Larry was chosen at centre-field on the Garda All-Star team of the twentieth century, while another great honour came on the occasion of the centenary All-Ireland football final between Kerry and Dublin at Croke Park on Sunday 23 September 1984. A presentation was made to Larry, then aged eighty-eight, by Paddy Buggy, GAA president. Larry was, at the time, the oldest-surviving captain of Gaelic games.

I am indebted to Frances Dillane of Ladytown, Newbridge, County Kildare, godchild of Larry (he was also best man for her father, Michael Casey) for her help with this article.

Larry Stanley, footballer, athlete, sportsman, gentleman, was born in 1896 and departed this life on 21 September 1987 – aged ninety-one.

A football selection

John McDonnell
(Dublin)

Matt Goff	Joe Barrett	Gus Fitzpatrick
(Kildare)	(Kerry)	(Kildare)

Paul Russell	Jack Higgins	Joe Synott
(Kerry)	(Kildare)	(Dublin)

Con Brosnan   John Murphy
(Kerry)   (Dublin)

Larry Stanley	John Joe Sheehy	Paul Doyle
(Kildare)	(Kerry)	(Kildare)

Frank Burke	Paddy McDonnell	John Joe Landers
(Dublin)	(Dublin)	(Kerry)

Larry Stanley.

1931–1940

Teams that participated in the
All-Ireland senior finals

COUNTY	FOOTBALL			HURLING	
	WON	LOST		WON	LOST
Cavan	2	1			
Clare					1
Cork				1	1
Dublin		1		1	1
Galway	2	2			
Kerry	5	1			
Kildare		2			
Kilkenny				4	4
Laois		1			
Limerick				3	2
Mayo	1	1			
Meath		1			
Tipperary				1	
Waterford					1

Fourteen counties participated in the senior finals.

The ten hurling finals involved seven counties with five counties successful.

The ten football finals involved seven counties with four of the counties successful.

Kilkenny contested eight of the ten hurling finals and won four.

A HURLING GAME:

Cork v Kilkenny, 1931 All-Ireland final

When Cork and Kilkenny paraded around Croke Park on Sunday 6 September, the 26,460 crowd was witnessing the prologue to the eighth meeting – if you include the Home final of 1903 – of these counties at the final stage.

To date Kilkenny were one win ahead. In 1893 and 1903 Cork trounced Kilkenny, while in 1926, in a most entertaining final, a second-half rally gave Cork a decisive win. Kilkenny's four wins were a different story. An objection and counter-objection to the 1905 final, which Kilkenny lost by three points, led to a replay which Kilkenny won. In 1904, 1907 and 1912 Kilkenny shaded it by just one point.

The roll of honour to date showed Cork in second place with ten titles. Tipperary, their Munster neighbours, headed the table with eleven successes. Kilkenny occupied third place with eight All-Ireland crowns.

As Seán Robbins of Offaly got the 1931 final under way, the question was: would Cork draw level in titles with Tipperary or would Kilkenny narrow the gap on them both?

This was to be a final of three acts, with drama, tragedy and fierce man-to-man combat, wonderful first-time hurling on the ground and overhead, near misses, great scores and deft touches. A hurling epic that brought honour to the ancient game.

The paths to the final were interesting. Kilkenny defeated Wexford, 8-8 to 1-1; Meath, 5-9 to 1-2; Laois, 4-7 to 4-2; and Galway 7-2 to 3-1. Apart from the game against Laois it was a comfortable programme for the Noresiders. That game was in the Leinster final, played at Nowlan Park, Kilkenny before 10,000 spectators. Laois were confident. They had beaten Dublin, the provincial title holders, and had defeated Kilkenny the previous year. At half time the O'Moore county trailed by 2-4 to 0-2. Then, in a sensational third quarter, Laois found the net on four occasions to go four points up. But a point by Lory Meagher and a Mattie Power goal brought Kilkenny level. In the last five minutes a goal and two points by Mick Larkin saw Kilkenny through.

Cork defeated Clare, 3-4 to 1-6; Tipperary, 3-5 to 2-3; drew with Waterford, 1-9 to 4-0; and got the better of Waterford, 5-4 to 1-2.

Cork had by far the tougher campaign. Clare, who were on the ascendancy, pushed them all the way, while the game with Tipperary, reigning All-Ireland champions, was a tense, teak-tough, torrid affair. All of Cork's goals came in the first half; the points came in the second half. In the Munster final against Waterford, Cork almost made their exit from the championship. It was deep into injury time when Jim Hurley got the equalising point. But they had learned well, and made no mistake in the replay. Victory was clear-cut and decisive.

Cork and Kilkenny, as they both faced the last hurdle, were captained by two great leaders – Eudi Coughlan of Blackrock and Cork; Lory Meagher of Tullaroan and Kilkenny. Indeed, Eudi had been a doubtful starter – he suffered a broken nose in the replay with Waterford.

In the first half Kilkenny defended the railway goal and faced the sun. Mattie Power, ace corner-forward, was back in the Kilkenny attack after a spell in the Dublin jersey. A 'Gah' Ahern goal put Cork ahead by four points at half time, 1-3 to 0-2. They increased their lead to six points early in the second half and with twenty minutes remaining looked as if they might pull away for a decisive win. But Kilkenny struck back. They won a 50-yard free. Lory stood over the sliotar. He failed to lift. Unfazed, he cut a beauty off the ground right to the square at crossbar height. Dan Dunne was there to finish it to the net. Kilkenny followed with four unanswered points – two from Lory – to go one point up. The game was in the balance. Eudi Coughlan gained possession. The angle was acute. On his knees, he struck the sliotar, which sailed between the posts for a sensational point. That ended the scoring at 1-6 apiece. Shortly before the finish, Dick Morrissey of Kilkenny was seriously injured. It took him four years to recover and he never hurled again. He was replaced by Jack Duggan.

Tom Ryall, in his book *Kilkenny: The GAA Story 1884–1984* (Kilkenny, 1984), said: 'The fare was superb, keen and skilful. It was a battle of giants.' The game, according to the *Cork Examiner*, 'played at top speed, and containing many thrilling personal duels, was from the first second to the last, a thrilling game'.

Act II

A classic of classics ... the pace was terrific and it was unabated from start to finish ... Beautifully accurate striking was witnessed on both sides; overhead play was superb; ground striking was swift and decisive.

Kilkenny People

With the football final scheduled for 27 September, the hurling replay did not take place until 11 October. Increased interest saw the attendance jump by almost 7,000 to 33,124. Seán Robbins of Offaly was again in charge. Before the throw-in the captains were introduced to Rev. Dr Hayden, archbishop of Hobart.

The replay was one of the greatest games in hurling lore. The sliotar moved up and down the field at great speed. First-time striking was the order of the day. Dinny Barry-Murphy, Cork's classy wing-back, reflecting afterwards on the game, said that for a while he didn't quite come to grips with what was happening around him and added that it was no place for handymen.

Scores were, as in the first game, at a premium – each one worth a king's ransom.

Morgan Madden of Cork, following an accidental stroke from Mattie Power, was carried off and replaced by George Garret, who proceeded to play a blinder.

Cork goals by Eudi Coughlan and Willie Clancy, and a Kilkenny goal by Dan Dunne, left the half time score 2-4 to 1-3 in Cork's favour – four points up as in the drawn game, despite having a goal disallowed.

Lory Meagher was magnificent – best man on the field. He played his heart out and pointed a 90-yard free in the second half. For most of the hour he played with three broken ribs, sustained in a clash close by the Hogan stand.

The story is told of a Kilkenny free, which Tommy Carroll of Mooncoin was about to take from a scorable position. Jim Regan, the Cork centre-half-back, was standing too close and the referee was ordering him back. Then Lory arrived and Tommy moved away as his captain said he would take the free. By now, however, the ribs were hurting. From Lory's effort no score resulted.

With a quarter of an hour to go Kilkenny led by 2-5 to 2-4. As in the first game, Cork had to come from behind to save the day. Paddy Delea shot the equaliser – incredibly Cork's only score of the second half. And at the final whistle, stalemate again.

The two drawn games had been energy sapping. Extra time was suggested, but this was turned down. With a view to finding a solution and avoiding a third game, it was proposed at a Central Council meeting by Bob O'Keeffe of Laois – seconded by Paddy McDonnell of Dublin and supported by Seán Gibbons of Kilkenny – that both counties be declared joint champions. The proposal was defeated by ten votes to five. If it had been successful, the likelihood of giving each player a half medal was in prospect.

Act III
There was no mistaking where one was ... on every side you could recognise the strong unchiselled faces which are distinctly Celtic type. You saw them again on most of the players on the field.
Gertrude Gaffney, *Irish Independent*

When the ball was thrown in, the hurlers were flashes of lightning rather than men ... the game was so swift throughout that one's eye was not quick enough to follow it.
Irish Independent

The third game took place on 1 November, before an official attendance of 31,935. There was a change of referee, with Willie Walsh of Waterford now in charge.

Cork fielded the same team that started the two drawn games. However, as in the second game, George Garret was called into action, this time in place of the injured Peter O'Grady.

Kilkenny had many changes. Dick Morrissey, Paddy Larkin, Lory Meagher and Billy Dalton were all on the injured list. Martin White, centre-forward in the first game, was replaced by Paddy 'Skipper' Walsh for the second. Martin went on to win three All-Irelands with Kilkenny in the 1930s. As I write he is in his 100th year, and is the only survivor from the heroes of 1931.

The odds were heavily stacked against Kilkenny. Their captain, the majestic Lory Meagher, was an immense loss. His absence was not revealed until the last minute, as it was feared supporters might not travel if they knew he was not playing. Accordingly, arrangements were made to ensure Lory was seen boarding the train at Kilkenny with his hurley and boots.

Coming up to half time it was nip and tuck with Kilkenny adopting a more physical approach than in the two drawn games. With two minutes to go to the break, the score stood at Cork 0-5 Kilkenny 1-2. Then Cork struck twice. A Kilkenny lapse in defence saw 'Gah'

Ahern find the net, and moments later Paddy Delea had the green flag waving again. Half time, Cork 2-5 Kilkenny 1-2.

Kilkenny, aided by the breeze, added 1-2 in the second half to come within a point of Cork, 2-5 to 2-4. However, the Rebel county went on to add 3-3 to a goal for Kilkenny. The game ended Cork 5-8 Kilkenny 3-4 – a final scoreline that did not quite reflect just how close the third game had been.

There was a moment of poignancy in the second half when a Kilkenny player went down injured. We are told that a girl in the crowd let her emotions overflow into tears as she and others begged Lory, with chants of 'Lory, Lory, Lory' to respond to Kilkenny's need, but the great captain could only smile as he watched helplessly with his injured ribs.

Pádraig Puirséal described the scene:

> ... and three cracked ribs keeping him out of the third game, sitting grey-faced in the Kilkenny dug-out, clinching and unclinching his hands in quiet despair, tears of frustration coursing down his cheeks.

Eudi Coughlan, the Cork captain, played the game of his life. He had the sliotar from each of the three games with the score inscribed on them; they rested on the sideboard in his living room. I held them in my hands when I visited him in 1981.

Dan Dunne of Kilkenny was the only player on the field to have found the net in each game. Central Council presented wristlet watches to both teams in appreciation of their contribution.

The All-Ireland victory of 1931 brought the curtain down on a great Cork era. Between 1926 and 1931, the county had won four All-Ireland titles – 1926, 1928, 1929 and 1931; five Munster crowns – 1926, 1927, 1928, 1929 and 1931; and two National League titles – 1925/26 and 1929/30.

For Kilkenny, it heralded the beginning of a second golden era. Between 1931 and 1940 they would contest all ten Leinster finals and lose only two, 1934 and 1938, and these only after replays. As well as eight provincial titles, they harvested four All-Irelands and one National League and made a major contribution to three Railway Cup successes.

Three times in all, Cork and Kilkenny crossed camáns for the championship. Men say that the first replay must stand as the classic final of all time. Then in the third, as the November evening drew to an early close, Cork came out winners. Even to a Cork man it was regrettable to see these Kilkenny lads being beaten – a great pity.

John Power, *A Story of Champions* (1941)

Eudi Coughlan, whose county career stretched from 1919 to 1931, was interviewed in 1984 by Declan Hassett for an article in *The Rockies: A Centenary Year Publication* (Cork, 1984). Eudi gave his views on the present-day game.

There is not enough man to man marking. You can't interfere with a man if he has the ball. In my time you'd get a shoulder or a crack of a hurley – you'd get it (the ball) out of your way quickly. There is too much protection nowadays ... you'd want the heart of an ox when we played – your ribs would be black and blue for a fortnight after.

The game was faster than it is now. In my time you'd hit the ball first or second time. Now they stop the ball, catch it, and throw it up and strike it – that's four movements; only two movements in my time.

Lory Meagher with the horse-drawn reaper and binder performing in a different 'field'.

Eudi Coughlan – photographed after the 1931 All-Ireland win
over Kilkenny, wearing a skull cap bearing the year.

A HURLING PERSONALITY:

Johnny Quirke (Cork)

Big Liam Murphy of Ballincollig, shook his black locks as he swung the puck-out. The like of it was never seen since Andy Fitzgerald's days. The crowd roared as the ball sailed in the breeze and dropped 140 yards away – on the 21-yard line. John Quirke was on it in a flash. Ted Sullivan cleared the way and Quirke's ash swept the ball to the meshes – two strokes from net to net.

'Carbery' on the 1941 hurling final, Cork v Dublin

Are hurlers born or made? The question is often debated. Perhaps 'Carbery' came closest when he wrote that 'hurling was largely a game of the spirit'. I put Johnny Quirke in that category.

Johnny was born in Milltown in County Kerry in 1911 – four miles from Killorglin, football country, home of the famed Laune Rangers. He wasn't yet one year old when the family moved to Blackrock, County Cork, where his father got a job as a steward in the Ursuline convent.

When I visited Johnny in 1981 he told me that he 'grew up play-ing hurling on the road and any field you could take a chance in'. By 1929 his talents were beginning to blossom, and he was selected on the Cork junior team. They beat Waterford in the Munster final but failed to Offaly in the All-Ireland final. He was now on the Blackrock senior panel and went on to win three county titles in a row – 1929, 1930 and 1931.

Johnny got his place on the Cork senior team in 1932, a baptism of fire in the Munster final on 31 July when they faced Clare before 25,000 people. Cork were reigning All-Ireland champions and the team was full of household names, including George Garett, Jim Hurley, 'Gah' Ahern, Jim Regan, Dinny Barry-Murphy, Tom Barry and their captain 'Marie' O'Connell. Clare, however, had no fear of Cork. They had beaten them in 1930 when Cork were All-Ireland title holders and only failed by four points in 1931.

Clare struck in the first half and led by 3-2 to 1-0 at half time.

Fierce Cork onslaughts in the second half were thwarted by Tommy Daly in goal, Pa 'Fowler' McInerney, John Joe 'Goggles' Doyle and Larry Blake. Johnny Quirke got the last score – a goal – but it was not enough to save Cork, who lost by 5-2 to 4-1. He was playing at corner-forward and marking the Clare captain, John Joe Doyle, a prince of corner-backs. It was a difficult task. 'John Joe cost me my place on the Cork team for a while after that game,' Johnny would later recall.

Cork hurling ran into a lean spell. Some time around the mid-1930s, the story goes, Johnny suggested to Seán Óg Murphy that he could manage Mick Mackey. Seán Óg looked at him and said: 'I think you are getting notions.' Well, in 1938 and 1939 Johnny did play on Mick and performed with distinction.

Johnny had to wait until 1939 for the Cork breakthrough, when they won a Munster title after an epic contest with Limerick. Johnny at centre-half-back was marking Mick Mackey. However, disappointment was Johnny's lot when Cork went down to Kilkenny by a point in the All-Ireland final, in a game that became known as 'the thunder and lightning final'.

Johnny was now entering the autumn of his hurling days. The past had yielded little, but Munster titles came in 1939, 1942, 1943 and 1944. He won four All-Ireland titles in a row, 1941 to 1944, and joined a select band of players to have such a distinction, for never before or since has any county won four hurling finals in a row. He won National League titles in 1940 and 1941. For ten years in a row, 1936 to 1945, he was on the Munster Railway Cup hurling selection – losing only in 1936 and 1941. He led his province to success in 1945. To be chosen for your province in those days was a tremendous honour. Just look at the names of those in the photograph of the 1943 Munster team (see p. 127) – each a master of the hurling craft.

Johnny played many great games, both as forward and defender, during a county career that spanned sixteen years. His greatest hour? It has to be the drawn Munster final of 1944 against Limerick. Archbishop Kinnane threw in the ball and Cork broke at lightning pace. This is how 'Carbery' described Johnny Quirke's contribution:

> ... *Quirke placed Morrisson ... Cork one goal up. Cork away again and John Quirke's eye was dead in – he pulled on a hard ground ball that gave Mickie Walsh no chance at all ... Cork forwards*

again sparkled. Kelly and Ring were moving fast and once more John Quirke's experience told – he dummied fast and pulled hard and low – net.

At half time Cork led by 4-3 to 1-5 and with the wind and sun in their favour after the break the game looked all over. Well into the second half, Cork had stretched their lead to eight points. Then Limerick struck. Points were swapped and then came goals by Dick Stokes and Mick Mackey to cut Cork's lead to two points. 'Carbery' describes the scene:

Clohessy fastened on one and crashed it home for Limerick's lead, and pandemonium outside the lines – 20,000 swaying. John Mackey set the score 24–22 in Limerick's favour. Broken time now. Then came John Quirke's greatest goal of his long career. Ring swung a pass to the old Rockie, Lynch helped to guard him. Quirke dummied twice and then shot. He knew a goal was the only rescue – he hit a beauty dead on the net, for a goal and for Cork's lead.

Dick Stokes, dead on time, made it a draw. Cork 6-7 Limerick 4-13.

In Cork's drawn game with Limerick
It looked a Limerick win,
With the Corkmen's backs against the wall
They fought Mick Mackey's men,
When victory seemed beyond their reach
No man was known to shirk
When the crowd roars,
They're even scores,
That great goal by John Quirke.
Cors O'Connell

For most of the replay, Limerick were in the ascendancy and were a point ahead in broken time. Then Johnny Quirke, who had a quiet game, came to the rescue with a beauty point. What followed is part of hurling lore – Ring's 'wonder' goal that kept the title in Cork.

Johnny, during a long hurling career, played with and against great men at club, county and interprovincial level. Outside of Cork he had special admiration for John Keane, Charlie Ware and Declan Goode of Waterford; Jackie Power, Paddy Clohessy and Mick Mackey of Limerick; John Maher of Tipperary; and indeed many others, some of whom appear in the Munster Railway Cup team of which Johnny was a member, playing at right-full-forward (see below).

Johnny loved to sing. One of his favourites was 'The Boys of Blackrock'. He sang it on television a few weeks before he died in 1983, aged seventy-two. I have chosen the following verses:

I met an old hurler now sixty and six,
Who played centre-forward and under the sticks.
He played with the Islands, the Redmonds, the Barrs.
He had medals to prove it with old battle scars.
He could play don't forget although an old crock
But the best men he met were the boys from Blackrock.

If you wanted a hurler you'd find him for sure
Ballinlough, Ballintemple, and around Ballinure,
I don't care what they say but give me the old stock,
And stand up and hurl with the boys of Blackrock.
  Now all you young hurlers take pattern by me.
And don't waste your time by the banks of the Lee.
Just come down to Beaumont and meet the old stock
And we'll learn to hurl with the boys of Blackrock.

Munster Railway Cup Winners, 1943. *Back row (l–r):* John Keane (Waterford), Dick Stokes (Limerick), Batt Thornhill (Cork), Willie O'Donnell (Tipperary), Jack Lynch, captain (Cork), Andy Fleming (Waterford), Mick Mackey (Limerick), Billy Murphy (Cork), Jim Barry, trainer; *front row (l–r):* John Quirke (Cork), Jim Young (Cork), Tommy Doyle (Tipperary), Christy Ring (Cork, Jackie Power (Limerick), Paddy Cregan (Limerick), Jimmy Maher (Tipperary); *insets (l–r):* Mick Kennefick (Cork), John Mackey (Limerick).

A hurling selection

Paddy Scanlon
(Limerick)

| *Paddy Larkin* | *Peter O'Reilly* | *Paddy Phelan* |
| (Kilkenny) | (Kilkenny) | (Kilkenny) |

| *Mickey Cross* | *Paddy Clohessy* | *Garrett Howard* |
| (Limerick) | (Limerick) | (Limerick) |

Timmy Ryan   *Lory Meagher*
(Limerick)   (Kilkenny)

| *John Mackey* | *Mick Mackey* | *Jimmy Walsh* |
| (Limerick) | (Limerick) | (Kilkenny) |

| *Martin White* | *Paddy McMahon* | *Mattie Power* |
| (Kilkenny) | (Limerick) | (Kilkenny) |

Kilkenny and Limerick dominated the 1930s with outstanding hurlers and exceptional teams. Kilkenny won eight Leinster titles, four All-Ireland titles and one National League. Limerick won five Munster titles, five National Leagues, three All-Ireland titles and the inaugural Oireachtas in 1939.

I have dedicated the team of the 1930s to Kilkenny and Limerick – a decade, like all other decades, that produced several other great hurlers.

Paddy Phelan on his Confirmation Day with his sister Biddy.

Mick Mackey holding the McCarthy Cup at Heuston Station in 1936 after Limerick won the All-Ireland hurling final.

Mick Mackey.

A FOOTBALL GAME:

Galway v Kerry, 1938 All-Ireland final

On a beautiful September Sunday afternoon, the footballers of Galway and Kerry paraded around Croke Park before a record attendance of 68,950, prior to referee Tom Culhane of Limerick getting the All-Ireland final of 1938 under way.

In the commentary box was the late Micheál O'Hehir – then an eighteen-year-old student – who was about to undertake his first All-Ireland final broadcast.

This was the first time these counties had clashed at the final stage. The most recent championship meeting was the semi-final of 1919. That game ended in a draw, with Galway winning the replay.

All-Ireland final replays were a Kerry forte. They had taken part in four of the five All-Ireland final draws to date and won them all: 1903 v Kildare (Home final); 1914 v Wexford; 1926 v Kildare; 1937 v Cavan.

The 1938 final was destined to end in a draw. On the way Kerry had a runaway victory over Cork in the Munster decider, 4-14 to 0-6. They were fortunate to have two points to spare over a talented Laois team in the semi-final, 2-6 to 2-4. That game was played at Croke Park on 21 August on the occasion of the official opening of the Cusack stand.

Galway created a surprise in the west when overcoming Mayo – All-Ireland champions in 1936 and Connacht title holders in 1935, 1936 and 1937 – by 0-8 to 0-5. Monaghan were well beaten in the semi-final at Mullingar, 2-10 to 2-3.

Kerry felt confident on final day. They had twelve titles to their credit; Galway had two. As well, Kerry had earlier in the year beaten Galway at Listowel and again in a League game in Galway. On both occasions Kerry had under-strength teams. Tradition and logic were on their side. *Ach ní mar síltear bítear.*

The game was a thriller. Both sides favoured catch-and-kick and high fielding. The exchanges were physical and sporting. At half time Kerry led by 1-3 to 1-2, the goals coming from John Joe Landers and Brendan Nestor respectively. Galway's defence was standing solid; Kerry's attack had missed many chances. In the second half, Kerry defended the railway goal with the breeze at their backs but facing the sun. They added two points but a goal by Ned Mulholland levelled matters. Points were exchanged. Tim O'Leary put Kerry a goal up, but a Ramie Griffin goal had Galway back on terms. Time was running out. Kerry launched a traditional final assault, forcing three fifties, but Galway packed their defence and beat off each one. With a minute remaining, Kerry's John Joe Landers drove high between the posts for what looked like the winner. But too late. The final whistle had sounded. The replay was set for 22 October.

The attendance of 47,481, while still good, was down considerably on the first day. In the game itself, Kerry attacks – and there were many of them – perished on a rock-solid Galway rearguard, where Mick Connaire at full back and Bobby Beggs at centre-half were magnificent. The Galway forwards, with fewer chances, were more opportunistic, with Brendan Nestor very much to the fore. Galway led by 1-3 to 0-4 at the interval.

Immediately on resumption Kerry scored a point. Galway responded with a scrambled goal following a well-taken free by their midfielder John Burke. Indeed, there were so many bodies around the ball that no-one seemed to know who exactly got the touch that took it over the line. With three minutes remaining both sides had added a point to leave the score Galway 2-4 Kerry 0-6.

A free to Kerry led to unprecedented confusion. As the Kerry man took the free, the referee, observing a Galway player standing too close, blew for a further free to Kerry. Galway supporters took it to be the final whistle, however, and surged jubilantly onto the pitch. The referee tried to restore order, aided by an announcement over the loudspeakers requesting people to return to their seats.

It took some time to clear the pitch. The Galway team was ready to resume; however all but two of the Kerry players had retired to the dressing room. And many of those had departed to the Central Hotel, where they had originally togged out. After much confusion, Kerry lined out to resume play with what was left of the team, supplemented by an assortment of substitutes.

A free to Kerry brought a point by Seán Brosnan – one of the two Kerry men who had remained on the pitch. Shortly afterwards, the real full-time whistle blew. Galway's third title; Kerry's invincibility in replays shattered. And for those with a superstitious mind there was a lesson too – if your winning score in an All-Ireland final is disallowed, then you will not win in extra time or in the replay, as was proven to Wexford's cost in the hurling final of 1891 and Cavan's in the football final of 1937. 'Green Flag', writing in the *Irish Press* the following day, had this to say:

> *The Kerry centre field had the best of the exchanges for most of the hour, but the Western backs negated this by as grand a display of defensive football as we've seen for some years in an All-Ireland final.*

I knew one of those Galway players, their full-forward Martin Kelly. He was a member of the Garda Síochána and served in my native Ardagh in west Limerick for many years. He was a rangy, well-built man, quiet spoken and gentlemanly. He was top scorer in the Connacht final of 1934 against Mayo with 1-1 of Galway's 2-4.

Sometimes my brother Aodán and myself would visit his house. We knew of his All-Ireland successes in 1934 and 1938, and on one occasion he showed us his medals. On one of our visits he told us a fascinating story about the closing moments of the 1938 All-Ireland final. When play resumed after the 'false' final whistle, I don't think anyone knows what fifteen finished the game for Kerry. Anyway, Martin cast his eye around the field and concluded that Kerry had sixteen on the pitch. He turned to Murt Kelly, who was one of Kerry's 'new' players and said: 'Murt, go off, there are sixteen of ye.' 'Ah, 'tis alright', said Murt, 'sure ye have the game won.' 'That's all very fine', replied Martin, 'until ye get scores to go ahead and then ye'll disappear one of the players.'

I contacted Martin's daughter, May O'Connell, who very kindly supplied the following:

> *Dad was born on 25 November 1906 in Cloncannon, Ahascragh, County Galway. He played with the local football team. He excelled at the game and his football skills were mentioned in his application to join the Garda. He was appointed to the force on 17 January 1929. He spent the first few years serving in Dereen, Beaufort and Killarney in County Kerry and was transferred to depot headquarters on 16 December 1932.*
>
> *Dad was captain of the Garda football team when he married Nora Walsh of Asdee, County Kerry, on 25 April 1935. But because the Garda team were winning all the tournaments, they were all sent down the country – Dad to Patrickswell, County*

Limerick, on 8 November 1935 where he spent a little over a year before going to Ardagh.

I think it was 1939 that the Galway team went to America. There they won many championships, including the world championship. Though very young, I remember it well. I can still see him coming into the room, the day he came home, carrying a playpen for me that he brought all the way from the US.

Dad did a lot for football during his life. He trained teams in Ardagh and also in Ballingarry where he was appointed sergeant on 17 December 1956. He retired on 26 November 1969 with an exemplary service record.

I remember well the crowds in our house in Ardagh. We had a wireless. That was rare at the time. All the men were sitting on the floor.

All his medals were divided among his grandchildren. His All-Ireland medals of 1934 and 1938 were given to his first two grandsons – now cherished possessions of Nigel Mulleady (Derry's son) and Martin O'Connell (my son). Dad died on 25 May 1985. He was special.

This is the team that halted Kerry's replay successes:

Jimmy McGauran

Mick Rafferty   Mick Connaire   Dinny O'Sullivan

Frank Cunniffe   Bobby Beggs   Charlie Connolly

John Dunne (captain)   John Burke

Jack Flavin   Ramie Griffin   Mick Higgins

Ned Mulholland   Martin Kelly   Brendan Nestor

That 1938 defeat by Galway was to cost Kerry a possible five-in-a-row. The previous year, 1937, they beat Cavan after a replay. And after 1938 Kerry won three in a row – all close calls as the following scorelines indicate: 1939 v Meath, 2-5 to 2-3; 1940 v Galway, 0-7 to 1-3; 1941 v Galway, 1-8 to 0-7.

The Kerry team that lost to Galway in the 1938 football replay. *Back row (l-r)*: C. O'Sullivan, P. Kennedy, W. Casey, Myers, S. Brosnan, P. B. Brosnan, M. Doyle; *front row (l–r)*: M. Regan, D. O'Keeffe, J. Walsh, T. O'Leary, W. Kinnerk (captain) with mascot, W. Dillon, T. McAuliffe, T. Connor.

Martin Kelly in his early days in the Garda Síochána.   Martin Kelly in later years.

A FOOTBALL PERSONALITY:

Gerald Courell (Mayo)

I had the pleasure of meeting Fr Gerry Courell – son of Gerald – in August 2007, when he was home on holidays from England. From him, I learned much about his father – a most unassuming man, a great GAA supporter and a brilliant footballer.

Gerald belonged to a family steeped in Gaelic games. His father Tom was a founder member, and first president, of Ballina Stephenites in 1886. The club colours, red and green, were adopted by Mayo as the county colours. Gerald's oldest brother Frank, who shone in many positions, particularly in defence, won Croke Cup medals with Mayo in the early years of the twentieth century. He captained Mayo in 1916 when the county reached the All-Ireland final, only to be defeated by a great Wexford combination. Two others brothers, Bertie and Joe, also played with Mayo in their time. Fr Gerry is now a lifetime patron of Ballina Stephenites, thus creating an unbroken link with the club and the Courell family since the club's foundation.

Gerald's county career started around 1925. In 1932, the year Mayo lost the All-Ireland final to Kerry by 2-7 to 2-4, he was the only Mayo man chosen on the Tailteann Games team to play America – a team of star footballers captained by Joe Barrett of Kerry and including Jack Higgins of Kildare, Martin O'Neill of Wexford, Jack Delaney of Laois, Johnny McDonnell of Dublin and Jim Smith of Cavan.

The same year, the Mayo football team went on a US tour. Gerald was in deadly kicking form. An American cartoonist was captivated by his accuracy from play and from placed kicks. Comments and headlines included: 'He can do anything with a football except kick around corners'; 'Wotta drop-kicker' and 'Gerald Courell possesses the most amazingly educated toe in Gaelic football'.

The management of an American football team was so taken by Gerald's accuracy that they made him an offer to turn professional and be their place-kicker. All he would have to do was come on during a game and take the place kicks. Gerald declined. He was a Ballina man through and through, the place of his birth. On alighting from the train following the US tour, one of Gerald's first questions to the greeting party was: 'Did Fitzgerald's [a local team] win?'

Reporting on Mayo's second game during the US tour, 'Wedger' Meagher of Tipperary said:

> *Courell, who was on the sideline in the first contest, was the star scorer for the Irish visitors, accounting for the major portion of the points and kicking with deadly accuracy.*

Gerald played for Connacht in the Railway Cup. They lost the 1933 final to Leinster by the narrowest of margins, 0-12 to 2-5. A year later, with a team consisting of eight Mayo players and seven Galway players, the western province gained revenge, winning by 2-9 to 2-8. Gerald collected his only Railway Cup medal.

In 1934 an *Irish Independent* supplement commemorated the golden jubilee of the GAA. It profiled some of the great hurlers and footballers, including Gerald Courell:

> *His pace, craft, elusiveness, and deadly shooting made him the terror of backs. With the Mayo team who toured America in 1932 Gerald was the star, scoring the amazing total of twenty-eight points from five games. Even this record was eclipsed in Ireland in 1933. Against Sligo he kicked 1-7 in a single game; and at Castlebar against Kerry he went one better, running up the astonishing total of 1-8.*

Gerald was part of a great Mayo era, beginning in 1934, that saw the county win six consecutive National League titles. On 13 May at Castlebar, before an attendance of 10,000, Mayo and Dublin drew in the final. The replay took place at Croke Park on 15 October. A goal and a point by team captain Gerald Courell saw Mayo ahead at half time by 1-1 to 0-3. They won by 2-4 to 1-5. Gerald became the first Mayo man to hold aloft a senior national trophy. Talking about it afterwards, he used to say 'how cold the cup felt' when he grasped it on that autumn afternoon.

Gerald was again captain the following year when Fermanagh were beaten by 5-8 to 0-2. He showed his class by scoring three great goals.

For the third year in a row Gerald led Mayo to victory in the 1936 League. In all three successes he played at right-full-forward. He was a sub on the winning team of 1937 and was still part of the panel that was again successful in 1938.

In 1936 Mayo won their first All-Ireland senior football title. In the Connacht final, which went to a replay with Galway, Gerald scored Mayo's two goals in a 2-7 to 1-4 win. Before the All-Ireland semi-final against Kerry at Roscommon Gerald was told, just as he was about to take the field, that he was not on the first fifteen. According to Fr Gerry it was a 'political' decision. However, following a 1-5 to 0-6 win over Kerry and an easy victory over Laois in the final, Gerald became the proud possessor of an All-Ireland medal.

In 1935 Mayo beat Galway by 0-12 to 0-5 in the Connacht final. According to a press report of the game:

> *The game provided a personal triumph for Gerald Courell, whose marksmanship was remarkable. Every shot he got from free kicks near goal were converted with the greatest of ease.*

In seven out of the nine Connacht finals from 1928 to 1936, Gerald was top scorer. Little wonder then that 'Carbery' referred to him as 'the most prolific scorer of his period'.

Gerald retired from club football in 1943, after which he became active in club administration. He was also active at provincial level, chairing the Connacht Council for three years. He refereed the All-Ireland minor final of 1949 between Armagh and Kerry when the Ulster county won its first title. With his friend and footballing colleague Jackie Carney of the 1930s he helped train the Mayo senior football team between 1948 and 1952. They were rewarded with four Connacht titles between 1948 and 1951 and two All-Ireland crowns in 1950 and 1951.

Gerald Courell died after a protracted illness in September 1983 aged seventy-five. His son, Fr Gerry, gave an appreciation at his requiem Mass: 'I don't know how I did it – Dad was dying for three months, Mam died in five minutes.' He continued:

> *The awe with which people used to point him out, when as a child I went to games with him, always amazed me ... His love for the GAA, his love for football, had nothing to do with the fame and success he gained, his love was for the game itself.*
>
> *He had no time for the cruder aspects of our game, foul language and foul play ... He was a gentle, sincere, humble man, who always looked on the bright side of things ... He lives on in the inspiration he gave us, in the heritage he left us.*

A football selection

Tom Burke
(Mayo)

Mick Rafferty   Eddie Boyle   'Purty' Kelly
(Galway)   (Louth)   (Mayo)

Frank Cunniffe   John Joe Reilly   Georgie Ormsby
(Galway)   (Cavan)   (Mayo)

Bob Stack   Bill Delaney
(Kerry)   (Laois)

Gerald Courell   Josie Munnelly   Tim Landers
(Mayo)   (Mayo)   (Kerry)

Danny Douglas   Paddy Moclair   Martin Kelly
(Laois)   (Mayo)   (Galway)

Tim Landers, one of the three
famous Landers brothers.

(L-r): Paddy Moclair, Jackie Carney and
Gerald Courell, Mayo teammates, all three.

1941–1950

Teams that participated in the
All-Ireland senior finals

COUNTY	FOOTBALL		HURLING		
	WON	LOST	WON	LOST
Antrim				1
Cavan	2	3		
Cork	1		5	1
Dublin	1			4
Galway		2		
Kerry	2	2		
Kilkenny			1	3
Laois				1
Louth		1		
Mayo	1	1		
Meath	1			
Roscommon	2	1		
Tipperary			3	
Waterford			1	

Fourteen counties participated in the senior finals.

The ten hurling finals involved seven counties, with four successful.

The ten football finals involved nine counties, with seven successful.

A HURLING GAME:

Cork v Limerick, 1944 Munster final

By the time Limerick and Cork, with victories over Clare and Tipperary respectively, had qualified for the Munster hurling final of 1944, the Allied landings in Normandy had been successfully executed. However, the war would drag on for another year. Rationing was the order of the day, with food, fuel, clothing, footwear, electricity – indeed everything – in short supply. The GAA, too, continued to suffer, with many of its competitions remaining suspended.

The clash of Cork and Limerick scheduled for 16 July gripped the imagination. A rip-roaring contest was anticipated – and with good reason. In 1939 the meeting of these teams in the final at Thurles before a crowd of 41,000 delivered a hurling epic. One press report described it as follows (from *The Mackey Story* by Séamus Ó Ceallaigh and Seán Murphy [Limerick, 1982]):

> *It was a glorious, thrilling all-exciting game, an event that set hearts throbbing madly and blood pulsating wildly … Class hurling at any time is the fastest ball game on earth – Sunday last at Thurles it was 'grease lightning' – and of such play adequate description is impossible.*

In a game of fluctuating fortunes, it was anybody's game. As the seconds ticked away Limerick held a one-point lead. Then a Cork raid yielded a goal. The umpires consulted before waving the green flag. Cork were Munster champions, 4-3 to 3-4.

The following year, 1940, the teams met again at Thurles at the final stage. 'Carbery' wrote (from *The Mackey Story*):

> *Many of us thought the 1939 Munster final had reached hurling meridian. Yet this year's vivid memories switched 1939 to 'the limbo of forgotten things' and 'battles long ago'. Scribblers are bankrupt of phrases. Our vocabulary is exhausted. We must invent a new language to describe modern hurling.*

The game ended all square, Limerick 4-3 Cork 3-6. For once the replay exceeded the drawn game in thrills and excitement. Half time showed a rare scoreline: Cork 0-3 Limerick 0-0. Early in the second half, in a ten-minute electrifying spell, Limerick swept in on the Cork defence to register 3-1 – Mick Mackey a point, followed by a goal each from Jackie Power, Paddy McMahon and Dick Stokes. Ten points in ten minutes – Limerick seven points to the good. Cork rallied but just failed to pull the game out of the fire. It ended Limerick 3-3 Cork 2-4.

Pitch invaded with two minutes left to play in 1940 Munster final replay between Limerick and Cork at Thurles. Order was restored and the game finished.

These games were Christy Ring's introduction to Munster final clashes. He would look back on them and describe them as 'frightening'.

They met again in Limerick in the 1942 Munster semi-final. Jim Young, Cork's wing-back, always claimed it was the greatest game of hurling he ever played in. Con Murphy, a Cork defender of those years, put it second after the 1947 All-Ireland final between Cork and Kilkenny. For a while it looked as if Cork's All-Ireland crown might topple. Heading towards injury time it was level pegging. Then Charlie Tobin with a one-handed stroke put Cork a point ahead. Another point followed. Cork were on their way, 4-8 to 5-3, when the final whistle heralded the end of yet another Cork–Limerick hurling epic.

Against such a backdrop, it is little wonder that the 1944 clash of these counties turned Thurles into a hurling Mecca. Cars were off the road because of wartime restrictions, so every other mode of transport was put to use – mainly the bicycle. As in 1940 we had a draw and a replay. For both games hurling fans descended on Thurles in their hordes, many as early as Saturday afternoon. Some slept in hay-barns and outhouses and even under the summer sky.

Jim Hurley, hero of many a Cork game of earlier years, cycled from Cork, staying overnight with the Leahys of Boherlahan. Many old veterans left Limerick city on Saturday and walked. Among them was 65-year-old Peter Ryan, who covered the 35-mile journey from his home in Lisnagry. The late Joe Cooper, a cyclist from Belfast, headed south with a few of his cycling and hurling enthusiasts.

'Carbery' painted the scene in his inimitable style:

> On the roads from Cork, Limerick and Kilkenny, perspiring cyclists were plugging their way in. From the top of a low hill outside Thurles town I saw them coming in happy droves along the straight roads like ants on the move.

Archbishop Kinnane of Cashel threw in the ball the first day. Mick Mackey of Limerick was the hero of both games – magical, majestic, memorable. He celebrated his thirty-second birthday on 12 July, four days before the drawn game. Johnny Quirke of Cork, the Kerry-born Blackrock hurler and veteran of a hundred battles, was Cork's saviour in both games. Christy Ring of Glen Rovers and Cork, whose hurling buds had yet to burst forth into brilliant blossoms, set off on a controlled solo run as the clock in the replay ticked towards the final whistle, and finished with a cracking goal.

The last advice to Cork before both games was to keep the game fast, for their mentors knew there were ageing limbs in sectors of the Limerick team. Cork broke at lightning pace and went two goals up, a lead they held at half time. They faced into the second half with the wind and sun in their favour.

Entering the last quarter Limerick launched assault after assault on the Cork lines. Goals by Dick Stokes and Mick Mackey brought them within two points. Limerick were now moving like mowers in a meadow. And when young Clohessy from St Patrick's sent Limerick into the lead for the first time, with a smashing goal, it was pandemonium. Johnny Mackey put them two points up, sending the excitement levels even higher. And when all seemed lost for Cork, Johnny Quirke came to the rescue with as good a goal as he scored in a long career, before Dick Stokes levelled for Limerick on the call of time.

'Carbery' summed it up:

> *The game was beautifully controlled, the pitch a picture and the hurling hearty, clean and fair ... we had to wait for the second half for the fireworks, the heavy thud of crashing body to body and splintering ash – winding up in a crescendo of excitement.*

Day 2 – 30 July
Very Rev. Dr O'Dwyer, superior general to the Maynooth Mission for China, threw in the ball. In a game of hectic man-to-man exchanges, watched by a crowd of 20,000, Limerick were in the ascendancy from the third minute. They led by a goal at half time and, entering the final quarter, had stretched the lead to five points. Then came a crucial moment and a decision that probably decided the game. Mackey got possession and headed for goal. Din Joe Buckley, alert to the danger, fouled Mackey, who kept going and goaled. But the referee had blown for a free, which was sent wide.

Cork rallied and a goal by young Morrison, as injury time was being played, cut the Limerick lead to one point. Johnny Quirke delivered the equaliser, and then came Ring's goal of goals, described by 'Carbery':

> *Referee looks at his watch – we make it a minute to go – Christy Ring gets the ball; it glues to his hurley as he sprints up the wing like a shadow – away she goes – dead straight, fast and through to the Limerick net for so sensational a win that we are silent until the whistle blows.*

Writing in the *Irish Press* the following day, 'Green Flag' said:

> *It was one of those goals that a man gets in a lifetime and it came at the right minute when a score was worth a King's ransom ... it was a brilliant feat and only a player like Ring could bring it off after a gruelling game.*

Christy Ring – 'young, slim and brimming with hurling potential'.

The *Irish Independent* reported:

> *To those who were not there it will be recited for many a year to come how the Glen Rovers man ran from his own half almost into the Limerick line with the ball bouncing merrily on his hurley and then smacked it across for the goal that won the day.*

We will leave the final word on that goal to two great hurlers who played on opposite sides that day. Din Joe Buckley, teak-tough Cork defender, recalled the goal for journalist Tom Morrison in later years.

> *Christy got the ball out on the right wing about 20 yards from the sideline and he must have travelled at least 60 yards before hitting his shot. Joe Kelly came thundering in and harassed the Limerick goalie Malone while the ball went directly to the net.*

Jackie Power's account is told by Seán Murphy in his book *The Life and Times of Jackie Power* (Limerick, 1996).

> *The ball that led to the goal was the only clean possession that Christy got as he was good and truly held by Tommy [Cregan]. He lofted the ball in and to my amazement up goes Joe Kelly's hurley and tapped the goalie's hurley, letting the ball into the net. I always felt that the goal should have been disallowed but I would pity the poor umpires if they did cross the flags, because of the tension that prevailed at that precise moment.*

The following four lines, which tell the story of that goal, are taken from 'Castleconnell's Darling Boy', a ballad to the memory of Mick Mackey by 'Éire Óg'.

> *That July day, when the Lee held sway,*
> *You burst the net three times;*
> *But Christy Ring, with a lovely swing,*
> *Won the match on the call of time.*

A GLIMPSE AT HURLING
OVER HALF A CENTURY AGO:

Ahane v Sarsfields, 1947

Despite changes in the scoring area, score values, team numbers, size and weight of the sliotar, coupled with the elimination of the third-man tackle, hurling has remained basically the same since the foundation of the GAA in 1884.

Coaching, however, has changed the emphasis. Optimum use of possession is now regarded as paramount. This can, however, be overdone. The ground stroke with and against the approaching sliotar, the overhead pull with and against the flying sliotar – both so thrilling from a spectator's point of view – are slowly disappearing. It is a negative aspect of evolution. It is important to have it reassessed.

The physical aspect, which applied in bygone decades and which has altered with the passage of time, can be gleaned from an account of a club game in the 1940s.

The match took place at Newport in May 1947. It was the final of the Ryan (Lacken) Memorial Park Tournament. The contestants were Ahane of Limerick and Sarsfields of Tipperary – two of the leading club teams in Ireland at the time. Hurling followers expected a stirring struggle and poured into Newport for the occasion. There was much at stake – individual honour, team pride, parish glory. The game would be a test of hurling ability and physical endurance – a contest of fierce man-to-man combat, where stamina, discipline and sportsmanship would be tested to the very limits.

The teams lined out as:

Sarsfields

Gerry Doyle

Mickey Byrne   *Ger Cornally*   *Neil Condon*

Michael Maher   *John McGuire*   *Tommy Purcell*

Tommy Doyle   *Tommy Mason*

L. Hickey   *J. Dwyer*   *Tommy Ryan*

Pat Mockler   *Nicholas Mockler*   *M. Doyle*

Ahane

Paddy Creamer

Mick Herbert   Tom Conway   Paddy Enright

Seán Herbert   Jackie Power   Paddy Kelly

Timmy Ryan   Thomas O'Brien

Eddie Stokes   Jack Mulcahy   Jimmy 'Butler' Coffey

Mick Mackey   John Mackey   Dan Mescall

Both teams had household names – players with county titles, Railway Cup medals, provincial and All-Ireland honours. One of the players, Jimmy 'Butler' Coffey, wing-forward on the Ahane team, had won Munster and All-Ireland honours with his native Tipperary in 1937. Jimmy, God willing, will celebrate his 100th birthday on 27 October 2009.

The local parish priest, Fr Ryan, threw in the ball between the midfielders and the forwards, all of whom, in those days, lined up at centrefield for the throw-in. Right away Mick Mackey was up to his tricks. 'Take it easy boys, this is not the real throw-in,' he said. But it was. And away dashed Mick with the sliotar to score the opening point – the only easy score of the game.

Ahane led at half time by four points. As the final minutes ticked away it looked like a draw. But two late points to Sarsfields gave them victory.

Tommy Doyle, in his book *A Lifetime in Hurling* (London, 1955), as told to Raymond Smith, had this to say:

> Ahane ... set a sizzling pace from the outset and our backs ... stood their ground against the unrelenting efforts of the Mackeys ... Did we spare the ash? I should hardly think so ... [It was] as hard an hour's hurling as I ever played in.

'Winter Green', writing in the *Tipperary Star*, called it 'a struggle devoid of mercy and compassion, a struggle dear to the hearts of oldtimers, a struggle that brought the best or the worst out of a man'.

Fast-forward that game into the present day. I can see yellow and red cards all over the place. I can see not enough players left on the pitch to finish the game. And yet in that game in 1947 no one wore a helmet, no one left the field injured, largely because the training of those days engendered in each player the art of self-protection, even in the fiercest of honest exchanges, in the heat of battle.

Jimmy 'Butler' Coffey (left) and Johnny Ryan (right) in O'Connell Street, Dublin the day after St Patrick's Day 1938. Jimmy assisted Munster in their 6-2 to 4-3 win over Leinster in the Railway Cup final while Johnny was a sub. Both won All-Ireland medals with Tipperary in 1937.

Jimmy 'Butler' Coffey, Tipperary v Limerick 1937 Munster final, about to whip on a ground ball as Jackie Power attempts to hook. Paddy Scanlon in the Limerick goal is on full alert.

A HURLING PERSONALITY:

Dick Stokes (Limerick)

Dick was a native of the parish of Pallas in east Limerick, born on 12 March 1920. At an early age his talents as a sportsman were in evidence in the local GAA pitch and at Doon CBS.

He was selected on the Munster Colleges team of 1939 that defeated Leinster Colleges by 5-6 to 2-4 in the final. Also on that team were Vin Baston, who would later excel on Munster Railway Cup teams and win an All-Ireland title with Waterford in 1948; Harry Goldsboro, who played for Tipperary at midfield on their All-Ireland winning side of 1945; Tony Herbert, brother of Seán and Mick of Limerick fame, who came on as a sub on Limerick's All-Ireland winning team against Kilkenny in 1940 and subsequently played with Faughs and the Dublin hurling team for many years; and finally Paddy Mackey, full forward on the Colleges team, brother of Mick and John, whose untimely death a couple of years later deprived hurling of a potentially great player. Full-forward on the Leinster Colleges team was the mighty Nicky Rackard of Wexford.

By 1940, Dick Stokes' hurling skills were well known to the Limerick selectors, and he was chosen on the county senior team for the championship. Limerick's golden era in hurling was still alive. Dick was joining the company of hurling gladiators – legendary names such as Paddy Scanlon, Paddy Clohosey, Paddy McMahon, Peter Cregan, Mick Mackey, John Mackey, Jackie Power, to name but some. And the opponents he would encounter were of similar ilk.

In the championship of that year, Dick found himself pitched into a hurling cauldron. He once said to me: 'We didn't start off a good team but we finished the championship a good team.' It took a draw against Waterford, followed by a thrilling replay, to advance to the Munster final against Cork. Another draw and another replay.

And what hurling! A journalist in recent times wrote that when Mackey and Ring won their All-Irelands the game was played at half the pace. Not true, not true at all.

Writing on the drawn game with Cork, Séamus Ó Ceallaigh said it was:

> ... *played at top speed ... the pace was indeed a cracker ... the speed of the game never slackened ...*

'Carbery' gave his view:

> ... *fiercely earnest and packed with pulsating passages ... Limerick were racing like red deer on Knockfierna.*

The following excerpt from a report summed up the replay: '... the pace was a cracker right from the start. Speed was the keynote, with perfect first-time striking and bouts of scientific overhead play' (from *The Mackey Story* by Séamus Ó Ceallaigh and Seán Murphy (Limerick, 1982)).

A semi-final win over Galway and victory over Kilkenny in the final gave Dick a Munster and All-Ireland medal in his first year in senior championship hurling. He emerged with reputation enhanced following some grand hurling displays in the wing-forward position. Dick was of medium height and strongly built. He had the physique, speed and craft to perform with distinction at the highest level. 'Carbery' described a fleeting moment from the drawn epic: 'Then, young fair-haired Stokes of Pallas flashed in, like a Kingfisher on a stream, for a Limerick minor.'

Dick's performances were well noted by the Munster Railway Cup selectors. Every year, from 1941 to 1946, he was chosen on Munster's Railway Cup team – always at wing-forward, except in 1943 when he was chosen at midfield with Jack Lynch. That brought Dick five Railway Cup medals – losing only in 1941 to Leinster by one point when Mick and John Mackey were not available for selection because of the untimely death of their brother, Paddy. In those years too, Dick never failed to deliver first-class performances for his native Limerick – when he showed himself to be a hurler of speed of thought and action, opportunist, free-taker, fleet of foot and a goal-getter. His departure to England, to pursue his medical career, deprived him of further opportunities to play for Munster.

Dick was in England when Limerick reached the League final of 1946/47 against Kilkenny, the reigning All-Ireland champions. Dick told me about his trip home for the game, which was played at Croke Park on 9 November.

*I was in Bolton as a GP ... I travelled by boat on the morning of
the match, 9 November. I thought a storm was blowing up, but
the steward said it was only a bit of a swell. I got sick three times.
When I got off the boat I went to bed for a couple of hours. I lined
out at centre forward. I was as weak as a tráithnín – no energy.
I moved into corner forward. A ball came across – I pulled – it
finished in the net. I got a couple of points as well.*

The game, a thriller, ended in a draw – Limerick 4-5 Kilkenny 2-11.

The replay took place on 7 March 1948. This time Dick flew
home. The game was another thriller, matching the All-Ireland final
between Cork and Kilkenny the previous September in excitement
and brilliant hurling. Among the stars was Dick Stokes, who at
centre-half-forward gave an exhibition of vintage forward play. It
was Dick's first and only National League medal – all the sweeter
for being at the expense of Kilkenny, All-Ireland champions.

Dick played football too. On 10 June 1945, Limerick met Kerry
in the second round of the Munster senior football championship
at the Gaelic Grounds. A report in *The Kerryman* stated: 'Dick
Stokes was the best of the thirty in a grand, all-round display.' And
that field contained many household football names.

In 1950, Dick played on the Limerick junior football team that
beat Cork by 3-6 to 1-6 in the Munster final. Derry ended their
All-Ireland ambitions in the semi-final at Magherafelt.

During Dick's days at UCD he played both hurling and football
with the college. He had Fitzgibbon Cup triumphs in hurling in
1941 and 1944 and a Sigerson Cup success in football in 1944. I
believe Dick is the only player to have won with UCD a Dublin
county senior title in both hurling (1947) and football (1943).

As neighbours in Wexford I often had a chat with him about
GAA affairs. He was always loathe to single out individuals above
others because, as he used to say, 'there were so many'. But he did
concede that he hadn't seen a better full-back than Nick O'Donnell
of Wexford, and that Paddy McMahon of Limerick, whose career
was cut short by knee injuries, was, at full-forward, 'as good as any
of them'. In football he saw Eddie Boyle, the Louth full-back, as
'special'. In 1990, Eddie was honoured with the All-Time All-Star
Football award. Not surprisingly, his childhood heroes were 'the
Limerick team of the thirties and in particular Mick Mackey and
Timmy Ryan'.

A Munster GAA correspondent wrote about Dick in 1951:

> *In seeking the outstanding player of 1951, I am not looking for the individual that thrilled Croke Park crowds or proved the main factor in bringing great success to his club or county. Rather I am seeking the man who by his example and self sacrifice did most for the games of the Gael during the season just concluded.*

In 1973 Dick was a member of the management team that guided Limerick through a successful Munster campaign and an All-Ireland title with victory over Kilkenny.

I saw Dick in action on the hurling field in his latter playing days, by which time he had moved back to the full back line. There, I witnessed a cool, composed, confident defender – a tight marker, deft touches, first-time, well-measured pull, short sprint and, when the occasion demanded, a word of encouragement to his young colleagues.

His career at county level lasted from 1940 to 1953. He was very versatile, for he played in his time in defence, at midfield and in attack. He was a fine footballer too. But above all, and at all times, Dick Stokes was the ultimate in sportsmanship.

Dick Stokes enjoying retirement in his latter years.

A hurling selection

Jim Ware
(Waterford)

Willie Murphy   Con Murphy   Andy Fleming
(Cork)   (Cork)   (Waterford)

Tommy Doyle   John Keane   Willie Campbell
(Tipperary)   (Waterford)   (Cork)

Harry Gray   Paddy Gantley
(Laois)   (Galway)

Jimmy Langton   Jack Lynch   Terry Leahy
(Kilkenny)   (Cork)   (Kilkenny)

Josie Gallagher   Jackie Power   Johnny Quirke
(Galway)   (Limerick)   (Cork)

Terry Leahy

A FOOTBALL GAME:

Cavan v Kerry, 1947 All-Ireland final at the Polo Grounds, New York

Far from an Irish homeland our heroes sailed away,
By ship and plane they crossed the main to grand old USA
They left behind an eager land from Donegal to Cork,
When they went to play the final at the Polo Grounds, New York.
* We pledge the men of Breffni; we pledge the Kerry team;*
We pledge to fame the Gaelic game that e'er shall reign supreme;
We pledge the land that bore them from Donegal to Cork,
As they played the football final in the Polo Grounds, New York!

Bryan MacMahon

Only once in the history of the GAA has a senior final been played outside the country. That was in 1947 when the football final, between Cavan and Kerry, was played at the Polo Grounds, New York. Even in the early years of the twentieth century, when London teams of exiles contested All-Ireland finals, the question of playing the final other than in Ireland never arose.

When the suggestion was originally made to play the final in New York not many took it seriously. It seems that efforts to have the 1946 final between Kerry and Roscommon played there came to naught. It may well be that wise heads in the GAA were conscious of the US 'invasion' of Irish hurlers and athletes in 1888 and the financial flop it turned out to be.

Prime movers behind the 1947 campaign were John 'Kerry' O'Donnell, a leading figure in New York GAA circles, and Canon Michael Hamilton, the Clare delegate to the GAA. It was suggested that it would be a worthwhile way to commemorate the centenary of the Famine of 'black '47' and the immigration to the US that ensued. The point was also made that Gaelic games in New York and other American cities had gone into decline and that their future would be greatly boosted. Some took the view that it would be a very special treat for 'the Gaels beyond the wave'.

Throughout the globe, on every soil,
Where human foot has trod,
You'll find the hardy sons of toil
From this old verdant sod:
And 'neath the friendly 'Stars and Stripes'
That oft they died to save;
They are here and there and everywhere
The Gaels beyond the wave!
                    'The Gaels Beyond the Wave' by 'Sliabh Ruadh'

By the end of May, despite the reservations of many in the GAA, including the general secretary Pádraig Ó Caoimh and Vincent O'Donoghue of Waterford, who would later become president in 1952, the decision to go ahead was carried by twenty votes to seventeen.

It was now full steam ahead with preparations for the New York venture. Micheál O'Hehir would travel and do the broadcast – a massive undertaking in those days. The game would be refereed by Martin O'Neill of Wexford – a lifelong devoted servant of the GAA. For those teams remaining in the football championship, a place in the All-Ireland final suddenly took on an added dimension.

Meath defeated Laois in the Leinster final. Kerry overcame Cork in Munster. Roscommon got the better of Sligo in the west and up north Cavan disposed of the Antrim challenge.

The semi-finals were played on 3 August – Cavan v Roscommon, which attracted a crowd of just over 60,000 – and 10 August, when Kerry and Meath played before an attendance of almost 66,000. The results produced a Cavan v Kerry final, the second time the counties would clash at this level. They first met in 1937 when Kerry won following a replay.

It was decided that some of the travelling party would go by sea and some by air. Those going by sea set sail on 3 September from Cobh on the SS *Mauretania* and arrived in the US on 8 September. The remainder flew from Rineanna – now Shannon. They had a 45-minute stop for refuelling in Santa Maria in the Azores, a Portuguese possession, and nine hours later they landed in Gander in Newfoundland. After two hours there they continued on for Boston, and following another delay there they continued en route to New York. They touched down on 9 September, some twenty-nine hours after leaving Rineanna.

The preliminaries included a ticker-tape parade down Broadway in a large fleet of cars with a police escort; a reception at City Hall, hosted by Mayor Bill O'Dwyer, a native of Bohola, County Mayo; and a meeting in St Patrick's cathedral with Cardinal Spellman. Among those present were the team captains, Dinny Lyne of Kerry and John Joe O'Reilly of Cavan, Pádraig Ó Caoimh, general secretary of the GAA, Martin O'Neill, secretary of the Leinster Council, Seán McCarthy, secretary of the Munster Council, and from Roscommon the GAA president, Dan O'Rourke.

On the Friday before the game, Micheál O'Hehir, with his usual attention to detail, went to the Polo Grounds to view the surroundings. To his consternation, he discovered that nobody knew anything about the broadcast and that no lines had been booked. Frantic activity followed, and with the support of Mayor Bill O'Dwyer arrangements were put in place.

Came the big day, 14 September, and all was in readiness. The broadcast lines were booked from 3.30 p.m. to 5 p.m. New York time. Heavy rain fell on Saturday evening and kept the attendance down to a disappointing 34,941 – about two-thirds of the ground's capacity. Receipts totalled $153,877, which, at the exchange rate at the time, converted to £38,469. The ground was rock hard, with little grass. The pitch, by home standards, was tight – it measured 137 yards by 84 yards. The heat registered 85 degrees Fahrenheit. Kerry wore white jockey caps as a shield from the sun.

Extended preliminaries saw the game start ten minutes behind schedule at 3.40 p.m. – what with the playing of 'Faith of our Fathers', the US anthem, the Irish anthem and the ceremonial throw-in by Mayor O'Dwyer.

At home in Ardagh in west Limerick we gathered in the kitchen to listen to the match, joined by a few neighbours. It was about 8.30 p.m. Irish time. We had the electricity, so there were no concerns about wireless batteries going dead. There was a sense of awe as we heard the unmistakeable voice of Micheál O'Hehir. It seemed like a kind of miracle – Micheál's voice from 3,000 miles away. The reception was not loud or very clear – there was some crackling and atmospherics.

Moments from what turned out to be a thrilling and exciting game still remain in my mind. A not fully fit Paddy Kennedy lined out for Kerry, not in his usual position of midfield but at corner-forward.

Kerry opened in blitz fashion. They were all over Cavan. Batt Garvey was flying on the wing; Eddie Dowling was dominating midfield. After a quarter of an hour Kerry were eight points up. They had scored two goals and had two more disallowed. It looked as if the reigning champions would coast home.

Then Cavan made a switch – P. J. Duke from midfield to his more usual wing-back position, in a direct swap with John Wilson. The team steadied and put some points on the board. Then, before half time, they struck. First Joe Stafford found the net, quickly followed by another goal from New York-born Mick Higgins. At half time it was Cavan 2-5 Kerry 2-4. My father looked pleased. The family farm, on which he grew up in County Longford, bordered County Cavan.

The second half was nip and tuck. Kerry levelled early on, but Cavan were never headed. Entering the closing stages the excitement was unbearable. Cavan led by a point. Tim Brosnan, who had come on as a sub for Kerry, struck the crossbar. Perhaps now the heat began to tell on Kerry as Cavan landed three unanswered points.

And then there was more drama. It suddenly dawned on Micheál O'Hehir at 4.55 p.m. New York time that there were ten minutes left in the game but that only five minutes 'booked line time' remained. During the broadcast he made an impassioned plea for 'five minutes more' to the US 'lines' authorities. He was begging, but did not know if anyone was listening. Well, listening someone was – perhaps with Irish blood in the veins. Micheál got his five minutes, and we got the final result: Cavan 2-11 Kerry 2-7. Cavan's third title.

Peter Donohoe, dubbed the 'Babe Ruth' of Gaelic football by the American press, scored eight of Cavan's points. Dan O'Keeffe in the Kerry goal was as brilliant and as eagle-eyed as when first he manned the gap for his county in 1931.

We talked about the match for a good while. The general consensus was that Cavan would be popular champions. Mother, a Kerry woman, was philosophical as she prepared a cup of tea for all: '*Beidh lá eile ag Ciarraí.*'

Mick Higgins was a survivor from that historic occasion – now fit and sprightly in his eighty-sixth year. He was Cavan's top scorer from play at the Polo Grounds, with 1-2 from his position at centre-half-forward. It was around the time of that game that I cut his photograph from the *GAA Digest* and placed it in my album of footballers.

I decided to make contact with Mick, who very kindly responded with details of his career and some recollections of the '47 final.

Mick was born in New York on 19 August 1922 to John, a native of Kiltimagh, County Mayo, and Mary (née Farrelly) from Kilnaleck in County Cavan. The family returned to Ireland in 1927. Mick's football days began as a minor at Marist College, Dundalk, and his county senior career stretched from 1943 to 1953. He was a member of the Gárda Síochána.

Mick won every honour in the game; two county senior titles – 1946 with Mountnugent, 1952 with Bailieboro; seven Ulster titles in an era dominated by Cavan between 1943 and 1952; two Railway Cups and two National League titles. He won three All-Ireland medals, in 1947, 1948 and 1952, captaining the side in his third success. That final went to a replay, with Cavan winning by nine points to five. Seven of those points came from the boot of Mick Higgins. It was one of the many great days he had in the blue jersey of Cavan. In 1949 Cavan and Mick Higgins set forth in search of three-in-a-row All-Ireland titles. They beat Armagh in the Ulster final by 1-7 to 1-6 and Cork in the All-Ireland semi-final by 1-9 to 2-3. But they fell at the final hurdle to neighbours Meath, 1-10 to 1-6.

In 1987 Mick was honoured with the Bank of Ireland All-Time All-Star award. That was followed in 1989 by the Hall of Fame award. Mick was the third footballer to receive the Hall of Fame award, following in the footsteps of John Joe Sheehy of Kerry in 1963 and Larry Stanley of Kildare in 1970.

Mick was chosen on the Ireland teams to play the Universities in 1951, '52 and '53 – the only Cavan man in 1951 and '52; he was joined by Séamus Morris in goal and Victor Sherlock at midfield in 1953. Mick also played club football in Kilnaleck, Drogheda and Celbridge.

On the 1947 final itself, Mick said it was very special to beat Kerry, who had some wonderful players, including his immediate opponent Willie Casey. The occasion, the atmosphere and the welcome in New York were unforgettable. Then there was the trip home by boat and the journey back to Cavan by bus, following a visit to the Mansion House and Áras an Uachtaráin. It was all so special, a parcel of memorable moments – unique for Mick, who had won his first All-Ireland senior medal in the city of his birth,

3,000 miles from the land of his parents.

But even great occasions evoke sad memories. Mick recalled that two outstanding Cavan footballers that had played with him at the Polo Grounds died a little later in the prime of life – P. J. Duke from pneumonia and John Joe O'Reilly following an operation.

'Our sweetest songs are those that tell of saddest thought' (Shelley)

The men of Breffni that made GAA history in 1947 were:

Val Gannon

Willie Doonan   Brian O'Reilly   Paddy Smith

John Wilson   John Joe O'Reilly   Simon Deignan

P. J. Duke   Phil Brady

Tony Tighe   Mick Higgins   Columba McDyer

Joe Stafford   Peter Donohoe   T. P. O'Reilly

In the course of the game the Cavan mentors made no substitutions.

Mick Higgins

A FOOTBALL GAME:

Cavan v Mayo, 1948 All-Ireland final

This was an extraordinary final – remembered, not because of the quality of the football, but for the many twists and turns the game took.

'It was a grim, rugged battle between fit and determined men', wrote 'Carbery'.

I heard and visualised every moment of this football final through the golden voice of Micheál O'Hehir. And to this day I remember the many names that played. Immediately there comes to mind the Cavan full-back line of Willie Doonan, Brian O'Reilly and Paddy Smith, the same line that played at the Polo Grounds in 1947; the half-back line of P. J. Duke, John Joe O'Reilly, both of whom died young, and Simon Deignan, who later refereed All-Ireland finals. At midfield there were two big men, Phil Brady and Victor Sherlock, and a forward sextet of Tony Tighe, Mick Higgins, Peter Donohoe, Joe Stafford, Edwin Carolan and J. J. Cassidy.

From Mayo I recall a fine full-back line – Peter Quinn, who went on for the priesthood, Paddy Prendergast, one of the great full-backs of the game, and Seán Flanagan, a master of corner-back play. There was big Pat McAndrew at centre-half-back, all 6 foot 4 of him; the Gilvarry brothers, John in defence and Joe in attack; John Forde, the captain; midfielders Éamon Mongey and Pádraig Carney; and the remaining five forwards, Tom Langan, Tom Acton, Peter Solan, Bill Kenny and Seán Mulderrig.

And, of course, not forgetting the two goalkeepers – Tom Byrne of Mayo and J. D. (otherwise Des) Benson of Cavan, who also played in the 1943 final which was lost to Roscommon.

The game ended in a welter of excitement; a dramatic incident in the dying seconds would become the subject of debate for many a day.

This football final at Croke Park on 26 September was only the third involving a meeting of teams from the west and the north. In 1933, Cavan defeated Galway 2-5 to 1-4. Ten years later Roscommon had a 2-7 to 2-2 win over Cavan following a 1-6 apiece draw.

In 1948, Cavan were in search of a first two-in-a-row and a fourth title in all. Mayo were hoping to add to their only title of 1936.

It was Cavan's eighth appearance in a final, Mayo's fifth. Cavan were captained by their centre-half-back, John Joe O'Reilly, who had led his native county to All-Ireland victory the previous year against Kerry at the Polo Grounds, New York. He had been playing with Cavan since 1937 when his brother, 'Big Tom', was captain. That final was lost to Kerry following a draw.

Mayo were captained by their right-half-back, John Forde. On the path to the final, Mayo beat Galway in the Connacht final in extra time in a replay by 2-10 to 2-7, having drawn the first day, 2-4 to 1-7. They then demolished Kerry by thirteen points to three in the All-Ireland semi-final.

Cavan had a good win over Antrim in the Ulster final, 2-12 to 2-4. They were pushed all the way by Louth in the semi-final on the rather unusual scoreline of 1-14 to 4-2.

The unique pairing of Cavan and Mayo gripped the public imagination. Supporters descended on Croke Park in their hordes, and with close on 75,000 packed into the ground the gates were closed over an hour before Dr Walsh, archbishop of Tuam, threw in the ball.

The morning rain had cleared as the teams paraded behind the Artane Boys' Band. However, a gusty wind blowing from the city end would present problems.

Cavan won the toss and with the wind at their backs defended the canal goal in the first half. Mayo backs were marking tightly and with ten minutes to go to half time the only scores on the board were two points from frees for Cavan from the boot of their sharpshooter Peter Donohoe. Then suddenly, inspired by their wing man Tony Tighe, the Cavan forwards tore in on the Mayo goal. Not once, nor twice, but three times the Mayo citadel fell. Tighe scored twice and he was involved in the move that brought Victor Sherlock's goal. At half time, a relieved Cavan and a bewildered Mayo retired to the dressing room. The scoreboard read Cavan 3-2 Mayo 0-0.

Mayo faced an uphill struggle in the second half but had the wind at their backs. Seán Mulderrig pointed. Peter Solan followed with a goal. Croke Park hummed with excitement. Micheál O'Hehir conveyed the atmosphere to those of us listening on the wireless. Cavan's lead was now seven points. The intimidating look was gone from the scoreboard. There was plenty of time left. Cavan lost their captain, John Joe O'Reilly, injured, but were soon well on top. Peter Donohoe pointed a free. Mick Higgins swept in for a goal. Victor

Sherlock added a point. Fifteen minutes to go. Cavan now twelve points up, 4-4 to 1-1.

Somehow Mayo mustered up reserves. Tom Acton goaled. They swarmed in again and Tom Acton once more finished the leather to the net. And when Pádraig Carney despatched a penalty past Des Benson to leave the scoreboard reading 4-4 to 4-3, no words could describe the electrified atmosphere that engulfed Croke Park. The historic grounds were no place for weak hearts when Éamon Mongey sent over the equalising point with five minutes to go.

Players were now tiring after almost an hour of hectic exchanges. Cavan launched an attack. It brought a close-in free. Peter Donohoe pointed. Just a minute to go now. The script to date would have done justice to Alfred Hitchcock – yet more drama remained. Mayo forced a close-in free. 'Surely a draw now,' we said to ourselves. Cavan packed their goal. Their centre-forward, Mick Higgins, was back there too. Pádraig Carney's kick was charged down by Mick Higgins and in seconds the game was over and Cavan were champions. Whether or not Mick Higgins was standing closer to the Mayo free taker than the rules allowed mattered not. And even though controversy raged for many a day, it still mattered not. The final result stood: Cavan 4-5 Mayo 4-4. Never before had eight goals been scored in an All-Ireland football final.

Mayo's hour came soon afterwards. Their left-full-back, Seán Flanagan, led them to successive titles in 1950 and 1951 – their last to date. Cavan, captained by Mick Higgins following a draw with Meath, won their fifth crown in 1952 – also their last title so far.

A FOOTBALL PERSONALITY:

Jimmy Murray (Roscommon)

Jimmy Murray was born on 5 May 1917 to John and Susan (née Walls), the eldest of ten children. His father ran a business in Knockcroghery; his mother was a teacher and a native of Magherafelt, County Derry.

From early childhood, Jimmy was a football fanatic. He was destined to become Roscommon's most famous footballing son. Support from his parents was immense.

Jimmy worked in the family business that developed over the years into a thriving bar, grocery, drapery and hardware. And in due course he took over its management. When training with the Roscommon team, his parents would insist that he never miss a session, even though Jimmy knew his presence was badly needed in the family shop.

He first wore the Roscommon colours as a minor in 1934 and 1935, but success was not to come until 1939 when Roscommon won the Connacht junior football title with a 2-6 to 1-4 victory over Mayo. In the All-Ireland semi-final they met and defeated Munster title holders Limerick by 2-9 to 2-4 after a stirring struggle. That Limerick team contained a number of outstanding hurlers, including Jackie Power and the Mackey brothers, John and Mick, who formed the midfield partnership.

Roscommon lost the Home final to Dublin by one goal. However, they were back again the following year and Jimmy won his first All-Ireland medal with a fine win over Westmeath.

On the home front Jimmy enjoyed much success. In 1936 and 1938 he won two county junior football titles, while at senior level he won six county titles between 1942 and 1949 – the blank years being 1944 and 1947. He had successes with the camán too – a county junior in 1945 with St Patrick's and a senior title in 1938 with Roscommon Gaels.

In 1938 Roscommon were graded junior. So when they returned to senior ranks in 1941 only a super optimist would have foreseen success in the immediate future. They did however have something to build on. There were the All-Ireland minor successes of 1939 and 1941 at the expense of Monaghan and Louth and the Connacht junior successes of 1939 and 1940 – the latter leading to an All-Ireland title.

A remarkable breakthrough came in 1943. Jimmy Murray was captain. He was an inspirational leader – small of stature, totally dedicated, a 'will o' the wisp' figure on the field, speedy and illusive, tenacious, yet stylish and, perhaps most important of all, a most accurate passer of the ball. 'Carbery' said he 'sparkled and fed his wings with shrewd passes' and referred to him as 'the idol of the West ... the inspiration of Roscommon's attack – the brainy pivot on which all their winning attacking movements hinge'.

Roscommon lost the Connacht finals of 1941 and 1942 to Galway by just one point on each occasion. They turned the tables in 1943 with a 2-6 to 0-8 victory – Roscommon's first provincial crown since 1914. In a humdinger of a semi-final they disposed of a talented Louth team, and must have blinked in disbelief as Croke Park and All-Ireland final day beckoned on the fourth Sunday of September. Their opponents were the men of Breffni, kingpins of Ulster football in those days.

As Jimmy Murray led his team around Croke Park in the pre-match parade, before an attendance of just over 68,000 people, he must have thought to himself that this was the stuff of dreams or fairy tale. Here were Roscommon, their third year back in senior ranks, about to contest the All-Ireland senior final. And the men he was leading? Well, they were the product, largely, of the minor teams of 1939 and 1941 and the junior team of 1940 – Larry Cummins, J. P. O'Callaghan, Brendan Lynch, Bill Carlos, Owensie Hoare, Eddie Boland, Liam Gilmartin, Donal Keenan, Frank Glynn and Phelim Murray, his brother.

The game ended in a draw, 1-6 each, with Jimmy contributing 1-1 of the Roscommon total. So it was back to Croke Park again on 10 October for the replay. This game turned out to be a tough, hard-fought, uncompromising encounter. Ten minutes into the second half Joe Stafford, the Cavan full-forward, was sent off – believed to be the first sending-off in an All-Ireland football final. Minutes from the end, with lost time being played, a Cavan player assaulted the referee, and when the final whistle blew, referee Paddy Mythen

Dan O'Keeffe in action against Mayo in the 1936 semi-final.

of Wexford was escorted from the pitch by Gardaí and officials.

The Sam Maguire Cup was presented to Jimmy Murray by Séamus Gardiner, president of the GAA. It was going west to great celebrations in Roscommon.

That this Roscommon team was a talented outfit, and their All-Ireland win no flash in the pan, was proved the following year when they retained the Connacht title with a 2-11 to 1-6 win over Mayo, captained once again by Jimmy Murray. They trounced Cavan in the semi-final by 5-8 to 1-3. Now for the acid test. Their opponents on 24 September in Croke Park were Kerry, who, with fifteen All-Ireland titles, were joint leaders in the roll of honour with Dublin. Roscommon had one.

Roscommon had twelve of the 1943 team – the newcomers were John Joe Nerney, Hugh Gibbons and John Casserly. Kerry had household names – players such as Dan O'Keeffe, Joe Keohane, Bill Dillon, Eddie Walsh, Paddy Kennedy, Jackie and Dinny Lyne, Murt Kelly and Paddy 'Bawn' Brosnan.

The attendance was huge – 79,245, with thousands locked out, all undeterred by the transport restrictions of the wartime years. Only one train left Roscommon and only the 'ghost' train left Kerry. And of course private cars were off the road. Those lucky enough to get in were treated to a fine exhibition of football – fast end-to-end play, high fielding, lengthy kicking – played in a fine sporting spirit. When Paddy Mythen of Wexford blew full time, Roscommon prevailed by 1-9 to 2-4.

So the Sam Maguire Cup was going west again for the second year in succession. Going west, too, was the football used in that game; it became a lifelong cherished possession of Jimmy Murray's and to this day is displayed in the family shop.

Jimmy had every reason to feel proud. In 1943 and 1944, he led the footballers of Roscommon to victory over the best teams in Ireland at the time – Galway, Mayo, Cavan, Louth and Kerry. Two more Connacht titles followed in 1946 and 1947 under his captaincy. A Railway Cup title eluded him, however. He came closest in 1945 when Connacht went under to Leinster by 2-5 to 0-6. In 1993, Jimmy received a well-deserved honour, an All-Time All-Star award.

When I learned of the death of Jimmy Murray, which took place on 16 January 2007, a few months short of his ninetieth birthday, my mind went back in time. First to that October Sunday in 1946 when I sat in my kitchen in Ardagh listening to Micheál O'Hehir

Home of Jimmy Murray.

bringing me the drama of my first football final, between Kerry and Roscommon. I close my eyes and I can still hear the excitement of the last five minutes. It was an unexpected excitement, because Roscommon were leading by six points, 1-7 to 0-4, and seemed set for victory, even though their captain Jimmy Murray was on the sideline receiving treatment following a clash with Paddy 'Bawn' Brosnan. Suddenly, or so it seemed, Paddy Burke – 'lovely dark-haired Paddy Burke', as referred to in a later ballad – had the ball in the net. But time was ticking away. Kerry got a sideline ball, and in a twinkling Tom 'Gega' O'Connor had the ball in the net for another Kerry goal. What drama! A draw, and now to the replay three weeks later on 27 October. I am listening in again. It's well into the second half. The teams are level. Kerry bring on Gus Cremin, the captain they had dropped after the drawn game. He isn't long on when he fields a Roscommon clearance and from about sixty yards out sends over the lead point. Kerry finish with a goal that gives them a four-point victory. I had listened to one of the great finals of Gaelic football.

In my mind it is now the late 1960s and I am sitting with my neighbour, Brendan Lynch, on the wall outside his house in Lisbeg, Tralee. We are talking about the great Roscommon team of the 1940s – in which Brendan, a huge man, played a star role in the half-back line – and in particular about 1946. Brendan reminded me that the harvest was late, and the final was postponed as all efforts were concentrated nationwide on saving a harvest that was at risk. Following the draw, the replay was postponed for three weeks to facilitate the saving of the beet harvest. Roscommon's training programme was such that the postponements did not help their cause. A title that had Roscommon written all over it was let slip. And with it went an honour that would have made the name Jimmy Murray unique in senior football history as the only captain to have collected the Sam Maguire Cup on three occasions. As it was he was the first, at the time, to have collected 'Sam' twice in succession. Previously, Joe Barrett of Kerry had collected it in 1929 and 1932.

Jimmy Murray's death saw the oldest-surviving football captain depart the scene. Brendan Lynch heard of his captain's death with sadness. Speaking to journalist Liam Horan, he said:

> *He wasn't a big man, but he had an extraordinary way of getting up in the air. He led by example. He would never ask you to do anything he wouldn't do himself. I played on him in training and you'd be black and blue after him. He was like thorny wire.*

There was a nostalgic moment for the great captain, now old and feeble, in 2006 when the Roscommon minor football team, following their All-Ireland win after a replay with Kerry, called to Jimmy with the cup. *Captaen uasal go raibh a seal ar an saol seo beagnach tugtha.*

On our way back from the west of Ireland in August 2008 my wife, Mary, and myself, passing through Knockcroghery, stopped and took a photograph of the home place and business premises of the great man.

The football used in the 1944 All-Ireland final.

I decided to go in. We met his son John and I told him of my memory of Jimmy going away back to 1946. He produced two large albums full of nostalgic memories of games and 'battles long ago'.

I browsed through the albums and saw photographs of many of the giants of distant days – his brother Phelim, Bill Carlos, Eddie Boland, Liam Gilmartin, Donal Keenan, Frankie Kinlough, Bill Jackson and J. J. Nerney. I looked, too, at the photographs on the wall of the wonderful Roscommon teams of 1943, 1944 and 1946 together with action photographs of their encounters.

John reminded me of how close Jimmy came to collecting 'Sam' on three occasions – something that has so far eluded all captains. He also made mention of how astute Jimmy was at reading the flow of a game, whether as a player on the pitch or a mentor on the sideline. In particular, he mentioned observations – crucial ones – Jimmy made at half time in the 1943 final against Cavan. He recalled, too, that Jimmy is the only captain to have led his team around Croke Park on five All-Ireland final days – twice in 1943, once in 1944 and twice in 1946.

As I was leaving, John presented me with a CD of his late father. It was then I learned of Jimmy's love of music and singing. It was an inherited talent; both his parents came from very musical families. The CD was recorded for charity in November 2002 in Murray's Bar – thirteen lovely ballads.

We played the CD in the car on the way home and marvelled at the strength of the voice of a man in his eighty-sixth year. We sang along with Jimmy. It shortened the journey. Sing away in Heaven, Jimmy.

Glóire na n-Aingeal go gcloisidh tú.

A FOOTBALL PERSONALITY:

Tommy Murphy (Laois)

Laois defeated Kildare by 0-11 to 1-6 in the Leinster senior football final of 1946. A report of the game the following day read:

> *If ever one man carried his team to victory, Tommy Murphy, the Laois centre half back, did it in capital style at Croke Park yesterday ... when he kicked eight of his team's eleven points from frees, was mainly responsible for a ninth, and played a big part in stemming an all-out Kildare bid near the end.*

Tommy Murphy

Laois advanced to the All-Ireland semi-final against Roscommon, who had won the All-Ireland in 1943 and 1944. Laois lost by 3-5 to 2-6. It was around this time that I first heard of Tommy Murphy. It was his tenth year in senior football. I cut his photograph from a newspaper (see left) and placed it in an album. It was a hobby of mine to collect the photographs of hurlers and footballers.

The semi-final attracted over 51,000 to Croke Park. The game was a cracker. After fifteen minutes Roscommon led by 2-2 to 0-0, but Laois cut the deficit to five points by half time. Midway through the second half scores were level. Laois, now surging forward in waves, threw everything at Roscommon, but the western defence stood rock-like. A Roscommon goal by Dónal Keenan and a Laois point from a free by Tommy Murphy closed the scoring.

Tommy, as always, played masterly football. He sent over a screw-kick from the corner in the first half that brought cheers of appreciation from the crowd. He made the first Laois goal of the second half and fed his forwards ball after ball.

Tommy hailed from the parish of Graiguecullen on the Laois/Carlow border. He was still a student at Knockbeg College in Carlow when he lined out with Laois in the 1937 All-Ireland senior football campaign. Earlier that year, he had played county senior for the first time while not yet seventeen. His fame as a footballer was destined to match that of the four Delaney brothers from Stradbally – Jack, Bill, Chris and Mick – who he was now joining on the Laois team. Between them, from 1928 to 1946 the brothers won eighteen Railway Cup medals with Leinster. Bill received the Bank of Ireland All-Time All-Star award in 1994. Jack was chosen on the Tailteann Games football team that played the USA in 1932. Their Uncle Tom played full-back with them on the Laois team beaten by Mayo in the All-Ireland final of 1936. In 1981, Tommy was honoured with the Bank of Ireland All-Time All-Star award.

He won provincial titles with Laois in 1937, 1938 and 1946. The privilege of playing in an All-Ireland final, however, eluded him. Laois lost the semi-finals of those years to Kerry, Kerry and Roscommon respectively. All were close calls. The result in each case could have gone either way.

The 1937 semi-final took place at Cork. Laois dominated the outfield exchanges. In contrast to Kerry, their game was based on short passing movements. But because these were overdone, they reaped little reward from their superiority. Over the hour they had fourteen wides to Kerry's five. The game ended level, Laois 1-6 Kerry 2-3. Tommy Murphy got Laois's first point and made their goal. His performance gripped the imagination of all present. For Kerry, goalkeeper Dan O'Keeffe was magnificent. A marvellous one-hand save in the closing stages saved the day for his team.

The replay – a thriller – was at Waterford. Kerry led at half time by 1-1 to 0-1. On resumption, a Laois passing movement ended with Tommy Murphy crashing the ball to the net. Later, a very heavy charge on Tommy saw him removed from the pitch. The game ended Kerry 2-2 Laois 1-4 with the winning Kerry point coming in the closing minutes. Indeed, ten minutes from the end Laois led by three points. But a goal by Tim Landers and a late point by Mick Lyne gave Kerry victory. As in the drawn game, Laois squandered opportunities; they had sixteen wides to Kerry's six. General opinion was that Kerry had what luck was going. A feature of both games was the superb display of Dan O'Keeffe in the Kerry goal.

In 1938 Laois suffered the same fate against Kerry in the All-Ireland semi-final at Croke Park. They contributed to their downfall by overdoing the passing movements that either broke down or led to no score. In a game where they had the better of the outfield exchanges they lost by 2-6 to 2-4.

Tommy Murphy was brilliant in the air, a master of the solo run and a fine kicker of the ball. He won six county senior titles.

He was honoured by the Leinster football selectors on Railway Cup teams. He won two medals – the first as a midfielder with fellow countyman Bill Delaney in 1940 and the second in 1945 when he came on as a sub at centre field.

In the centenary year, 1984, a team was chosen of great players who never won an All-Ireland medal. Centrefield on that team was Tommy Murphy, with Jim McKeever of Derry as his partner.

A Millennium Football Team was chosen, and Tommy was again selected at midfield – this time with the Kerry maestro Mick O'Connell.

In an interview for the *Graiguecullen Centenary Yearbook* (Graiguecullen, 1984), Tommy described the footballing men of his era – the late 1930s to the early 1950s – as '... strong as horses. As tough as the divil. They were reared hardy. They had great determination and the pride was there too.'

Tommy died in May 1985. For a personal glimpse of this great footballer I contacted my brother Aodán, who wrote the following:

'Fond memory brings the light of other days around me'. The great Thomas Moore's line fits in beautifully with a very special memory that I have. I was born in 1935 and I remember as the 1940s rolled by, the hours of enjoyment brought by Micheál O'Hehir's broadcasts every Sunday when the hurling and football championships started. He made the games come to life as if you were actually looking at them and I had pictures of my heroes from those games. I am positive that, like myself, many wished to meet one or some of their heroes some day. I did.

I started my teaching career in Clogh boys' national school, a most unusual parish in north Kilkenny bordering County Laois. It was coalmining country. Clogh parish had another side, Moneenroe, and the two schools had an excellent under-14 football team. The same parish had a renowned history of football fame going back to the founding of the GAA. Our school team became unbeatable in Kilkenny for years on end and their fame spread to other counties. Graiguecullen, County Laois ran an under-14 football tournament every year and we took part and won the Perry Cup regularly. Huge crowds came to see the games.

It was in the early 1960s and we were in the final against Graiguecullen. I will never forget that year. I was in school and answered a knock at the door. A man, very well built, not too tall, greeted me with a handshake and a big smile. 'You are only wasting your time coming to Graigue on Friday evening. We are going to kick ye home,' he said. He was laughing heartily and I asked: 'Who, in the name of God, are you?' I got the land of my life when he answered: 'I am over the Graigue lads now. I am Tommy Murphy.'

I was stunned for a moment and wondered if it could be the great Tommy Murphy. 'Are you the real Tommy Murphy, the boy wonder?' I asked. 'That was a long time ago,' he replied, still laughing his head off.

I couldn't believe my luck. Tommy was a charming man and he called to me a few times that week with the usual message – don't bother coming – followed by a big laugh.

We travelled to Graigue. There was a huge crowd and the game was out of the top drawer. We won by a point. I remember, as if it were yesterday, Tommy Murphy running down the

Tommy Murphy in 1981 receiving his All-Time All-Star award from then Taoiseach Garret Fitzgerald.

sideline, hand outstretched and a huge handshake, a big laugh and his words – you have a super team.

I had met my hero. He was humble, unassuming and a man worth meeting. He never lost his interest in football and my final memory of Tommy is seeing him being pushed into Croke Park in his wheelchair. He was a man in a million. As the song says: 'memories are made of this.'

A football selection

Dan O'Keeffe
(Kerry)

Jim McCullagh   *Paddy O'Brien*   *'Weesie' Murphy*
(Armagh)   (Meath)   (Cork)

Willie Goodison   *Bill Carlos*   *Stephen White*
(Wexford)   (Roscommon)   (Louth)

Paddy Kennedy   *Tommy Murphy*
(Kerry)   (Laois)

Kevin Armstrong   *Alf Murray*   *Mick Higgins*
(Antrim)   (Armagh)   (Cavan)

Jack McQuillan   *Peter Donohoe*   *Tom Langan*
(Roscommon)   (Cavan)   (Mayo)

Kerry goalkeeper Dan O'Keeffe in the replay against Laois in 1937, which Kerry won by a point.

1951–1960

Teams that participated in the
All-Ireland senior finals

COUNTY	FOOTBALL		HURLING	
	WON	LOST	WON	LOST
Armagh		1		
Cavan	1			
Cork		2	3	1
Derry		1		
Down	1			
Dublin	1	1		1
Galway	1	1		3
Kerry	3	2		
Kilkenny			1	1
Louth	1			
Mayo	1			
Meath	1	2		
Tipperary			2	1
Waterford			1	1
Wexford			3	2

Fifteen counties participated in the senior finals.

The ten hurling finals involved seven counties, with five of these successful.

The ten football finals involved eleven counties, with eight of these successful.

A HURLING GAME:

Limerick v Wexford, 1957/58 National League final

Since the foundation of the GAA, every decade has produced great games at inter-club, inter-county and inter-provincial level. And those games could take place at any stage of the championship, sometimes even in the first round. In general, however, it is the great finals that tend to leave a lasting impression.

The hurling final of 1907, played at Dungarvan, between Kilkenny and Cork became the benchmark by which all future contests were measured. Then there was the memorable final of 1922 between Kilkenny and Tipperary, with Kilkenny snatching a victory that Tipperary seemed to have wrapped up. In the same decade spectators were treated to a classic contest in the first Railway Cup final between Leinster and Munster on St Patrick's Day 1927. The first replay of 1931 between Cork and Kilkenny was talked about for many a day, as was the 1947 All-Ireland final between the same counties. The list includes the Limerick v Kilkenny League final of 1935 and the unforgettable Munster championship contests of 1939, 1940, 1942 and 1944 between Limerick and Cork.

Side by side with all of those games stands proudly the Wexford v Limerick League final of 1957/58, played at Croke Park on 11 May 1958 before an attendance of over 26,000.

This was hurling to thrill the heart and send the blood pulsing. John D. Hickey of the *Irish Independent* described it as the greatest game he had seen – and he had witnessed many a spectacle. Mick Dunne of the *Irish Press* wrote:

> *The hurling was superbly exciting, the pace bewilderingly fast, an enthralling struggle was waged with intense vigour, yet the exchanges were scrupulously fair and sportsmanlike.*

Joe Sherwood in the *Evening Press* described it as 'a gripping pulsating combat', while Mitchel Cogley in the *Irish Independent* said it was 'a game that was a privilege to see'.

On the way to the final Wexford defeated Kilkenny, Cork, Waterford, Dublin and Antrim. Limerick accounted for Tipperary, Galway, Clare and Kerry. The Wexford team was backboned with several hurling stalwarts – Billy Rackard, Nick O'Donnell, Jim English, Jim Morrissey, Ned Wheeler, Padge Kehoe, Tim Flood, Martin Codd, Mick Morrissey and Séamus Hearne. In Pat Nolan Wexford had discovered a wonderful goalkeeper.

Limerick, with Mick Mackey as mentor, were less experienced in the big time. Dermot Kelly their captain, Vivian Cobbe and Jim Keogh had won a Munster title in 1955 when Limerick surprisingly beat a talented Clare team that had already disposed of Cork and Tipperary. Dermot Kelly, Tom McGarry, Jim Quaid, Vivian Cobbe and Mick Tynan were on the team that had Cork on the rack in the 1956 Munster final – that is until the closing stages when Ring ran amok and did the seemingly impossible. Some of the remaining players had won a junior All-Ireland title. It was a young team – fast, energetic, skilful and adept at ground play and first-time striking.

The scene was set from the throw-in, when referee and former Galway hurling star Josie Gallagher got the game under way in ideal weather conditions. Players, shoulder to shoulder and hip to hip, lashed the sliotar to and fro. The open spaces were being used. The pace was hectic. Who says that hurling was slower in the past?

Nicky Furlong in his book *The Greatest Hurling Decade* (Dublin, 1993) wrote: 'All I remember are the green leprechauns making joyful havoc, and the gold and purple jerseys desperately shoring up.'

Limerick struck early, but by half time Wexford had levelled 2-5 to 3-2. Nicky Furlong again takes up the story: 'Enchanted, exhausted, gasping, the crowd buzzed with excitement at half time. Could mortal men keep putting on shows of this intensity?'

I watched the game from behind the canal goal – standing room in those days. I was enthralled and bewildered by what I was witnessing. It was one of those games that sapped the energy of even the supporters.

The second half was a replica of the first. With less than ten minutes left the scoreboard read Limerick 4-7 Wexford 4-5. From then to the end it was drama heaped on drama. Wexford added 1-2. Limerick scored a point. Limerick pounded and pummelled the Wexford defence. Pat Nolan made two super saves. Billy Rackard and Nick O'Donnell performed heroics that bordered on the reckless.

It was a game that had everything – 'hurling in all its stern naked grandeur', played at speed with dash and fluency and in a sporting spirit that was exemplary.

As I write it is the spring of 2008 – just fifty years after the great game. I close my eyes and I can still see the scene at the final whistle as described by Nicky Furlong: 'I was overwhelmed with pity as I watched Wexford players consoling Limerick heroes down in the green sod in the midst of swirling Wexford revellers.'

Martin Codd, at left full forward for Wexford, was on the Limerick captain Dermot Kelly. A short time ago Martin very kindly recalled his memories of that great hour for me.

Sometimes I am asked which was the best game I ever played in. To some players, I am sure, this could be a difficult question to answer, but to me one game stands out above all others. Having played over a period of seventeen years for club and county, I would have played in many good games. Club hurling in the 1950s and early 1960s was much better than it is today. Mount Sion in Waterford, Glen Rovers in Cork, Thurles Sarsfields in Tipperary and Bennettsbridge in Kilkenny were all outstanding teams with many inter-county players. My own club, Rathnure, would play against these teams in tournaments every summer and these games would be of great quality, as the prizes would be valuable.

Games like the All-Ireland final of 1956, when we beat Cork, would stay in your mind for ever, but the League final of 1957/58 is the game that had everything. Wexford were a very experienced team with most of them having played in four All-Ireland finals and three League finals. For many of the Limerick team it was their first time to play in Croke Park. The final score was Wexford 5-7 Limerick 4-8.

It was a very free-flowing game with very few frees. Wexford's only score from a free was one point. I was playing at left-corner-forward. My instructions were to stay as close to goal as possible, so I spent much of the time watching the game from a distance. For three-quarters of the game our lads had great difficulty matching the speed of the Limerick men and we found ourselves three points down with seven or eight minutes to go. We fought back and got a goal and two points to go in front with about three minutes left. The goal came against the run of play.

You may ask what makes me think this was the greatest game I ever played in. It was fast and open with very few frees. The ball travelled up and down the field at great speed with some great ground hurling. The tackles were clean, skilful and very fair. Everyone was in a hurry to get on with the game which made the referee's job easy. I was the one who scored Wexford's last goal when I tapped the ball over the goal line after a fierce tussle in the Limerick goalmouth. This put me on a high for the last few minutes of the game, but there was no ball coming up to our end of the field.

Limerick went all out for a winning goal, which was a mistake as they had chances to score points. Ned Wheeler, who was playing at centrefield for us, was having a problem with his boots and sat down to sort the problem out. I felt I was doing nothing where I was, so I raced out to centrefield to help. Limerick were winning all over the field now and were bringing fierce pressure on the Wexford full-back line. Much of the last three or four minutes of the game was played inside the 21-yard line where Wexford were defending.

This gave Billy Rackard and Nick O'Donnell the opportunity to prove that they were two of the best defenders ever to play hurling. Billy's block on one of the Limerick forwards when he had a clear shot on goal is something I'll never forget. His hurl was knocked from his hands and with no time to pick it up he went in and blocked the Limerick man's stroke with his bare hands.

That one act of courage was the winning of the game. After contributing so much to a great game you would feel sorry for the Limerick men, but that's sport.

These are the players who served up a hurling special:

Wexford:

Pat Nolan

Billy Rackard   Nick O'Donnell   John Redmond

Jim English   Jim Morrissey   Mick Morrissey

Ned Wheeler   Séamus Hearne

Harry O'Connor   Padge Kehoe   Oliver Gough

Martin Lyng   Tim Flood   Martin Codd

Jimmy O'Brien and Oliver 'Hopper' McGrath came on as subs.

Limerick:

Gerry Casey

Dermot Kelly   Jack Enright   Jim Keogh

Tom McGarry   Jim Quaid   Séamus Quaid

Tommy Casey   Declan Moylan

Liam Hogan   Nicholas Stokes   Vivian Cobbe

Joe Shanahan   Mick Tynan   Liam Moloney

Willie Hogan came on as a sub.

Martin Codd died on 2 May 2008. *Solas na bhFlaitheas duit, a Mháirtín uasal.* His son-in-law, Niall Wall, wrote this lovely poem to Martin's memory:

Great Spirit of Askinfarney
You are Blackstair who watches over us
The streams that cleanse us
The mist that shrouds us
The purple and gold that unites us
And while we hold you in our hearts
We will never be alone.
You are the strength of trees
The laughter of children
The whisper of the wind
You are Wexford
And while we love each other
Your smile will beam.
Not age or illness
Nor even death
Can take away or dull nor fade
The singing heart
Who walks unseen
Yet by our side.
Farewell dear friend
Go to your rest
For you go not far
But even near
Each gentle breeze
Your loving touch.

Martin Codd

Action from the 1957/58 National League classic. (L–r): Martin Lyng (Wexford), Jim Keogh (Limerick), Padge Kehoe (Wexford), Tim Flood (Wexford) and Jack Enright (Limerick).

HURLING PERSONALITIES:

The boys of Wexford

For the twenty years prior to 1951, the hurling scene was dominated by Kilkenny (five All-Irelands, one National League); Cork (six All-Irelands, three National Leagues); Tipperary (four All-Irelands, two National Leagues); and Limerick (three All-Irelands, six National Leagues).

On the periphery, as it were, you had Dublin (one All-Ireland, one National League); Waterford (one All-Ireland); Galway (two National Leagues); and Clare (one National League), all capable of presenting, from time to time, a formidable challenge to the then four superpowers of the game.

Wexford players enjoy the minor game as they
await the 1955 senior final.

Suddenly, or so it seemed, Wexford arrived on the scene; their coming was not prophesied. After all, it was away back in 1910 that they had defeated a 'Tyler' Mackey-led Limerick team by 7-0 to 6-2 to win their first and only All-Ireland title. And their last appearance in an All-Ireland final was in 1918 when they were heavily beaten by a talented Limerick fifteen.

I remember listening to Micheál O'Hehir's broadcast of the 1950 Leinster final from Nowlan Park between Wexford and Kilkenny. The Kilkenny names were familiar. The Wexford ones were new – Rackard, Flood, Codd, Morrissey, Kehoe, names all destined for greatness in the decade ahead. Wexford lost that game by 3-11 to 2-11 – a game they could, and perhaps should, have won. Billy Rackard still remembers the green flag that waved for a Kilkenny goal for a ball that was on the Wexford goal line but not over it. And he remembers, too, the dying moments when his brother Nicky tore in on the Kilkenny goal. 'Diamond' Hayden, the Kilkenny full-back, averted a certain goal by tripping Nicky. Though young at the time, I remember feeling we were going to hear a lot more about the hurling men from the Model county – big, strong, fit athletic men whose style of play was 'lift and strike'.

In the decade that followed, the men in purple and gold adorned the hurling scene with displays of rare splendour. They left a lasting impression, defeating all the hurling powers. They were renowned for their sportsmanship. Pat Stakelum, brilliant Tipperary centre-half-back of those days, summed it up well:

> The arrival of Wexford gave the game a fabulous lift ... They were mighty men with a sense of fair play that was quite remarkable. The Rackards adorned the game, and so did Padge Kehoe, Ned Wheeler, Tim Flood and Nick O'Donnell.

Wexford brought to hurling a magic and romance that still lives in the memories of those of us privileged to have seen them in action.

More than three dozen players lined out for Wexford in the period 1951–1960. There was, however, a core of six players that were there in 1951 on All-Ireland final day when Wexford were valiant against Tipperary who were still going strong nine years later when Wexford again faced Tipperary in the All-Ireland final of 1960. I speak of Nick O'Donnell, Billy Rackard, Ned Wheeler, Jim Morrissey, Padge Kehoe and Tim Flood.

1951: Jimmy Finn (left) leads Tipperary; Nick Rackard (right)
leads Wexford, followed by his brothers Bobby and Billy.

Let us now glance at a few of the many highlights of those years.
In 1951, despite losing to Tipperary in the All-Ireland final, Wexford
served notice and gave evidence of the kind of hurling Gaeldom would
witness from the Model county in the years ahead. The lineout was:

Ray Brennan

Martin Byrne   *Nick O'Donnell*   *Mick O'Hanlon*

Sam Thorpe   *Bobby Rackard*   *Billy Rackard*

Ned Wheeler   *Jim Morrissey*

Padge Kehoe   *John Cummins*   *Ted Russell*

Tim Flood   *Nicky Rackard*   *Paddy Kehoe*

Between 1951 and 1955 Wexford hurlers drank many a cup of woe
as their efforts to win All-Ireland glory floundered, often unexpectedly, at different stages. At last in 1955, hurling's Everest was
conquered when Galway, who had a bye straight into the final,
were defeated. Ten of those who were there in 1951 remained.

Gone were Ray Brennan, Martin Byrne, Sam Thorpe, John Cummins and Ted Russell. In had come Art Foley, Jim English, Mick Morrissey, Séamus Hearne and Tom Ryan.

In 1956 Wexford made it two in a row with a magnificent victory over Cork. The departure of Mick O'Hanlon and Paddy Kehoe meant that eight of the 1951 team celebrated 1956. The lineout was:

Art Foley

Bobby Rackard   Nick O'Donnell   Mick Morrissey

Jim English   Billy Rackard   Jim Morrissey

Séamus Hearne   Ned Wheeler

Padge Kehoe   Martin Codd   Tim Flood

Tom Ryan   Nicky Rackard   Tom Dickson

Wexford swept all before them in 1956 – winning the Leinster title, the All-Ireland crown, the National League and the Oireachtas. And ten of them played on the Leinster team that won the Railway Cup – at that time a most prestigious competition. In a barber's shop in Wexford hung a picture of the 1956 team. The caption beneath the photograph was taken from Peadar Kearney's ballad, 'Down by the Glenside'. It read: 'We may have great men but we'll never have better'.

Onwards now to 1960 and one of Wexford's greatest moments. Nicky Rackard had retired after 1956 and Bobby Rackard was sidelined in 1957 following a farm accident. That meant that six of the 1951 team now remained.

There were no All-Ireland semi-finals in 1960, because Galway were playing in Munster and Ulster had no representative. Wexford reached the All-Ireland final with a two-point win over Noreside neighbours Kilkenny, 3-10 to 2-11, in the Leinster final. Tipperary qualified for the final with a two-point win over arch-rivals Cork, 4-13 to 4-11, in the Munster final. The contest at times was of battle proportions. For Tipperary, the result was a kind of pyrrhic victory.

To say that Tipperary were favourites for the All-Ireland title of 1960 would be an understatement. Micheál Maher, the Tipperary full-back, recalled the occasion:

1960: All-Ireland throw-in – Wexford v Tipperary.

We were absolutely sure of beating them. We were waiting for the ball to be thrown in and get on with the game, but as things turned out it was worse we were getting as the game progressed.

Liam Devaney, the Tipperary centre-forward, had memories of that day too:

We hit the field first and we were red-hot favourites. Then Wexford came out and Theo English and myself observed their two midfielders – Jim Morrissey and Ned Wheeler. Both were big men and looking very fit, but that didn't dent our confidence.

I watched the game from the Hogan stand on a day ideal for hurling. 'Hopper' McGrath pointed for Wexford within thirty seconds of the throw-in. After that Wexford were never headed and took a terrier-like grip on the game. A close-in free, to the left of the railway goal, was taken by Padge Kehoe. It finished in the Tipperary net, following a deflection off a defender's hurley. Wexford were now firing on all cylinders and playing some grand hurling. Their confidence grew. They hurled with flair and abandon. Against all expectations, they led at the interval by 1-7 to 0-8.

In the second half, as in the first, 'Hopper' McGrath struck early; he rounded the Tipperary defence and his rasping shot shook the net. Urged on by the crowd, Wexford grew in stature. The veterans of 1951were wonderful – Nick O'Donnell at full-back, Billy Rackard at centre-half-back, midfielders Ned Wheeler and Jim Morrissey and in the attack Tim Flood and Padge Kehoe.

The half-back line of Jim English, Billy Rackard and John Nolan was a defensive bulwark.

John Dowling's full-time whistle heralded one of the biggest shocks in hurling history: Wexford 2-15 Tipperary 0-11. It was the first time since 1922 that Tipperary had lost an All-Ireland final.

Wexford lined out as:

Pat Nolan

John Mitchell   *Nick O'Donnell*   *Tom Neville*

Jim English   *Billy Rackard*   *John Nolan*

Ned Wheeler   *Jim Morrissey*

Jimmy O'Brien   *Padge Kehoe*   *Séamus Quaid*

Oliver 'Hopper' McGrath *John Harding*   *Tim Flood*

'Battle of Ross'. Oireachtas semi-final, 9 October 1960 – game abandoned. Nicky Rackard, clothed, rushes on to the pitch after 'Hopper' McGrath was felled (Wexford v Cork).

Mick Dunne, writing in the *Irish Press* the following day, aptly described the result with a quotation from Lord Byron's poem 'The Destruction of Sennacherib':

> *The Assyrian came down like the wolf on the fold*
> *And his cohorts were gleaming in purple and gold.*

Wexford's Kilkenny-born captain, Nick O'Donnell, collected the McCarthy Cup for the second time. It was Wexford's fourth All-Ireland crown and their third since 1951.

Of the eight players of 1951 who played in the 1956 All-Ireland final and the six who played in the 1960 final, only two now remain: Ned Wheeler and Tim Flood. The others – Billy Rackard, Bobby Rackard, Nicky Rackard, Nick O'Donnell, Jim Morrissey and Padge Kehoe – are all *imithe ar shlí na Fírinne*, gone to the happy hurling ground: 'A bourne in Paradise, where all the hurlers go'. *Dia go deo leo*.

A hurling selection

Pat Nolan
(Wexford)

Bobby Rackard	Nick O'Donnell	John Barron
(Wexford)	(Wexford)	(Waterford)

Tom McGarry	Billy Rackard	Phil Grimes
(Limerick)	(Wexford)	(Waterford)

Ned Wheeler   Jim Morrissey
(Wexford)   (Wexford)

Christy Ring	Tom Cheasty	Jimmy Doyle
(Cork)	(Waterford)	(Tipperary)

Séamus Power	Nicky Rackard	Johnny Kiely
(Waterford)	(Wexford)	(Waterford)

The selection is dedicated, in the main, to the men of Wexford who took the stage at the beginning of the decade and those of Waterford who arrived on the scene towards the close of the decade.

Séamus Power (left) and Phil Grimes.

1960: Nick O'Donnell with President Éamon de Valera and Dr Joe Stuart, President of the GAA.

These are joined by three 'outsiders' – Tom McGarry, that gifted all-round sportsman, who fell foul of Rule 27 (the ban on foreign games); Jimmy Doyle, one of the game's most talented and sporting players; and Christy, himself, the hurling wizard from Cloyne, who was shouldered off the field by Nick O'Donnell and Bobby Rackard after Cork had fallen to Wexford in the 1956 All-Ireland hurling final.

A FOOTBALL GAME:

Galway v Kerry, 1959 All-Ireland final

The 1959 football final was the first one I witnessed. The contestants were Kerry and Galway. They had not met at this stage since 1941, when Tom 'Gega' O'Connor of Dingle got the only goal of the hour and Kerry made it three in a row with a 1-8 to 0-7 victory.

It was their fifteenth title. They now headed the honours list for the first time – one ahead of Dublin.

In 1959 Kerry had eighteen titles and Galway four. At the semi-final stage, Kerry accounted for reigning title holders Dublin by two points. Galway beat Down, who had won their first ever Ulster title by 1-11 to 1-4.

I took my place in the newly built Hogan stand well before the minor game so as to savour the full atmosphere of Croke Park on football final day. The meeting of Dublin and Cavan in the minor final ensured that all four provinces were represented. It was a fine game with Cavan, in the first half, shaping as if they would capture a title they had not won since 1938. However, Dublin finished strongly and took their fifth title in six years and their seventh in all.

About an hour before the senior game, the gates were closed. Officially, close on 86,000 had packed into Croke Park, with thousands of disappointed fans locked out.

Kerry's last title was in 1955. There were six survivors – Paudie Sheehy, Tadhgie Lyne, Jerome O'Shea, Seán Murphy, John Dowling the captain and Johnny Culloty, then at corner forward, now in goal.

Galway's most recent title was in 1956. They had eight survivors from that year – Jack Mahon, Joe Young, Seán Purcell, Frank

Stockwell, Frank Evers, Mattie McDonogh, Mick Greally and Jack Kissane.

The teams emerged to a tremendous reception. The biggest man of the thirty was Galway's midfielder Frank Evers, standing at 6 feet 2 inches. In weather conditions ideal for football, referee John Dowling of Offaly got the game under way. Despite the fact that half a century has now passed since that final, fleeting moments of that day remain vivid in my memory.

I was looking forward to seeing the footballing brilliance of Mick O'Connell, the Kerry captain from Valentia Island – a man who made his county senior debut in 1956. But it was not to be. In the semi-final against Dublin, he had given a majestic display of high fielding and long accurate kicking – a man who could kick with both feet, a man who aimed for perfection in all facets of the game. For days before the final, however, he was feeling unwell and probably should not have played. To add to his woes, he suffered a leg injury early in the game and after being switched to centre-forward had to depart the scene.

Big John Dowling from Tralee put Kerry ahead with two fine points. Then a Galway movement saw Frank Evers finish the ball to the net. The game – hard, fast and physical – was level at half time. Galway were dominating at midfield until Kerry made switches.

I was captivated by the speed and range of skills of Paudie Sheehy – son of the famous John Joe. His brothers Niall, Brian and Seán Óg would all, at some stage, play for Kerry.

A battle of wits, or so it seemed to me, was going on between Galway's 'terrible twins', Frank Stockwell and Seán Purcell, and their respective markers, Niall Sheehy and Kevin Coffey. The strongly built Kevin Coffey from Beaufort was doing a fine job at centre-back in containing the Galway captain Seán Purcell, while Niall Sheehy was having a solid game at full-back on Frank Stockwell. The Galway men alternated but their efforts were spiked by their markers and therein lay part of the story of Kerry's success.

Early in the game Mattie McDonogh and Frank Evers were lording it at midfield for Galway, but that changed when a Kerry switch brought Tom Long from centre-forward to cope with Evers.

Man of the hour was Kerry's Seán Murphy, from Camp in the Dingle Peninsula, at right-half-back. In the second half I was looking directly across at him. He made it all look so simple in a display that was impeccable.

For a while in the second half the game continued to hang in the balance. Then came three Kerry goals – two from Dan McAuliffe and one from substitute Garry McMahon from Listowel.

By a strange coincidence, as I penned these lines in spring 2008 I heard of the death of Garry. In his time with Kerry he won Munster and All-Ireland titles. He also played Railway Cup for the province. I saw him in action again in the 1962 All-Ireland final against Roscommon. It was the first minute of the game. Kerry got a free. Mick O'Connell took it and it floated goalwards to the unmarked Garry McMahon. With a flick of his right hand the ball was in the net. It seemed to knock the heart right out of Roscommon, who after that never really got into the game.

Back now to 1959. Those three goals were the difference between the teams in the end. Galway never gave up. Their forwards tore in on the Kerry goal, but too many of their efforts were wasted. I can still vividly see one of those attacks. Joe Young swept down the wing on the Hogan stand side and bore in on the canal goal. He let fly a mighty drive that curved and passed the right-hand goalpost on the wrong side. On another day the same shot would have been followed by the waving of the green flag.

At full time the scoreboard read Kerry 3-7 Galway 1-4. However, the outfield exchanges were closer than the scoreline might suggest. My first football final – memories of a fine game and some of Gaelic football's greatest exponents.

A FOOTBALL PERSONALITY:

Dermot O'Brien (Louth)

As we drove to Croke Park the final to see,
Our friend Dan O'Hanlon says: 'Listen to me!'
Look out for the Louth boys, for I'm telling you
They'll win this All-Ireland – it's long overdue!
The experts all say we are on the small side,
But the small man can humble the big fellow's pride,
And with Louth's fighting spirit – between you and me –
We could topple the giants from the Banks of the Lee!

Nicholas Craven

Dermot O'Brien was born on 23 October 1932 – son of Paddy and Nancy (née Dowdall). He had two great passions in life – football and music – both of which brought him fame and reward. They overlapped in his early life until he retired from competitive football in 1960 and became a professional musician in 1962. In subsequent years, however, Dermot did play charity matches with the Jimmy Magee All-Stars.

Dermot hailed from Ardee – Áth Fherdia, the Ford of Ferdia, a name famous in Irish mythology. With his club, St Mary's Ardee, he won a county minor title in 1949, followed by three senior titles in 1951, 1956 and 1960. In his minor days his talents were spotted by the county selectors and he played for Louth in 1949 and 1950.

Dermot made his county senior debut in 1952. Success came a year later when Louth defeated Wexford in the Leinster final. They then faced a reconstructed Kerry team in the All-Ireland semi-final. Late in the second half Dermot rose to field a high ball and in the process fell on his back and was badly injured. Kerry won by five points. Dermot took a three-year sabbatical from county football but continued to play at club level.

He was back in 1957 when Louth reached the All-Ireland final with victories over Carlow, Wexford, Kildare, Dublin and Tyrone. It was a tough campaign that carried a valuable learning curve. Their opponents, Cork, had easy victories over Clare and Waterford in Munster, before surviving the Galway challenge in the semi-final by just one point, 2-4 to 0-9.

Thus did it come to pass that Louth and Cork faced each other to do battle for the Sam Maguire Cup on Sunday 22 September 1957, the first meeting of these counties at this level. It was Ireland's smallest county, Louth – home of the legendary Setanta-cum-Cúchulainn – versus Cork, the largest county. Measured on a square-mile basis it was, indeed, a David and Goliath affair. But football isn't like that.

I was stationed in Ballyshannon and getting ready to listen to Micheál O'Hehir's broadcast. A year earlier I was in Clifden and listened to the final between Cork and Galway. Cork, it seemed to me, wasted many golden opportunities and it cost them. Unlucky losers, perhaps. Despite that, my heart was now with Louth, the underdog.

They were captained by Dermot O'Brien, who was playing at centre-half-forward. It was in some ways a captaincy by chance. Earlier in the championship his clubmate Patsy Coleman was captain, but following an injury the mantle fell to Dermot. Patsy was back to take his place at right-half-back for the final, and Dermot offered to step down as captain. The selectors, however, felt that the fairest way was to toss a coin. Dermot won.

As I awaited the broadcast I couldn't help wondering what thoughts had gone through Dermot's mind in the build-up to the final. He would have been well aware that down the decades Louth had produced many wonderful footballers – names like Tom Burke, Jim Smith, Eddie Boyle, Seán Boyle, Jack Bell and Paddy Markey. And yet success was limited; Leinster was a hard province to emerge from. Eight Leinster titles would, to many, seem a poor reward. Three of those titles were won in the early years of the twentieth century – 1909, 1910 and 1912. Louth lost the 1909 final to Kerry, were awarded a walkover in the 1910 final from Kerry and defeated Antrim in the final of 1912.

Provincial crowns were won in 1943 and 1948, but on each occasion Louth were beaten in the semi-final, by Roscommon and Cavan respectively. The All-Ireland final was reached in 1950 after a great semi-final win over Kerry, 1-7 to 0-8. They lost to a fine Mayo team in the final, 2-5 to 1-6.

As already stated, Dermot played his part in the provincial successes of 1953 and 1957. And as he led his team in the pre-match parade he knew it was only the fourth time that Louth were contesting a final on the pitch – 1909, 1912, 1950 and 1957. There were three survivors from the 1950 campaign – Tom Conlon, the then captain, Stephen White and Jim McDonnell.

The game was a close, tense, vigorous affair – never much between the teams on the scoreboard. Each had periods of dominance. Cork seemed to have the better-balanced outfit and led at half time by two points – it could have been more. It was nip and tuck in the second half. With about five minutes left on the clock Cork led by a point. Then came the Louth winner – out of the blue, you might say. Kevin Behan took a sideline kick. It was beautifully placed. The Cork defence seemed to have it well covered, but Louth's corner forward Seán Cunningham rose, fisted, and the ball was in the net. Louth 1-9 Cork 1-7.

Dermot O'Brien collected the Sam Maguire Cup in the Hogan stand from GAA president Séamus McFerran of Antrim. He made a fine speech in the Irish language, but we did not have television in those days to capture it, as was the case in 1980 with Galway's Joe Connolly and in 1995 with Clare's Anthony Daly. Dermot had a special *grá* for the Irish language. He saw it as a badge of identity and used it whenever the opportunity presented itself, and even spent time in the Gaeltacht to enhance his knowledge.

Dermot captained the Leinster Railway Cup team in 1958. They lost to Connacht in the semi-final at Ballinasloe, 1-11 to 0-7.

Dermot was an extremely successful musician. It is probably true to say that music was in his blood, and he mastered many instruments. His name and the accordion were synonymous, and his father was bandmaster of the Ardee Brass and Reed Band. At the age of fourteen Dermot came under the watchful eye of Sister Malachy, a music teacher, who was his piano tutor for four years. He never forgot her. In later years when he formed a céilí band he named it after her – St Malachy's Céilí Band.

Before turning professional in 1962, Dermot spent some time playing with the Emerald Céilí Band and after that with the Vincent Lowe Trio. In the 1960s and 1970s he had his own show on television – the Dermot O'Brien Show. He toured the UK, the US, Canada and Germany, and played as far afield as the United Arab Emirates.

Dermot's final years were spent in his native Ardee. He died on 22 May 2007, having earlier that year attended the reunion celebrating the All-Ireland victory of fifty years earlier. *Imíonn na daoine …*

Dermot O'Brien leads Louth in 1957 All-Ireland semi-final v Tyrone.

A football selection

Thady Turbett
(Tyrone)

Micheál O'Brien   Paddy Prendergast   Seán Flanagan
(Meath)   (Mayo)   (Mayo)

Gerry O'Reilly   Gerry O'Malley   Jim McDonnell
(Wicklow)   (Roscommon)   (Cavan)

Jim McKeever   Seán Murphy
(Derry)   (Kerry)

Paudie Sheehy   Seán Purcell   Packie McGarty
(Kerry)   (Galway)   (Leitrim)

Tom Long   Frankie Stockwell   Kevin Heffernan
(Kerry)   (Galway)   (Dublin)

1961–1970

Teams that participated in the
All-Ireland senior finals

COUNTY	FOOTBALL		HURLING	
	WON	LOST	WON	LOST
Cork		1	2	1
Down	2			
Dublin	1			1
Galway	3	1		
Kerry	3	3		
Kilkenny			3	2
Meath	1	2		
Offaly		2		
Roscommon		1		
Tipperary			4	2
Waterford				1
Wexford			1	3

Twelve counties participated in the senior finals.

The ten hurling finals involved six counties with four of these successful.

The ten football finals involved eight counties with five of these successful.

A HURLING GAME:

Kilkenny v Waterford, 1963 All-Ireland final

As I travelled to Croke Park from Wexford on Sunday 1 September 1963, I had time to reflect on the two thrilling All-Ireland finals of recent times between the 1963 finalists Kilkenny and Waterford.

In 1957 I had journeyed from Ballyshannon to see these counties contest that year's final. And what a final it was – exciting, heart-stopping, swaying fortunes, delightful passages of hurling, pulsating stuff.

I was standing under the Hogan Stand close to the canal end. I saw Ollie Walsh in action for the first time. I have never forgotten his magnificent goalkeeping display.

Entering the last quarter, Waterford led by 3-10 to 2-7 and looked as if they would be crowned All-Ireland champions for the second time. But at full time the scoreboard read Kilkenny 4-10 Waterford 3-12, Kilkenny one point to the good. Waterford supporters, and indeed many neutrals too, felt a sense of bewilderment. For this was a game Waterford could have won and certainly should have drawn. For the fourth time in succession Kilkenny had taken the title by just a point – 1935, 1939, 1947, 1957 – all epic encounters.

1935: It was a wet, miserable day – a sodden sliotar. Yet, Kilkenny and Limerick were serving up a classic. Picture the final moments. The score stood Kilkenny 2-5 Limerick 2-4. Referee Tommy Daly of Clare awarded a 21-yard free to Limerick. Their captain Timmy Ryan stood over the sliotar – full time beckoned. Up came Mick Mackey and said: 'Timmy, I'll take it.' Mick went for the goal. Kilkenny saved. Full time and the Noresiders were hurling champions.

1939: Another classic encounter. In the second half there was thunder, lightning, torrential rain and hectic hurling. Time was ticking away and the final whistle approached. The scoreboard read Kilkenny 2-6 Cork 3-3. Excitement was fierce. Kilkenny won a disputed seventy. Paddy Phelan landed it short. Jimmy Kelly of Carrickshock was on hand to gather and send over the winning point for a dramatic win.

1947: This time the weather was kind. In broken time the scores were level, Kilkenny 0-13 Cork 2-7. Terry Leahy, hero of the hour, latched on to a Cork clearance. Then a swerve and a glance and away went the sliotar for a sensational winner. Another classic contest.

1957: Kilkenny came from six points down to, in the words of the late Micheál O'Hehir, pull the game out of the fire and literally steal an All-Ireland crown by one point.

It is worth recalling that in the pre-match parade of 1957 – well, for part of it – there were sixteen Kilkenny men. Not many had spotted that film star John Gregson was in the parade. He was taking part in a film called *Rooney* whose hero was an enthusiastic hurler. Shots from the All-Ireland final were used in the film.

Now to 1959. We witnessed two finals – a draw, described by the *Irish Independent* as 'a struggle of breathtaking splendour, astonishing pace and nerve-shattering intensity', and a replay. It took a goal by the stout-hearted Séamus Power in the closing seconds to snatch a draw for Waterford. The final score tells something of the nature of the game – Waterford 1-17 Kilkenny 5-5.

In the replay, Waterford fell six points behind early on. Then they proceeded to take a grip of the game. Tom Cheasty was in great form. He scored 2-2. Frankie Walsh, the captain, was deadly accurate – eight points in all, six from frees.

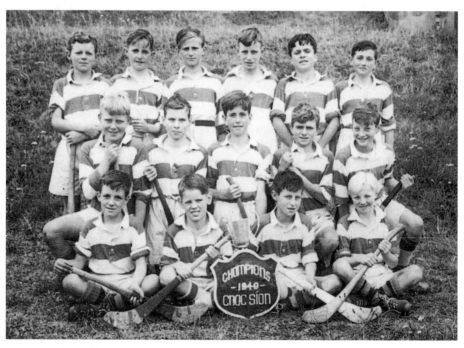

Frankie Walsh, second from right in front row (1949).

In 1963 Kilkenny and Waterford were in action for the third time in seven years – indeed, for only the third time in the championship up to then. The curtain-raiser to the senior game was the minor final between Wexford and Limerick. It was a delightful contest – thrilling, free-flowing, high-scoring. Victory to the Model county, 6-12 to 5-9. There were many players in action that day who in later years would play at senior level and win highest honours – among them Tony Doran and Vinnie Staples of Wexford who would win a senior title in 1968, and Éamon Grimes and Éamon Cregan of Limerick whose moment of ultimate glory would come in 1973.

An attendance of over 73,000 watched as Jimmy Hatton of Wicklow, in charge of his first final, got the game under way.

Kilkenny had just five survivors from 1957 – Ollie Walsh in goal; Billy Dwyer and Denis Heaslip in the same positions of full-forward and right-half-forward respectively; Seán Clohessy, now switched to midfield from left-full-forward; and Johnny McGovern, at left half-back in 1957 and now operating at centre-forward.

Waterford had nine of the 1957 team in action. John Barron had moved from left full back to full forward, Séamus Power from left-half-back to right-full-forward, and Phil Grimes from centrefield to left-full-forward. The remaining six played in their original positions – Tom Cunningham, Austin Flynn, Martin Óg Morrissey, Mick Flannelly, Tom Cheasty and Frankie Walsh.

At half time Waterford trailed by seven points, 3-6 to 1-5; before the second half was five minutes old they had fallen eleven points behind, 4-7 to 1-5. Waterford, however, did not die. Between then and the final whistle they scored 5-3 as against Kilkenny's ten points.

Playing a blend of Munster and Kilkenny hurling, as indeed was their wont, the Waterford forwards found a rhythm and were a delight to watch. With Power, Walsh and Grimes adding to the Waterford tally, the Déise were only two points behind as the clock ticked to the last minute. The balance, however, tilted Kilkenny's way when Eddie Keher sent over a point from a free. Final score: Kilkenny 4-17 Waterford 6-8. Kilkenny's fifteenth crown.

The four corner-forwards were in rare scoring form – for Waterford Séamus Power 3-0, Phil Grimes 1-2; for Kilkenny Tom Walsh 2-0, Tommy Murphy 2-1. Waterford's other big scoring forward was Mick Flannelly with two goals.

The Kilkenny captain Séamus Cleere gave a classical display at left-half-back. At centre field Seán Clohessy and Paddy Moran held sway and therein lay the key to victory. The occasion, however, belonged in many respects to Eddie Keher, who got fourteen of Kilkenny's seventeen points – ten from frees. His name brought a new meaning to free-taking accuracy. He was flawless – neither distance nor angle presented any problem – the product of painstaking practice. For Eddie, 1963 was the launch of a glittering career – a career that began at senior level when he came on as a replacement for Johnny McGovern in the closing stages of the All-Ireland final replay of 1959 – the day he also helped in the minor final against Tipperary and lost by one point.

I decided to contact Eddie to get some of his memories of All-Ireland final day 1963.

At the time I was a banker in Dublin staying in a flat in Frankfort Avenue, Rathgar. A lot of my training was done in Dublin and occasionally I travelled down to Kilkenny with Seán Clohessy and Billy Dwyer to train with the rest of the lads.

At the time my frees were not going too well and in practice Martin Walsh, Tom's brother, would say to me: 'What used Fr Tommy Maher tell you?'

We had extra coaching before meeting Waterford, who were firm favourites. They had several experienced players who were around for quite a while. We were young, apart from a few players like Seán Clohessy, Billy Dwyer, Johnny McGovern and Ollie. For me it was a very big occasion – my first senior All-Ireland really.

The team came up and stayed in a hotel the night before the match. I stayed in my flat. Seán Clohessy came to collect me on the Sunday morning. He told me that he went to the pictures the previous night to relax and get away from it all. At that time cinemas were full of smoke, so he could have been inhaling anything. At the interval the lights went on and a man in the seat in front of Seán had one of the Sunday papers (they were always available on Saturday nights in Dublin). The heading read 'Waterford Will Win'.

We all met in the hotel on Sunday morning. Fr Maher went around to speak to each of us, giving us a boost and letting us know what was expected of us. For the match I felt relaxed and had the feeling everything was right on the day. We were young and full of enthusiasm. I remember Waterford slapped in a rake of goals in the second half. Towards the end the score was down to two points in our favour. A lot of the frees I had taken during the match were out on the sideline. Then with time running out we got a free that was straight in front of goal. It was the easiest one of the day. But trying to be sure I was lined up right and doing everything right it was the worst I hit, but it did go over the bar to give us a three-point margin. And the strange thing is, it is the only game I played in that I still remember the score: Kilkenny 4-17 Waterford 6-8.

A HURLING PERSONALITY:

Tom Walsh (Kilkenny)

The name Walsh has been associated with Kilkenny hurling since the early days of the Association. The records show John Walsh of Tullaroan in action in 1893; John Walsh and Willie Walsh from the same club were there in 1895.

In the 1897 All-Ireland final against Limerick, the Noresiders were captained by Jackie Walsh of Tullaroan. Also on the team which lost to Limerick by 3-4 to 2-4 was Dick Walsh of Mooncoin – not to be confused with Dick 'Drug' Walsh of later days.

'Drug' Walsh of Mooncoin arrived on the hurling scene in 1904, and by 1913 had won seven All-Ireland hurling medals. He captained his native county to three of those titles – an honour he shares with Mikey Maher of Tipperary and Christy Ring of Cork.

Jim 'Builder' Walsh played with Kilkenny in the 1916 All-Ireland final against Tipperary. Subsequently, he won All-Ireland titles with Dublin in 1920, 1924 and 1927 playing at wing-back.

Paddy 'Skipper' Walsh played in the second and third games of the epic All-Ireland contests with Cork in 1931. Jimmy Walsh, the farmer from Carrickshock, won four All-Ireland medals in the 1930s. He was captain in 1932 and 1939 with wins over Clare and Cork respectively.

Bill Walsh was on the losing All-Ireland teams of 1946 and 1950, giving second best to Cork and Tipperary respectively. He came on as a sub in 1957 against Waterford to claim an All-Ireland medal on the field. Kilkenny finished the game with five Walshs on the pitch. In goal was the great Ollie, at right-full-back was Tom and beside him in the full-back position was his brother Jim 'Link'. Mick was at centre-back and Willie came on to replace midfielder John Sutton.

And so we arrive at the 1960s and Tom Walsh, and my visit to him in mid-October 2007.

I started hurling in under-14 age group with my school in the parish of Thomastown at age ten. Our school won four County Kilkenny finals during my time. I came to inter-county prominence as a minor in 1961 and 1962 winning two All-Ireland medals. In the next five years I played in four senior All-Ireland finals, with two wins in 1963 and 1967 and two losses in 1964 and 1966. In the 1967 final I sustained an injury which resulted in the loss of my left eye and the end to my hurling career at the age of twenty-three.

God confers gifts in many different ways. In my case, the friendship and goodwill that has followed through my life from the GAA fraternity has been astonishing to comprehend. I am extremely grateful to all those wonderful people who after forty years still acknowledge their memory of my short hurling career.

The two most memorable games for me had to be my first and last All-Ireland winning medals in 1961(minor) and 1967 (senior). In both of these games Kilkenny beat Tipperary, and in each case I happened to be in the right place at the right time to score decisive goals.

I considered it a privilege to compete with and against some of the following names: Billy Rackard, Ned Wheeler, Dan Quigley, Des and Lar Foley, Mick Bermingham, Tom Cheasty, Séamus Power, Austin Flynn, Frankie Walsh, Jimmy Doyle, John Doyle, Donie Nealon, Mick Roche, Denis Murphy, Justin McCarthy; also my fellow parishoner and friend Ollie Walsh, Séamus Cleere, Pat Henderson and Eddie Keher.

Some are deceased and may their holy souls rest in peace.

From the outset the GAA had a common goal to travel a journey with a set of ideals which would transcend every parish in Ireland and also create self-confidence through their commitment to succeed, pride in an ability to play unique sporting games that

Irish people would enjoy and show dignity and respect to the authority of the GAA.

Long may these ideals underpin the foundations of the GAA.

Tom Walsh.

Tom was born in 1944 to Patrick and Kathleen (née Cassin) – the youngest of a family of four boys and two girls. From an early age hurling became part and parcel of his life. He had a unique presence on the field – described by Enda McEvoy of the *Sunday Tribune*: 'To the Kilkenny supporters he was a complement to Eddie Keher, and in terms of raw electric excitement arguably Keher's superior'. To which Enda could have added that he was blessed too with the silken skills and deft touches of the delightful-to-behold Billy Fitzpatrick.

As Tom hurled in the county minor training sessions at Nowlan Park, he was watched and admired by Angela, daughter of Paddy Grace, a legend and folk hero in Noreside hurling circles. Love blossomed. Tom and Angela married on 7 August 1968.

Tom made his county debut as a minor in 1961. They met Tipperary in the final, the third successive meeting of the counties at that level. The game was a battle royal. Tom Ryall in his book *Kilkenny: The GAA Story 1884–1984* (Kilkenny, 1984), tells us about it:

> *It was one of the best minor finals ever ... fine overhead striking, crisp ground play, plus the ebb and flow of battle ... the vital goal came when Peter O'Sullivan, the Munster goalie, had his clearance charged into the net by Tom Walsh ... Pierce Freaney and Tom Walsh were the heroes.*

They scored 1-4 each and Kilkenny won by 3-13 to 0-15.

Tom was still a minor the following year. In the Leinster final, in which Kilkenny beat Wexford by 5-7 to 5-4, he scored 3-4. Tipperary were, yet again, their All-Ireland final opponents. Tom had a great first and final quarter. He contributed 2-2 to their 3-6 to 0-9 victory. It was the third year in a row that Tipperary had fallen to Kilkenny in an All-Ireland minor final.

The county senior selectors were quick to spot Tom's hurling talents. So at the age of nineteen he found himself playing in the 1963 All-Ireland senior final against Waterford. He was now in the company of hurling giants, playing with and against great men – Waterford names like Austin Flynn, Larry Guinan, Martin Óg Morrissey, Tom Cheasty, Frankie Walsh, Séamus Power, John Barron, Phil Grimes and Mick Flannelly. And on a Kilkenny team that lined out as:

Ollie Walsh

'Fan' Larkin   *Cha Whelan*   *Martin Treacy*

Séamus Cleere   *Ted Carroll*   *Martin Coogan*

Paddy Moran   *Seán Clohosey*

Denis Heaslip   *Johnny McGovern*   *Eddie Keher*

Tom Walsh   *Billy Dwyer*   *Tom Murphy*

Tom Walsh (right) in action against Tipperary.

Kilkenny won that final on the rather unusual scoreline of 4-17 to 6-8. Tom Walsh contributed two goals.

Following the 1963 All-Ireland final, Kilkenny selector Tom Waldron told Tom that he had 'a most wonderful career ahead of him'. Tom had a very clear and definite picture in his mind regarding how he wanted to play hurling. In his pursuit of excellence, in all facets of the game, he used as his benchmark team colleague Eddie Keher, three years his senior, as he aimed for first-touch mastery, anticipation, instinctive positional sense, speed of thought and action and a radar-like reading of the game.

From 1961 to 1967 Tom played in an All-Ireland final every year except 1965, winning two senior titles, 1963 v Waterford and 1967 v Tipperary; an Oireachtas title; and four Leinster medals. He won a National League in 1965/66 when arch rivals Tipperary were beaten in the Home final and New York in the final. The provincial selectors noticed his talents and he became a regular on the Leinster team, winning Railway Cup medals in 1964, 1965 and 1967.

The 1967 championship for Kilkenny got under way at Carlow, when Dublin were easily defeated by 6-10 to 1-5. In the Leinster final, they had a seven-point victory over Wexford, and a date with Tipperary beckoned in the All-Ireland final on 3 September.

The two teams had met in the final in 1922. In a great game, Tipperary seemed to have the title won, but Kilkenny staged a late rally to win by 4-2 to 2-6. Four times after that the counties met in the All-Ireland final: 1937, 1945, 1950 and 1964. And each time the Premier county won. The blue and gold jersey of Tipperary seemed to put the hex on the black and amber of Kilkenny. So when the counties met in the 1967 final all kinds of honour and pride were at stake. Tipperary were going through a golden era. They were a vastly experienced outfit, having won in the 1960s the All-Ireland titles of 1961, 1962, 1964 and 1965.

The 1967 final, played in blustery conditions, was a tough, uncompromising encounter. Aided by the elements, Tipperary led at half time by 2-6 to 1-3. However, at the finish, Kilkenny were All-Ireland champions for the sixteenth time: 3-8 to 2-7. Their goalkeeper, Ollie Walsh, gave a fantastic display and was honoured later in the year with the Texaco Hurler of the Year award. The six backs in front of him were magnificent. They held the Tipperary forwards scoreless in the second half until the last minute, when they conceded a point. John Teehan played a stormer at midfield. Eddie Keher retired midway through the second half with a fractured wrist. Tom Walsh was at centre-forward. He faced one of the game's great centre-half-backs in Tony Wall. Tom's speed throughout the game was a constant thorn in the Tipperary defence. Of the Kilkenny total of 3-8, Tom contributed 1-2. His goal came just before the final quarter – a sweet first-timed ground ball that finished in the net at the railway end. It tipped the scales in Kilkenny's favour. But in the closing moments of the game tragedy struck for Tom Walsh, when an injury he incurred led to the loss of his left eye.

> *There were four minutes left when it happened. I knew imme-diately I was hurt. I put my hand up to my eye and when I saw blood, I said, Oh Jesus, I'm in trouble. Dr Kieran Cuddihy came onto the pitch to take a look. I asked him if he could put a patch on it. He started flailing his arms. I knew then it was serious. The first-aid people came on. I walked to the dressing room. My brother Martin joined me there. The ambulance arrived to take me to the Eye and Ear Hospital at Adelaide Road.*

Tom has no recollection of being in pain between the time he got the injury and his arrival in hospital. 'I think the adrenalin was flowing and that took care of the pain. At the hospital I probably got a "shot".'

Words cannot describe the trauma Tom suffered when it was conveyed to him by surgeon Francis McAuley, when he woke up after the operation, that the injured eye had to be removed, in order to protect the other eye. Tom was discharged within two weeks. There was trauma of a different kind as he came face to face with his father.

> *Walking down the hall to meet him was tough for me. I felt his pain far more than he felt mine, because he was surely thinking of the future that lay ahead of me and that my life, as it had been up to then, was now over. He wasn't a sentimentally demonstrative man. But at that emotional meeting, he threw his arms around me – something which he had probably never done before.*

It was an embrace that sealed the ending of the hurling career of a gifted player of immense potential.

A hurling selection

Ollie Walsh
(Kilkenny)

Jimmy Brohan   Austin Flynn   John Doyle
(Cork)   (Waterford)   (Tipperary)

Séamus Cleere   Tony Wall   Martin Coogan
(Kilkenny)   (Tipperary)   (Kilkenny)

Mick Roche   Joe Salmon
(Tipperary)   (Galway)

Donie Nealon   Des Foley   Frankie Walsh
(Tipperary)   (Dublin)   (Waterford)

Liam Devaney   Tony Doran   Tom Walsh
(Tipperary)   (Wexford)   (Kilkenny)

A FOOTBALL GAME:

Galway v Meath, 1966 All-Ireland final

For the first time ever in the history of the senior football champion-ship, Galway and Meath faced each other in the final at Croke Park on Sunday 25 September before a crowd of over 71,500. Meath had two All-Ireland titles to their credit, Galway had six.

In the 1966 campaign, Meath beat Kildare by 1-9 to 1-8 in the Leinster final and captured their tenth provincial crown. In the All-Ireland semi-final they had a cracking 2-16 to 1-9 win over a fine Down team. They entered the final as slight favourites.

Galway beat Mayo by 0-12 to 1-8 in the Connacht final to collect their twenty-fifth title. A narrow 1-11 to 1-9 win over Munster champions Cork put them into the final.

Galway were now playing in their fourth final in a row and in search of a three-in-a-row win. They were a vastly experienced team and battle-hardened; they knew what it took to survive in close finishes.

In 1963 they beat Kerry by 1-7 to 0-8 in the semi-final. A late

Dublin goal, following a sideline kick on the Cusack Stand side and close to Hill 16, saw them lose the final by 1-9 to 0-10. Better days lay ahead.

In 1964, captained by John Donnellan, Galway survived a Meath challenge in the semi-final by 1-8 to 0-9 and went on to beat Kerry in the final by 0-15 to 0-10.

The following year they were captained by Enda Colleran. The fates were kind to them in Connacht – they were very fortunate to survive Mayo by a point and Sligo by three points in the western final. Down ran them close in the All-Ireland semi-final, 0-10 to 0-7 and they beat Kerry in the final by 0-12 to 0-9. It was the third year in a row that Galway had beaten Kerry in the closing stages of the championship. And it was the second year in succession that Kerry had been beaten in a final – a fate that never previously befell them.

As the teams paraded around Croke Park for the 1966 final, I wondered how Galway would cope with the high fielding of several of the big Meath men. But they had the experience and the craft to do it, as I would soon learn. The nucleus of the 1963 team was still there – ten in all. And only three changes had been made from the 1965 final lineout.

Galway won the toss and their captain Enda Colleran decided to play with the breeze. They kept the ball low. It was obviously a planned tactic, and denied Meath any height advantage they might have. Throughout the field Galway were excellent. The defence was rock-like; the attack moved as a unit.

The half-time score did not really reflect Galway's superiority; 1-6 to 0-1. Meath did better in the second half. Over the hour they were best served by Jack Quinn at full-back, Peter Moore at midfield and Pat 'Red' Collier at right-half-back. I can still see 'Red' Collier racing down the wing on a solo run, from his half-back position, in an attempt to get an attacking movement going. The full-time score of 1-10 to 0-7 cloaked the gulf that existed between the teams on the day.

Noel Tierney at full-back was majestic. Johnny Geraghty in goal was flawless; Mattie McDonagh at centre-forward was magnificent. Mattie never played a better game; he scored 1-1. He was the only survivor from the 1956 team, captained by goalkeeper Jack Mangan, that defeated Cork in that year's final.

The 1966 win gave Mattie a fourth All-Ireland medal – the only footballer from Connacht to be so honoured. The record still stands. At midfield, teenager Jimmy Duggan had a fine game. He was following in the footsteps of his father Joe, who was on the losing All-Ireland final Galway teams of 1940, 1941 (both lost to Kerry) and 1942 (lost to Dublin). Jimmy's partner, Pat Donnellan, did Trojan work.

It was the first time a Connacht team had won three All-Ireland titles in a row. Indeed, not since Kerry in 1939, 1940 and 1941 had such a feat been achieved.

For team captain Enda Colleran, from the Mountbellew club (later to be chosen at right-full-back on the Team of the Century and the Millennium Team), it was a very special day. In receiving the Sam Maguire Cup for the second year in a row he was joining a select band – Jimmy Murray of Roscommon, 1943 and 1944; John Joe O'Reilly of Cavan, 1947 and 1948; Seán Flanagan of Mayo, 1950 and 1951.

1966: Galway's Mattie McDonagh in action against Meath.

In subsequent years the honour fell to Tony Hanahoe of Dublin (1976 and 1977) and Declan O'Sullivan of Kerry (2006 and 2007).

When Enda retired from Gaelic football he took up rugby. He played with Corinthians, at full back, and won a Connacht League and Cup.

The Galway lineout on that historic day in September 1966 was:

Johnny Geraghty

Enda Colleran   Noel Tierney   John Bosco McDermott

Colie McDonagh   Seán Meade   Martin Newell

Jimmy Duggan   Pat Donnellan

Cyril Dunne   Mattie McDonagh   Séamus Leydon

Liam Sammon   Seán Cleary   John Keenan

Galway made one substitution. In the closing stages of the game Seán Meade was replaced by John Donnellan, brother of Pat.

A FOOTBALL PERSONALITY:

Paddy Doherty (Down)

I first saw Paddy Doherty in action in the All-Ireland final of 1960 against reigning All-Ireland champions Kerry – a game that attracted a record attendance at the time of 87,768. He was wearing the number 12 jersey and playing at left-half-forward, a position he played in throughout the bulk of his footballing career. And in that position he excelled. Paddy, a left-footer, always played with style and skill and with an art that concealed art. He would advance to an incoming ball, timing his jump to gather the ball chest high, then swerve and go at speed to launch an attack on goal. Paddy was a thinking player who always aimed at turning possession to advantage. He was in many respects the complete footballer – gifted in his skills, possessed of an ideal temperament, and displaying at all times a touch of class in all facets of his game.

In the 1960 final against the Kingdom, Paddy was top scorer with 1-5. His goal came from a penalty after he himself was fouled. It sealed Kerry's fate and the Sam Maguire Cup was heading north of the border for the first time.

It was Down's first time contesting an All-Ireland final. As they paraded, their mien conveyed the impression of men on a mission. Kerry's full-forward John Dowling, meanwhile, was limping as he marched behind the Artane Boys Band.

It was a game of hard physical exchanges, tense and furious. The *Irish Independent* the following day said: 'There was no room for ornate endeavour in this football furnace.' At half time, it was Down 0-7 Kerry 0-5. Then a little more than ten minutes into the second half, a harmless looking high ball from James McCartan from about 40 yards out came into the Kerry goalmouth at the railway end, where an unimpeded Johnny Culloty in goal reached under the crossbar to field it, only to see the ball fall from his attempted grasp into the net. Minutes later came Paddy Doherty's penalty, putting Down two goals up.

For Down, victory was a team effort where each man hounded his opponent. Éamon McKay in goal had a fine game and kept a clean sheet. George Lavery was brilliant at right-corner-back. James McCartan at centre-half-forward operated like a tank. Joe Lennon and Jarlath Carey had the better of the midfield exchanges. Their captain, Kevin Mussen, kept the fleet-of-foot Paudie Sheehy well in check.

It was Kerry's biggest All-Ireland defeat up to then, 2-10 to 0-8. The jubilation with which the presentation of the cup to Kevin Mussen by Dr Morris, archbishop of Cashel, was greeted was a moment to cherish.

So let us recall the Down lineout on that historic day, Sunday 25 September 1960.

Éamon McKay

George Lavery   *Leo Murphy*   *Pat Rice*

Kevin Mussen   *Dan McCartan*   *Kevin O'Neill*

Joe Lennon   *Jarlath Carey*

Seán O'Neill   *James McCartan*   *Paddy Doherty*

Tony Hadden   *Patsy O'Hagan*   *Brian Morgan*

In the course of the game Kieran Denvir replaced Joe Lennon.

In that year's semi-final against Offaly, Paddy also scored a vital penalty. With less than ten minutes to go, Down were three points adrift. The penalty was a real pressure kick, but Paddy made no mistake. Down lived to fight another day. Paddy had scored 1-7.

Paddy scored many goals, and points too, during an illustrious career that began at county level in 1951 when he played with the Down minors. He was still a minor the following year when Down lost the Ulster final to Cavan by two points. In 1953 Paddy played junior for the county, and the following year made his senior debut in the Dr McKenna Cup – a senior career that lasted until the Ulster final of 1969 against Cavan. In that game, which Down lost, Paddy scored a goal that Owen McCann in *Greats of Gaelic Games* (1980) described as one of the four best he had seen.

> *Doherty, playing in the number 15 jersey, took a pass from Rooney, and then went off on a solo of about 10 yards, a well-controlled and pulse-raising run. Then, from 30 yards he sent a left-footed ground shot to the net. A wonderful goal, and a precious moment that, from many glorious instances watching Gaelic games.*

Paddy Doherty also played soccer for Lincoln City and Ballyclare Comrades. He found the net in that game, too, with his deadly left foot. However, the lure of Gaelic football was magnetic. He returned to the game having served a period of suspension.

In a senior career that spanned sixteen years, Paddy reaped a rich harvest of awards and honours. Down won their first Ulster title in 1959 and between then and 1969 contested all eleven Ulster finals, winning seven – a nice provincial haul for Paddy in a province where competition was very stiff.

He played in five National League finals and was successful in three. He was captain in 1961/62 and led Down to a one-point victory, 2-5 to 1-7, in a thrilling and furiously contested final against a Dublin team captained by Kevin Heffernan. The attendance exceeded 56,000. The other wins were in 1959/60 v Cavan, 0-12 to 0-9 before a crowd of over 49,000; and 1967/68 v Kildare, 2-14 to 2-11 – a game that attracted almost 48,000 spectators.

Paddy won seven Railway Cup medals – his first in 1956 and his last in 1968 as a substitute. He was captain in 1964 when Leinster were beaten by 0-12 to 1-6. Other Down players on that victorious team were Leo Murphy, Dan McCartan, Joe Lennon, Seán

O'Neill and Jim McCartan. In the 1965 final against Connacht, Ulster won by 0-19 to 0-15. Two players dominated the scoring. Cyril Dunne scored ten points for the Westerners, all from frees. Paddy Doherty is credited with twelve for Ulster – five from play, seven from frees.

Three times in the 1960s Down footballers scaled the Everest of the football world – 1960, 1961 and 1968. Paddy Doherty was part of all three successes, together with Dan McCartan and Seán O'Neill. In each of those years the Down men defeated Kerry – in the finals of 1960 and 1968 and in the semi-final of 1961. Paddy was captain in 1961. That honour was bestowed on him after the

ddy Doherty.

Ulster final against Armagh, when Kevin Mussen, the reigning captain, lost his place on the team. The final against Offaly attracted a crowd of 90,556 – the largest ever to attend an All-Ireland final.

When Paddy called it a day in 1969, the Ballykinlar club man, born on 28 March 1934, left those of us who saw him in action with many memories – memories of a footballing genius and prolific scorer.

Indeed, Ballykinlar reminds me of more than just Paddy Doherty. For my father, James, spent eight months or so in an internment camp there, following the serving of an order of 2 December 1920, from which I quote:

Whereas on the recommendation of a Competent Military Authority, appointed under the Restoration of Order in Ireland Regulations, it appears to me that for securing the restoration and maintainence of order in Ireland it is expedient that James Fullam of Granard in the County of Longford should, in view of the fact that he is a person suspected of acting, having acted, and being about to act in a manner prejudicial to the restoration and maintenance of Order in Ireland, be subjected to such obligations and restrictions as are hereinafter mentioned.

*Now **I HEREBY ORDER** that the said James Fullam shall be interned in Ballykinlar camp and shall be subject to all the rules and conditions applicable to persons there interned and shall remain there until further orders ...*

A group of prisonsers in Ballykinlar Camp in 1921. In the back row, 2nd from right is James Fullam. In the third row are Martin Walton of music fame (1st from right), Seán Lemass, a future Taoiseach (3rd from right), and Ernest Blythe, a future Minister for Finance (5th from right).

A football selection

Johnny Geraghty
(Galway)

Enda Colleran   Noel Tierney   Bosco McDermott
(Galway)   (Galway)   (Galway)

'Red' Collier   Dan McCartan   Mick O'Dwyer
(Meath)   (Down)   (Kerry)

Colm McAlarney   Mick O'Connell
(Down)   (Kerry)

Seán O'Neill   Mattie McDonagh   Paddy Doherty
(Down)   (Galway)   (Down)

Liam Sammon   John Dowling   Brian Morgan
(Galway)   (Kerry)   (Down)

1971–1980

Teams that participated in the
All-Ireland senior finals

COUNTY	FOOTBALL			HURLING	
	WON	LOST		WON	LOST
Armagh		1			
Cork	1			3	1
Dublin	3	3			
Galway		3		1	2
Kerry	4	2			
Kilkenny				4	3
Limerick				1	2
Offaly	2				
Roscommon		1			
Tipperary				1	
Wexford					2

Eleven counties participated in the senior finals.

The ten hurling finals involved six counties, with five of these successful.

The ten football finals involved seven counties, with four of these successful.

A HURLING GAME:

Kilkenny v Limerick, 1973 All-Ireland final

Kilkenny were reigning All-Ireland hurling champions when they opened their 1973 campaign against Dublin. They won well, 2-19 to 2-11.

They then defeated a talented Wexford in the Leinster final by 4-22 to 3-15. That win earned Kilkenny a place in the All-Ireland final.

Down south, Limerick met Clare in the first round. In a teak-tough thriller at Thurles on 24 June the Shannonsiders won by 3-11 to 3-9. Richie Bennis will still tell you it was the toughest game he ever played in.

The Munster final on 29 July saw Limerick meet Tipperary at Semple Stadium on a sweltering hot, energy-sapping day. The two teams served up an epic contest that left the players physically exhausted and the supporters emotionally drained.

After just ten minutes Limerick had raced into a seven-point lead, 2-1 to no score, but by half time Tipperary were four points ahead, 2-9 to 3-2.

Limerick went on a goal spree in the first half of the second half. As the game entered the final twenty minutes, of the eighty-minute contest, the scoreboard read Limerick 6-4 Tipperary 2-13 – the Shannonsiders three points to the good. As the minutes ticked away, the tension became unbearable. Tipperary drew level. Then they went ahead. Limerick added two points to regain the lead. But with less than two minutes remaining Tipperary equalised.

Hitchcock could not have scripted a more dramatic finish. With scores level Limerick won a seventy. Referee Mick Slattery of Clare told Richie Bennis that time was up and that he must score direct – no-one else could touch the ball. Well, score Richie did and jubilant Limerick supporters in the attendance of almost 42,000 went wild. The players too went wild – Limerick's first Munster crown since 1955.

London were defeated in the All-Ireland semi-final at Ennis on 5 August, and in the All-Ireland final it would be Shannon v Nore. The last time the two counties contested a final was in 1940 when Limerick won by 3-7 to 1-7. At the time Kilkenny were reigning All-Ireland champions, having defeated Cork in 'the thunder and lightning final' of 1939.

In the intervening years Limerick produced many a fine hurler and some very good teams. However, glory days were few; League titles in 1947 and 1971; Munster titles in 1955 and 1973; an Oirechtas title in 1971.

Kilkenny, on the other hand, had much to celebrate – six All-Ireland titles, 1947, 1957, 1963, 1967, 1969 and 1972; sixteen provincial crowns; two National Leagues and six Oireachtas titles.

Limerick entered the final with the benefit of two gruelling games in Munster, while Kilkenny faced final day with the loss of key players – Eddie Keher and Jim Treacy injured, Kieran Purcell recovering from an appendix operation (he did enter the fray early in the second half), and Éamon Morrissey, who had emigrated to Australia. Despite their woes, Kilkenny had some great hurlers – among them Noel Skehan, 'Fan' Larkin, Pat Lawlor, Pat Henderson, Frank Cummins, Liam O'Brien, Claus Dunne, Pat Delaney, Brian Cody and Mick Crotty.

Heavy rain before and during the game made conditions difficult but did not diminish the quality of the hurling. Throughout the first half it was nip and tuck, with Limerick recovering from an early deficit of 0-3 to 1-5 to lead at half time by 0-12 to 1-7.

Early in the second half Kilkenny levelled. It was then that Séamus Horgan in the Limerick goal brought off a superb save from a hand-pass effort by Mick Crotty, deflecting the ball over the bar. It was, almost certainly, a turning point.

In the tenth minute of the second half, Limerick got a key score. Liam O'Donoghue sent in the ball, Frankie Nolan crossed it, Moss Dowling got the finishing touch and the green flag waved.

In the last quarter Limerick were in full flow and scored points with abandon. For two spells, one of ten minutes and the other of thirteen minutes in the second half, Kilkenny were held scoreless.

At the call of time Limerick had taken their seventh All-Ireland crown, 1-21 to 1-14. It had been a great team effort. For two of Limerick's mentors, the 1973 success was very special. I refer to Dick Stokes and Jackie Power – both gone now, God rest them. Dick and Jackie were in action when Limerick beat Kilkenny in the All-Ireland final of 1940. And they were in action too for the National League final of 1947 when Limerick again beat the Noresiders after a thrilling draw and an equally exciting replay. It was Dick and Jackie who, when the team was being selected, masterminded the switch of Éamon Cregan from attack to centre-half-back to cope with Pat

Delaney at centre-forward for Kilkenny. It was one of the corner-stones of victory. Éamon was magnificent as he held the centre with consistently long clearances and a masterly reading of the game.

Seán Foley at left-wing-back was viewed by many as man of the match. Séamus Horgan in goal was excellent, as, indeed, he had been all through the championship. It took a goalkeeper of the calibre of Noel Skehan to deny him an All-Star.

Richie Bennis capped a regal display with ten points – seven from frees and three beauties from play from long distance. Éamon Grimes at midfield rampaged all over the place and was a wonderful captain.

One journalist wrote: 'The triumph had its cornerstones in the splendour of the half-back line [Phil Bennis, Éamon Cregan, Seán Foley] and the efficiency and gluttony of the midfield [Richie Bennis and Éamon Grimes]', while other reports called it 'a very entertaining game that was marked by many superlative passages of play' and 'a game of intense endeavour, graced by passages of elegance and many memorable individual displays'.

President Erskine Childers, attending his first hurling game, was enthralled by the occasion. 'This was the greatest game I have seen in my lifetime and I am speaking of all games', he said.

Ned Rea was full-forward on the Limerick team that day. Ned was associated with sport, and particularly hurling, since his early years. At St Munchin's College in Limerick he played rugby. He won a Limerick county minor hurling title with Kilmallock in 1961. During his time at UCC he won Fitzgibbon Cup titles in 1966 and 1967. In 1965 he was on the UCC team beaten in the county final by St Finbarr's.

Ned went to Dublin in 1968 and two years later joined the Faughs club and won county titles in 1970, 1972 and 1973. The club honoured him with the captaincy in 1977. Ned became chairman of Faughs in 1985 and occupied the position for sixteen years.

His grand-uncle Matt won All-Ireland senior football titles with Dublin in 1898 and 1899. Ned's brothers were also fine hurlers. Jack played with Faughs, as did Matt, who also hurled with Limerick and won League titles with the county in 1984 and 1985. Gerry hurled full-back for London for fifteen years.

Ned grew up hearing about Mick Mackey and Christy Ring and other heroes of those days. He had a special *grá* for Nicky Rackard and the Wexford team of the 1950s. Tom McGarry of Limerick was one of his favourite hurlers – 'one of my favourite people – very special.'

> *I played my first senior county game with Limerick in a League match against Dublin in 1963. The first inter-county player I marked was Jimmy Shields – a native of Limerick who was playing in the Dublin colours. The next inter-county man I marked was 'Hopper' McGrath of Wexford. You couldn't leave him out of your sight. He was very elusive. I spent the first ten minutes running after him. I played on Jimmy Smyth too. He was a handful – very cute – he'd get frees for fouling you. Ray Cummins was a team-mate in college – a great man to reach for a ball – a handful. I played on Christy Ring in his last game for the Glen in 1967. It was a great honour. He was forty-seven but he had the enthusiasm of a seventeen-year-old. The Glen got a goal and he ran to the crowd with delight. And finally there is my good friend Frankie Walsh of Waterford. I always tell him he was cranky when he won and cranky when he lost.*

The most memorable year in Ned's hurling career was 1973. He was at full-back when Limerick lined out in the National League final against Wexford at Croke Park on 13 May. In a rip-roaring con-test – tempestuous at times – with Pat Nolan in the Wexford goal bringing off several wonder saves, Wexford won by 4-13 to 3-7.

When the Limerick team to play Clare in the opening round of the 1973 championship was selected, Ned was out of favour. He watched the game from the embankment in Semple Stadium. 'It was tough and tense. Jim O'Donnell gave an exhibition at centre-half-back – he won the match for Limerick.'

A combination of circumstances led to Ned being asked if he would play at full-forward as Limerick prepared for the Munster final against Tipperary. Ned agreed: 'It would take the pressure off me. I hated full-back. My favourite position was left-full-back.' Ned was given a trial in a game against Waterford. He found the net a few times and impressed. 'I wanted to play in that Munster final, wouldn't anyone? It would be such an honour. In the training sessions I was laying into Pat Hartigan. Jackie Power, our mentor, got concerned for Pat and told me to take it easy – that I would be playing against Tipperary.'

And what were the training sessions like? They were 'animal', ac-cording to Ned. They were presided over by Mick Cregan, an army man – Éamon's brother. This is how Éamon described them to Enda McEvoy in an article in the *Sunday Tribune* on 19 January 2003.

> *To warm up, six laps of the field, which had to be completed in a certain time (exceed the time and you had to make up for it on the next lap). Ninety minutes of hurling training. Then the real killer, forty-five minutes of physical work: ten press-ups, eight tuck jumps, six squats and sprint the width of the pitch, 90 yards. Repeat another nine times. A two-minute recovery period ensued, followed by short sprints called doggies. And we did that from the first week in January to the Thursday week before the final.*

And to think there are those who believe it was Ger Loughnane and Brian Cody who introduced commando training methods for hurlers.

So Ned took his place in the Munster final, wearing number 14 against Tipperary. At 6 foot in height and 15½ stone, his physical presence created havoc. He won frees and made scoring openings for his colleagues – Frankie Nolan 2-1, Éamon Cregan 2-0, Moss Dowling 1-0. Liam O'Donoghue 0-1, Richie Bennis 1-5. A total of six goals and seven points. Tipperary scored 2-18. There was just one point in it. No sweeter way to win a Munster crown.

Limerick were free at last from the tyranny of the Munster championship. So many times since 1940 they had been ambushed when prosperous days loomed on the horizon. Now in 1973 they faced the remainder of the championship campaign with a newly found confidence.

The semi-final produced the rather bizarre situation of brother marking brother. Ned at full-forward was opposed by his brother Gerry playing full-back for London. 'He held me scoreless,' Ned recalls. But Limerick won to set up a final meeting with Kilkenny.

> *I was already living in Rathmines. I met the team as they arrived from Limerick. We went by bus to the hotel, where we had dinner. Four of us were sharing a bedroom – Séamus Horgan, myself and two others – the sensible with the non-sensible. I slept well and went to Mass the following morning. Soon it was time to go to Croke Park. So far I had no feeling of nerves. It was all so fantastic – the thought of playing in Croke Park on All-Ireland final day. From the bus, with our police escort, we saw our supporters*

waving as we drove along. It was then I began to feel the butter-
flies. It was raining heavily. There they were getting drenched. We
can't let these supporters down, I said to myself. From then on I
wanted to concentrate – to be left to my own thoughts – I didn't
want to be distracted. I was no longer listening to others.

In the dressing room, as we prepared, Jackie Power didn't need
to say too much. There was something about his presence that
was calming. It made you feel good. Among the players there
was great camaraderie.

Those over us saw that we got anything we wanted from the
County Board. Mick Cregan had warned us about the 'almighty
roar' that would greet us as we emerged from the dressing room.
I didn't mind the drawn-out ceremonies beforehand. For me it
was just great to be in Croke Park – great to be playing in an All-
Ireland final. So many would give their right hand to be there.
The only time I really worried was when Kilkenny put on the
pressure early in the second half. Séamus Horgan made a vital
save – a turning point. But I wasn't happy until the game was
over. Against Kilkenny you never know. Then it was a case of 'let
the celebrations begin'.

Ned Rea.

A HURLING PERSONALITY:

Denis Coughlan (Cork)

I was born in Blackpool (Glen Rovers/St Nicks) and so grew up listening to the great feats of 'Fox' Collins, Jack Lynch, Jim Young and many more.

My father was a great influence on me. Being an only son, he took me to all the Glen Rovers games and especially to the great Cork v Tipperary games in Limerick in the 1950s. Mind you, I only saw glimpses from his shoulders, from time to time, but have never forgotten the excitement of it all.

I clearly recall my first senior hurling game for 'The Glen', in 1962. I was seventeen and we played Faughs of Dublin in Banagher, County Offaly. Christy Ring was the main attraction and I was marking Billy Dwyer, the well-known Kilkenny hurler.

I played for the next twenty years for the Glen senior team, while also playing football with St Nicks for most of that time too.

My career with Cork hurlers and footballers ran concurrently with my club career; needless to say it was a very busy stage in my life.

Winning county championships was very important to the club and the two that stand out for me were hurling 1969 and football 1965.

Of course captaining the Glen team to their first All-Ireland club final was very special.

Playing with Cork hurlers and footballers was a great honour and I especially looked forward to Munster final day.

In football, [playing in] Killarney against Kerry was always a special day, while strangely enough Limerick was my favourite for hurling finals. I suppose it reminded me of the days my father would take me on the train to those games.

I enjoyed every moment of my career. I had great help and advice along the way, and met some lovely people.

Some of my opponents made life difficult for me, but it was
a pleasure to have been on the same field in football with Mick
O'Connell, Jimmy Duggan (Galway), Pat Griffin (Kerry), while
Christy Ring, Jimmy Doyle, Eddie Keher, Babs Keating and Mick
Roche in hurling were wonderful sportsmen.

Winning and losing is all part of sport and I have absolutely
no regrets or disappointments. I would love to be able to do it
all again.

Denis was born on 7 June 1945 to John and Margaret (née
O'Flaherty). His father played club hurling with St Mary's and
Brian Dillon's and won a county junior title with the latter in the
early 1930s.

Denis was one of the great dual players of Gaelic games – blessed
with talent, rewarded with honours. The hurling days stretched
from 1965 to 1981, the football era covered 1964–1974. 'Of the two
games I preferred hurling, no hesitation – and no regrets, absolutely
none.' His career reads like a litany of awards and successes. He
belongs to a small elite band – probably less than a score – that won
All-Ireland honours at senior level in both hurling and football. The
first dual medallist was Nenagh-born William J. Spain, who won a
football title with Limerick in 1887 and a hurling title with Dublin
in 1889. The most recent dual winner was Teddy McCarthy of Cork,
who also happens to be the only player to have won his medals in
the same year – 1990.

Denis won his hurling titles in 1970, as one of the subs, followed by a rare three-in-a-row in 1976, 1977 and 1978. He won
his football medal in 1973. In the 1970s Cork produced a number
of outstanding dual performers. For the three-in-a-row in hurling
and the football win of 1973, Denis was joined by Brian Murphy,
Jimmy Barry-Murphy and Ray Cummins. To these you can add
Bill Mackessey, Jack Lynch, Derry Beckett, Denis Walsh (hurling
in 1986, football in 1989 as a sub), Paddy Healy (hurling in 1944
and 1946, football as a sub in 1945) and Teddy O'Brien (football in
1973 and hurling in 1976 – as a sub in both years).

In football, Denis first wore the Cork senior jersey in a National
League game against Carlow in 1964. 'The first medal I ever won
was a football one – we beat London in the All-Ireland junior final
of 1964. That day I played at left-full-back.'

Denis was very versatile. He manned one of the midfield positions in the 1965 under-21 All-Ireland final – a game lost to Kildare by 2-11 to 1-7. In 1967 he was captain of the senior team and played at centre-half-back. Following one point victories over Kerry and Cavan, Cork narrowly lost the final to Meath 1-9 to 0-9. Denis made his name in 1971 as a potent football forward. In the campaigns of that year he scored a remarkable six goals and seventy-four points in fifteen games.

Railway Cup honours came his way in 1972 when chosen at centre-forward for Munster. On St Patrick's Day, Munster drew with Leinster in the final at Croke Park, 1-15 each. The replay took place at Cork on 23 April, when Munster won by 2-14 to 0-10, the first time since 1949 that the province won the competition, and their seventh title in all.

The crowning glory of Denis's football career – an All-Ireland title – came in 1973. Operating at midfield, he was a key figure in a talented Cork lineout captained by their goalkeeper, Billy Morgan, and containing seven players who had won Railway Cup honours with Munster the previous year. The results were:

v Clare, 1st round, 2-14 to 0-3
v Kerry, Munster final, 5-12 to 1-15
v Tyrone, All-Ireland semi-final, 5-10 to 2-4
v Galway, All-Ireland final, 3-17 to 2-13.

It was Cork's fourth title – their first since 1945.

Other football honours include four Munster titles and two county titles with his club, St Nicholas – a club founded back in 1898.

However, it is Denis the hurler, a member of Glen Rovers (founded in 1916), I remember best. I saw him in action in the Munster final in 1969 against Tipperary at the Gaelic Grounds in Limerick, when Denis gave a vintage display of hurling. Time and again he cleared his lines and treated us to some delightful ground striking. Always in command, he made it all look so easy.

And then there was that lovely sunny May afternoon in Thurles in 1972 when Cork and Limerick clashed in the National League final – a game that had everything to thrill the 30,000 hurling fans. Denis, assisted by his partner, Justin McCarthy at midfield, gave an immaculate display. Their contribution was a key factor in Cork's 3-14 to 2-14 win. That year Denis collected his first All-Star trophy.

He had a role in six All-Ireland finals. He was at midfield in 1969 and 1972 when the Leesiders lost to Kilkenny. In 1970 he was a sub on the team that beat Wexford. Then came the three-in-a-row between 1976 and 1978. In all those campaigns, operating at left-half-back in the number 7 jersey, Denis turned in many wonderful performances, perhaps none more so than in the 1977 final against Wexford.

Little wonder then that Denis was chosen as Texaco Hurler of the Year in 1977 and that for each of the three years 1976–1978 he was selected as an All-Star in the left-half-back position – giving him four in all.

Other hurling honours include eight Munster titles, five county titles, two All-Ireland club titles and four National Leagues – the first as a sub in 1970 and the others in 1972, 1974 and 1980.

In 1977 he captained an Ireland side that defeated a team from Scotland in a hurling/shinty game played at Páirc Uí Chaoimh.

Growing up, his heroes were Johnny Clifford, a third cousin (Johnny scored the only Cork goal of the 1954 All-Ireland final in the closing stages of the game and ended Wexford's hopes), the Cork three-in-a-row hurlers of 1953 to 1955 and the Glen Rovers trio of Josie Hartnett, Dave Creedon and John Lyons. All gone now, God rest them.

Outside of Cork the following players got special mention.

> *Francis Loughnane of Tipperary was the most difficult wing for-ward I marked – he had an unorthodox style; John Connolly was a fine midfielder; Frank Cummins and any Kilkenny forward; Tony Doran was a great leader – everything gravitated towards him; at centre-back Mick Jacob played some great games; but the best hurler I saw in my lifetime, anywhere, was Mick Roche of Tipperary – and he was out on his own at midfield.*

Some moments stand out as very special for Denis.

> *I first wore the Cork jersey in senior hurling in an Oireachtas game against Kilkenny at Páirc Uí Caoimh in 1965. I was mark-ing Paddy Moran. Beating Tipperary in the Munster final of 1969 was very special. Cork hadn't done it since 1954. It was a great day – one of my better ones.*
>
> *In 1971 I was sensationally dropped from the Cork football team to play Kerry in the Munster final. I came on as a sub after twenty minutes and scored ten points.*

No wonder Denis remembers it. Cork went on to beat champions Kerry by 0-25 to 0-14. And, finally, there was a memory of the maestro himself.

> *I played with Christy [Ring] for four years from 1964 onwards. I remember one evening in training with the Glen. Finbar O'Neill was in goal. At one stage Christy set about testing him. He began at the 40-yard line. He worked his way into the 21-yard line, belting ball after ball at Finbar. We all just stood aside and watched in admiration.*

Denis' last game in championship hurling was the Munster final defeat by Limerick at Thurles in 1980. He was thirty-five. He did play in the early stages of the 1981 National League but before the game with Waterford, 'Frank Murphy beckoned, via Johnny Clifford'. He was being rested, he was told – permanently as it transpired.

Denis Coughlan in training.   Denis (left) in the 1977 county semi-final v Bandon.

A hurling selection

Noel Skehan
(Kilkenny)

'Fan' Larkin   Pat Hartigan   John Horgan
(Kilkenny)   (Limerick)   (Cork)

Mick Jacob   Éamon Cregan   Denis Coughlan
(Wexford)   (Limerick)   (Cork)

Frank Cummins   John Connolly
(Kilkenny)   (Galway)

Jimmy Barry-Murphy   Pat Delaney   Mick Crotty
(Cork)   (Kilkenny)   (Kilkenny)

Eddie Keher   Ray Cummins   Seánie O'Leary
(Kilkenny)   (Cork)   (Cork)

A FOOTBALL GAME:

Cork v Galway, 1973 All-Ireland final

A betting man would have got very attractive odds, at the start of the 1973 football championship, on Cork and Galway reaching the final. It had happened only once in the history of the game. That was in 1956, when Galway won by 2-13 to 3-7.

The 1973 final attracted an attendance of 73,309. Captained by their brilliant goalkeeper Billy Morgan, Cork lay waste to all before them on the road to the final. Clare, trained by former Cork star Éamon Young, fell in the first round at Cork Athletic Grounds by 2-14 to 0-3.

On a wet 15 July, again at Cork Athletic Grounds, Cork faced arch-rivals Kerry, reigning provincial title holders and All-Ireland finalists of 1972, in the Munster final. In an incredible first half performance that had Kerry on the rack, Cork ran in five goals – two from Jimmy Barrett and one each from Billy Field (a penalty), Jimmy Barry-Murphy and Denis Long. They led at half time by 5-4 to 0-6. At one stage in the second half, Kerry cut the lead to five points but their comeback efforts were thwarted by the magnificent Billy Morgan. Final score: Cork 5-12 Kerry 1-15.

The All-Ireland semi-final featured Cork v Tyrone – the first ever such pairing. Cork were victorious by 5-10 to 2-4, their goals coming from Ray Cummins, Declan Barron, Jimmy Barry-Murphy (2) and Seán Coughlan (a sub for Ned Kirby).

Galway had a tougher passage – two points to spare over Mayo in the Connacht final and the same margin of victory over Offaly, All-Ireland title holders of 1971 and 1972, in the All-Ireland semi-final.

Let us now take a glance at the Cork forward line-up on final day that ran in thirteen goals in their three games to date.

Ned Kirby	*Declan Barron*	*Dave McCarthy*
Jimmy Barry-Murphy	*Ray Cummins*	*Jimmy Barrett*

Absent was Billy Field, who fractured a leg in the game against Tyrone.

Cork, seeking a fourth title, had not won since 1945. Galway, with the memory of the three-in-a-row of 1964, 1965 and 1966 fresh in their minds, were in search of an eighth crown.

The two teams served up an excellent game of football. An opportunist goal by Jimmy Barry-Murphy put Cork ahead by 1-10 to 0-6 at half time. In the second half Cork lost their centre-half-back John Coleman; Galway rallied and cut the lead to one goal. Cork made switches. Jimmy Barry-Murphy got a second goal, while Billy Morgan in goal excelled and inspired his outfield colleagues. When John Moloney of Tipperary sounded the final whistle Cork were deserved winners.

Billy Morgan received the Texaco Footballer of the Year award. Seven of the team were chosen as All-Stars – Billy Morgan, Frank Cogan, Brian Murphy, Kevin Jer O'Sullivan, Denis Long, Jimmy Barry-Murphy and Ray Cummins.

There was, however, something else about that win that has remained in my mind – the presence on the Cork team of four dual players who will rank with the all-time greats of Gaelic games – Brian Murphy, Denis Coughlan, Jimmy Barry-Murphy and Ray Cummins.

Remarkably, all four subsequently won three successive All-Ireland hurling medals in 1976, 1977 and 1978. Brian Murphy won all his medals as a corner-back; Denis Coughlan was at centre-field in football and at left-half-back in hurling; Jimmy Barry-Murphy played at top of the right in football. He won his hurling medals as a wing-forward; Ray Cummins won all his medals playing at full-forward.

So, in the space of six years, we find a quartet of Gaelic players – dual players – from the same county, and playing on the same team, taking home four All-Ireland medals each. A unique achievement that may never be replicated. I have had the pleasure of meeting all four – gentlemen off the field, gentlemen on it.

People sometimes wonder why this really talented Cork football team did not win more with young players coming on stream from successful minor and under-21 teams. Was it a case of players over-celebrating the 1973 victory? Were the pressures on dual players their undoing? Or was it simply that there appears to be a hex that haunts Cork football and deprives it of its potential?

A FOOTBALL PERSONALITY:

Paddy Cullen (Dublin)

I attended St Laurence O'Toole's national school, Seville Place, Dublin [inner city]. Grew up playing for the school teams organised by our Christian Brother teachers. They were fantastic. The 'boot room' for football boots was on the top floor, and it was a major rush each Wednesday to get a decent pair, first come first served; after that, pot luck!

I played in only one final for the school in Croke Park against Larkhill school, Whitehall, and lost by three points. I found out in later years that Jimmy Keaveney was on the Larkhill team.

I joined O'Connell Boys club from school and played for them all my football life. The club had billiards, TV, board games, table tennis, a small gym in the basement for basketball, etc.

Big event in the club was two weeks' holidays to Warrenstown College, County Meath each year for games and fun and trips.

Each member had to save for this each week in the club.

I also played soccer in goal and this is how I came to play in goal for Dublin as I never played there for my club. Jimmy Keaveney arranged it.

My childhood heroes were the Dublin football teams of the 1950s and 1960s and Wexford hurlers of the same era.

My brother in law Johnny Greene, was the man who brought me to 'Croker' every Sunday as a young boy, lifting me over the stile – simple days!

I write this in the hope that Mikey Sheehy will read it some day.

Paddy Cullen cut a fine athletic figure as he stood on his goal line – 6 feet 3 inches and 13 stone 10 pounds. He was born on 18 October 1944. His father James, a carpenter by trade, was a native of Monageer in County Wexford. His mother Elizabeth (née Kennedy) was Dublin born. Paddy was one of a family of six boys and four girls. 'My sisters Betty, who is still alive, and May, God rest her, both played camogie at club level.'

Paddy wore the Dublin jersey for the first time in 1966.

As a trainee electrician at the time, I was playing soccer in goal for McNaughtons. I was contacted one Friday night and asked if I would play full-forward against Derry at Parnell Park. Dublin were stuck, as John Timmons had the flu. I broke my ankle after ten minutes and was out of action for months. The following year they were looking for a goalkeeper to play against Offaly in a 'Corn na Cásca' game on Easter Sunday. Jimmy Keaveney, who followed all sports, had seen me in action on the soccer field. He said to the selectors 'I know a fella playing soccer' – illegal of course in those days for any GAA player. All hell broke loose at the idea. However, when things subsided I got a white postcard calling on me to play. At the same time I had an offer from Drumcondra soccer club to join them and play against Drogheda. I decided on the Dublin jersey. When I heard that Drumcondra had lost by six goals to one, I was glad I wasn't in goal.

Paddy's first trip to Croke Park for an All-Ireland final was in 1954 to see the hurlers of Wexford and Cork in action.

I was ten years old. Johnny Greene, my brother-in-law, took me.

He lifted me over the turnstile. The Wexford teams of the 1950s
and 1960s were my hurling heroes – all of them. I adored those
players. In later life I met Bobby and Billy Rackard and for that
I say thank God. It was an honour. The football heroes of my
youth were the Dublin players of the same era and in particular
Paddy Flaherty. He was my model goalkeeper – a lovely man
– he is still to the good. I was at the 1955 football final between
Dublin and Kerry. There were big expectations. The Dublin team
was seen as the football machine. It would take the long kick out
of the game. We were beaten by the catch-and-kick. My heroes
lost. Bad day!

In football terms, 1971–1980 belonged to Dublin and Kerry.
Between them, they won seven All-Ireland titles – Kerry four, Dublin
three; seven National Leagues – Kerry five, Dublin two; sixty-seven
All-Star awards – Kerry thirty-six, Dublin thirty-one.

One could pick an outstanding football fifteen from the players
who won those honours. So here goes:

Paddy Cullen
(Dublin)

Gay O'Driscoll   *John O'Keeffe*   *Robbie Kelleher*
(Dublin)   (Kerry)   (Dublin)

Páidí Ó Sé   *Tim Kennelly*   *Ger Power*
(Kerry)   (Kerry)   (Kerry)

Brian Mullins   *Jack O'Shea*
(Dublin)   (Kerry)

David Hickey   *Tony Hanahoe*   *Pat Spillane*
(Dublin)   (Dublin)   (Kerry)

Mikey Sheehy   *Jimmy Keaveney*   *Johnny Egan*
(Kerry)   (Dublin)   (Kerry)

Paddy Cullen played a key role. In the decade in question he won
six Leinster titles, three All-Ireland crowns and two National
Leagues. He got four All-Star awards and Paddy played in a Railway Cup final in 1976 but lost to Munster. He did, however, win a
Railway Cup medal 'on the bench in 1974'.

Paddy played in six successive All-Ireland finals from 1974 to 1979, a record, I believe, for a goalkeeper. In Wexford's great era 1913–1918, six of their outfield players played in six successive finals. Some might point out that Kerry's great custodian, Dan O'Keeffe, played in seven successive All-Ireland finals. True. But two of those were replays.

Paddy Cullen also played in four successive National League finals between 1975 and 1978. So in many respects, Paddy is unique.

Dublin emerged from the football doldrums in 1974. 'The county hadn't won an All-Ireland title since 1963 and their last provincial crown was in 1965. We surprised everyone, even ourselves – I was then twenty-nine.' The 1974 campaign was tough. Dublin grew in stature as the championship progressed. In Leinster they defeated Wexford, Louth, Offaly and Kildare before disposing of Meath in the final. Favourites, and reigning All-Ireland title holders, Cork fell in the semi-final.

The final against Galway was refereed by Patsy Devlin of Tyrone and attracted an attendance of 71,898. Dublin coach and team manager Kevin Heffernan, himself a footballing star of earlier years, had prepared his team well. Indeed, so impressive was his tactical approach and overall contribution that he received the Texaco Footballer of the Year award. Dublin's full-forward Jimmy Keaveney was top scorer on the day with eight points – five from frees. The game ended Dublin 0-14 Galway 1-6. Paddy Cullen produced a confidence-inspiring performance, in the process saving a second half penalty from Liam Sammon. For Dublin the future looked bright.

It was the highlight of my football career. Sure it had to be – my first All-Ireland title. Winning was incredible – isn't it what every child dreams of? My father died in 1958 so he never saw me play. He would have loved that moment. I was a great fan of Paddy Cole's. He was one of the first onto the pitch after the final whistle and he threw his arms around me. I don't think I ever had lows from the times I played – it's all good memories – being selected and pulling on the jersey was always a cause of elation.

Dublin reached the final of 1975, again captained by Seán Doherty, and were firm favourites to overcome a very young Kerry team. But Mick O'Dwyer, the Kingdom coach and star player of earlier times, had done his homework.

Kerry triumphed by 2-12 to 0-11 in a compelling contest. They were full of speed, stamina and defiance. They functioned as a unit and executed their movements with a precision that left their more experienced opponents baffled. All were stars in a famous victory, but none more so that Ger Power and Pat Spillane. Kerry lost their captain, Mickey O'Sullivan, who was having a great game, midway through the first half. He was concussed following a 'sandwich' tackle as he bore down on the Dublin goal and was removed unconscious from the pitch. In his absence, the Sam Maguire Cup was received by Pat Spillane.

Came 1976. The Dublin half-back line of 1974 and 1975 consisting of Reilly, Larkin and Wilson were gone and replaced by Tommy Drumm, Kevin Moran and Pat O'Neill. All-Ireland final day saw Dublin and Kerry in action again – Dublin forewarned after 1975 – no complacency this time. The attendance was 73,588. Dublin, led by Tony Hanahoe as captain, took the field as National League champions. In the final against Derry, Paddy Cullen had kept a clean goal. He did the same in the All-Ireland final. He had plenty to do, but was at all times rock-solid and inspiring. Dublin avenged 1975 and won by 3-8 to 0-10 – a seven-point margin of victory, the same margin they had lost by the previous year. Jimmy Keaveney at full-forward was top scorer with 1-2. Kevin Moran, new to the championship scene, had an outstanding game at centre-half-back.

The Dublin team with Paddy Cullen (back row, fourth from left).

In the opening moments he sallied upfield to set the tone for what was to follow.

From 1958 to 1976 a Gaelic games tournament was played each year at Wembley in London. Dublin played Kerry in the last football game at that venue in 1976. Paddy Cullen excelled between the posts for Dublin, who won by 0-10 to 0-7.

In 1977 Dublin and Kerry met again – this time at the semi-final stage. Earlier in the year in the League final at Croke Park Kerry won by 1-8 to 1-6. The rivalry was now intense. The semi-final was a classic. Dublin prevailed, 3-12 to 1-13. To date the score was even – Kerry in the 1975 final, Dublin in 1976, Kerry in the League of 1977, Dublin in the All-Ireland semi-final of 1977. There were other days to come.

In the All-Ireland final of 1977 against Armagh, Jimmy Keaveney got a memorable goal. His shot from far out on the Cusack Stand side travelled along by Hill 16 and unbelievably finished up in the Armagh net. For the second year in a row Jimmy was chosen as Footballer of the Year. Tony Hanahoe wore many hats in 1977. He was captain, manager and selector.

As the championship of 1978 got under way, Paddy Cullen had achieved a level of success that most footballers could only dream of: three All-Ireland medals, 1974 v Galway, 1976 v Kerry, 1977 v Armagh; two National Leagues, 1976 v Derry, 1978 v Mayo; three All-Star awards 1974, 1976 and 1977.

In 1978 Dublin, captained by Tony Hanahoe for the third successive year, reached their fifth All-Ireland final in a row. They were hot favourites to defeat Kerry and record a historic three-in-a-row and in so doing emulate the victories of their predecessors in 1906–1908 and 1921–1923. Dublin moved swiftly into a 0-6 to 0-1 lead. Then came a John Egan goal that steadied Kerry, followed by a piece of Mikey Sheehy magic. Paddy Cullen had advanced from his goal when the referee awarded a free to Kerry. A Dublin defender handed the ball to Mikey Sheehy, who promptly put it on the ground and chipped the retreating Paddy, who found himself retrieving the ball from the net. By half time the favourites tag had withered a little. Three times in the second half Paddy turned to take the ball from the net. That was five times in the course of the game. At the final whistle the scoreboard looked unreal – Kerry 5-11 Dublin 0-9. Paddy could appreciate the magic of the Mikey Sheehy goal. He got the boot from Mikey and hung it prominently in his lounge bar – a great subject for discussion and a reminder of how the fates can behave. For, to this day, there are those who will tell you that (a) there was no free; (b) the referee had his back to the action; (c) Paddy was being penalised, in response to booing from the crowd, for an alleged earlier foul that went unpunished; (d) there was no whistle to signify the taking of the free.

The 1979 final once again paired Dublin and Kerry, with Dublin again captained by Tony Hanahoe. Kerry won by 3-12 to 1-8. So from six successive All-Ireland finals Paddy and his Dublin colleagues won three, with victories over Galway, Armagh and Kerry. The other three were lost to Kerry.

Of the four successive League finals, two were won – v Derry 1976, v Mayo 1978; and two were lost – v Meath 1975, v Kerry 1977. That 1977 League final attracted an attendance of 43,456 to Croke Park. In 1979 Paddy Cullen received his fourth All-Star award. The 1979 All-Ireland final was Paddy's last championship game. It is interesting to note that he never played senior football at club level.

I asked Paddy to name some of the best forwards that confronted him in his playing days.

John Egan was a model team forward, a player's forward, unselfish, a forager, would lay off the ball, worked his socks off, took knocks but was up again and got on with it. And he could score.

Jimmy Barry-Murphy, a glamorous player, a cool opportunist, a thinking player, weighed up his options, the men around him did the work.

Tony McTague, what a player and what a place kicker.

Mick O'Connell. I played against him a few times towards the end of his days. He was usually a midfielder but he could play anywhere – a pure footballer.

Mickey Kearns – a Sligo man, a great wing-forward – got an All-Star in 1971 – was a regular on the Connacht Railway Cup teams from the mid-1960s to the mid-1970s when he got an opportunity to display his many footballing skills.

Mikey Sheehy, the man with the magic touch. He got goals even when they didn't seem on.

Paddy Cullen was fronted by the same full back line in his first five All-Ireland finals and in all four League finals. He kept them on their toes: 'watch this', 'mind that', 'pick up your man …' They were a formidable trio – Gay O'Driscoll, Seán Doherty and Robbie Kelliher.

Paddy Cullen.

A football selection

Paddy Cullen
(Dublin)

Gay O'Driscoll　*John O'Keeffe*　*Donie O'Sullivan*
(Dublin)　　　　(Kerry)　　　　　(Kerry)

Tommy Drumm　*Kevin Moran*　*Kevin Jer Sulli*van
(Dublin)　　　　(Dublin)　　　　(Cork)

Dermot Earley　　*Brian Mullins*
(Roscommon)　　　　(Dublin)

Tony Hanahoe　*Kevin Kilmurray*　*Mickey Kearns*
(Dublin)　　　　(Offaly)　　　　　(Sligo)

Jimmy Barry-Murphy　*Jimmy Keaveney*　*John Egan*
(Cork)　　　　　　　(Dublin)　　　　(Kerry)

1981–1990

Teams that participated in the
All-Ireland senior finals

COUNTY	FOOTBALL			HURLING	
	WON	LOST		WON	LOST
Antrim					1
Cork	2	2		3	2
Dublin	1	2			
Galway		1		2	4
Kerry	4	1			
Kilkenny				2	1
Mayo		1			
Meath	2	1			
Offaly	1	1		2	1
Tipperary				1	1
Tyrone		1			

Eleven counties participated in the senior finals.

The ten hurling finals involved six counties, with five of these successful.

The ten football finals involved eight counties, with five of these successful.

A HURLING GAME:

Galway v Kilkenny, 1987 All-Ireland final

As I settled down to watch, on television, the hurling final of 1987 between Galway and Kilkenny, I wondered how the men of the west would perform against one of the superpowers of hurling. I wondered, too, how the Fates would choose to behave. Historically, they tended to frown rather than smile on Galway.

And as I pondered, my mind went back to the days of my youth, and Micheál O'Hehir's broadcast from Birr of the All-Ireland hurling semi-final of 1947 between these two counties. Earlier that year, on 6 April, at Croke Park, Galway had beaten a richly talented Munster team in the Railway Cup final by 2-5 to 1-1. Galway had many class performers – among them, excellent net-minder Seánie Duggan, Donal Flynn, Willie Fahy, 'Inky' Flaherty, John Killeen, Paddy Gantly and Josie Gallagher. Their hurling future looked bright. And so it seemed at Birr as the game entered injury time and Galway held a slender lead. Sadly, there were no smiles from the Fates, as Jim Langton and Terry Leahy sent over points to give a final whistle scoreline of 2-9 to 1-11 in Kilkenny's favour. It seemed an injustice.

I reflected, too, on the All-Ireland finals of 1975 and 1979. In 1975 Kilkenny were going through a golden patch. Galway had beaten Tipperary in the League final and disposed of Cork in the All-Ireland semi-final. Few would have wagered that Kilkenny would have had twelve points to spare on final day. But they had, 2-22 to 2-10.

In 1979, Galway had 'Babs' Keating of Tipperary hurling fame at the helm. The odds favoured Galway. But two goals that might have been saved and a penalty that was not converted ended Galway's hopes, 2-12 to 1-8.

So let us now return to 1987. Galway were favourites, which can be a burden. They were reigning National League champions, and were appearing in their third final in a row, having lost narrowly to Offaly in 1985 and Cork in 1986. In the 1986 All-Ireland semi-final at Thurles, Galway, playing a two-man full-forward line, gave a scintillating display of hurling in outwitting Kilkenny by 4-12 to 0-13. So both Galway and Kilkenny had good reason to want to win in 1987.

Referee Terence Murray of Limerick got the game under way before an attendance of just over 65,500. Heavy rain had fallen before the game and a fairly strong breeze blew. The exchanges at the throw-in heralded what was in store. Con Houlihan wrote:

> Both sides were so bent on winning that some players weren't over-concerned about the means ... Terence Murray booked seven players – all were lucky to escape the shameful walk. And a few more were lucky to escape censure.

Galway, with the aid of the breeze, led at half time by five points to four in what had been a tense, tough, torrid encounter. Scores were at a premium. The quality of the hurling fell short of expectations. Kilkenny's shooting was uncharacteristically off beam.

In the opening moments of the second half, Galway brought on Noel Lane – goal-poacher supreme – in a move that proved inspirational. With about eight minutes to go he was on hand to finish a move – that had involved Steve Mahon, Éanna Ryan and Joe Cooney – to the net.

Shortly before that, John Commins in the Galway goal brought off two splendid saves in quick succession from Kilkenny's full-forward Liam Fennelly. Each was a turning point.

Until then it was nip and tuck in the second half, as the game hung in the balance. One felt during that period that a goal for either side would win the game. Kilkenny led only once. That was around the eighth minute of the second half when the score stood at 0-8 to 0-7. In that period they outscored Galway by four points to two.

But Noel Lane's goal, at a crucial moment, put Galway five points ahead. Tony Keady added a point and Galway were on the road to glory.

The half-back line of Pete Finnerty, Tony Keady and man of the match Gerry McInerney was superb – both defensively and offensively. Gerry came home from New York, where he had been living for some time, for the final. Joe Cooney was Galway's highest scorer with five points. Ger Fennelly, one of four brothers – Ger, Kevin, Seán and Liam – was top scorer of the day with seven of Kilkenny's nine points.

The final score was Galway 1-12 Kilkenny 0-9. It was a good year for the Tribesmen; All-Ireland winners, their third crown; National

League champions, their fourth title; Railway Cup winners, their sixth win; six All-Star awards, and it might well have been more; hurler of the year for Joe Cooney.

A HURLING PERSONALITY:

Eugene Coughlan (Offaly)

Living in Clareen, I knew from an early age I was going to be hooked on hurling as there was a great hurling tradition, both in my family and my club, Seir Kieran. My grandfather Edward was on the first team that won a junior hurling championship in 1912. My father, John, was a great hurler for the club; he won junior and captained the side to intermediate success and also wore the Offaly jersey. He was looked up to in the club. He played at centre-back and centre-half-forward. He was a great fan of the Wexford hurling team of the 1950s – lots of Offaly people were. My uncles Éamonn and Jim also played and won medals with the club. On my mother's side there was also a strong hurling tradition; her brothers Séamus and Johnny Guinan won senior hurling championship medals with Coolderry. So hurling was in my blood.

Growing up at home on the farm in Bellhill in the 1960s was different than it is today. At that time there was a lot of physical work like milking the cows, saving the hay, thinning turnips and harvesting the corn. There were no televisions, computers, Play-Stations or mobile phones, so it had to be the hurley. We played a lot of hurling between ourselves. We always went for the cows on time, but the hurleys and sliotar were also brought along, and as a result the cows were often late being milked. Saving the hay was a great time of the year, as we used the trams of hay as goalposts. The weather seemed to be great that time and there was also lots of time for the hurling. My father often dropped the fork for the hurley and played with us.

I have five brothers – Brendan, Seán, Michael, Noel, Liam – and two sisters – Bernadette and Carmel. Five of us played in county senior finals and my oldest brother, Brendan, played in an under-21 county final. Carmel was a very good camogie player and won a championship medal with Birr, and also played for Offaly. Michael was on the Offaly panel that won the All-Ireland in 1985. He played centre-back in 1988 when we beat Wexford in the Leinster final. Liam was on the Offaly panel in 1995 that lost to Clare in the All-Ireland final; he played in goal in the 1996 championship but was beaten by Wexford in the Leinster final.

I went to Seir Kierans national school. Every day during lunch break we used to play hurling; my last year in the school was the first time that we fielded a school team. I won a Leinster schools medal with the Presentation Brothers College, Birr. I played for the Offaly minors and went on to play for two years with Offaly under-21s. The highlight was playing a draw against Kilkenny on one occasion.

I joined the Offaly panel in 1976 – that year Westmeath beat us in the championship. I played my first game at senior level in the Offaly jersey against near-neighbours Laois at Birr in a League game in 1976. And by a strange coincidence my last game for Offaly was against the same opposition at the same venue in the National League of 1990/91.

1976 was a low time for Offaly hurling. But things started to improve as we won Division 1B of the League, which promoted us into Division 1A. That gave us a chance to meet the top teams, and we gained great experience and confidence from these matches.

In 1980 Diarmuid Healy joined the Offaly back-room team. His main focus was on the skills of the game, and he gave us the belief that we could be successful. Diarmuid was a brilliant coach and played a major part in Offaly's breakthrough. This was a great decade for Offaly hurling. Between 1980 and 1990 I played in eleven Leinster finals, winning seven, played in three All-Irelands, winning two. The highlight was winning my first All-Ireland in 1981. The homecoming was very special, and when the cup came to Seir Kieran, Pádraig Horan our captain handed me the cup on the outskirts of the parish and said to me: 'This is your night.' It was a great feeling to bring the Liam McCarthy Cup into the club for the first time.

In 1988 my club made the big breakthrough as we won our first Offaly senior hurling championship. It was a great honour for me to captain the side to victory, bringing back the biggest prize in Offaly hurling – the Seán Robbins Cup – to our club. I have fond memories of that team, which lined out as:

Liam Coughlan

Seán Coughlan   Eugene Coughlan   Paddy Mulrooney

Johnny Abbott   Michael Coughlan   Ger Connors

Pat Mulrooney   Kieran Dooley

Johnny Dooley   Jimmy Connors   Noel Bergin

Michael Mulrooney   Joe Dooley   Billy Dooley

There is something extra special about the club and club success. When you know all the people, approximately 400 in the parish, it makes it a very special occasion. This is the great thing about the GAA – it can be so big in such a small place.

John Harrington of the *Evening Herald* described Eugene as:

... an unusually skilled hurler for a back man. He seemed to have double-jointed wrists and extendable arms as he flicked, battled and drove balls away from danger.

Despite all the hurling played in the Faithful county down the decades, Offaly did not win a Leinster title until 1980. It was a great breakthrough. They had defeated Kilkenny, one of the superpowers of the game, against all the odds. The attendance confirmed this – just 9,613. Injury kept Eugene off the starting fifteen on that historic day, but he did come on as a sub at corner back to share in the glory.

In his playing days, Eugene stood 6 feet 2 inches and weighed around 13 stone. A first-class full-back with a commanding presence in front of goal, he was imperturbable in temperament and calm under pressure. He hurled on many of the leading full-forwards of his time; in the 1984 All-Ireland final Eugene held Jimmy Barry-Murphy scoreless. 'He was one of the great full-backs. He got the better of me that day'. There was also Joe McKenna, John Connolly,

P. J. Cuddy and Christy Heffernan, with whom Eugene had many clashes, and of course Tony Doran. 'I was a great admirer of Tony since my teens. I remember listening to the radio broadcasts and hearing his name mentioned. He used lift the crowd. I never thought that I would some day play on him.'

After the defeat of Kilkenny in the Leinster final of 1980 Offaly hurling entered on golden days. By 1990 they had won seven Leinster titles and two All-Ireland crowns. The hurling strongholds all knew that a new hurling force had arrived.

Eugene shared in all those successes. Although honoured by the Leinster Railway Cup selectors on a number of occasions, he never won a Railway Cup medal – it was a decade when the competition was dominated by Munster and Connacht. A National League title also eluded Eugene. On a windy afternoon in Semple Stadium in May 1981 Cork beat Offaly in the League final 3-11 to 2-8. Defeat was Offaly's lot too, in the League final of 1988 against Tipperary. Eugene played at full-forward and scored 1-1 but it was not enough. Final score: Tipperary 3-15 Offaly 2-9.

Eugene's hurling displays in the mid-1980s earned him the Texaco Hurler of the Year award in 1985 and All-Star awards at full-back in 1984 and 1985. However, he was still capable of vintage performances in the autumn days of his playing career. I am thinking in particular of the Leinster semi-final of 1990 against newly crowned National League champions Kilkenny. Offaly entered the fray as underdogs; they emerged victorious. Kilkenny suffered one of their heaviest defeats, 4-15 to 1-8. Man of the match was Eugene Coughlan.

After the 1981 final against Galway, it was evident the way Eugene dealt with the threat of John Connolly in front of goal that he had the temperament for the big occasion and the nous not to concede close-in frees. Following the semi-final win of 1990 over Kilkenny, Offaly went on to beat Dublin in the provincial final. It completed a three-in-a-row in Leinster for Offaly – another first for the county.

Eugene was born on 18 November 1956, one of a family of six boys and two girls. He grew up in Clareen, a parish that gave to top flight hurling Kevin Kinahan and the Dooley brothers, Joe, Johnny and Billy – a parish proud of its eleven All-Star awards. 'It is the smallest parish in Ireland. It is the only parish in Offaly with a link with Kilkenny. It is in the diocese of Ossory. Bishop Forristal used come on Confirmation day.'

After the club success at senior level in 1988, Eugene was given the management of the underage teams in the club. 'You get a great kick bringing on youngsters and seeing them moving to higher level in the club and even the county. Joe Bergin, now playing for the county, was one of my youngsters. I had a lot of success with the underage teams and felt very rewarded when we won the A under-21 county title in 2008.'

In his own mind Eugene had planned to hurl until he was fifty. He didn't see why he couldn't. The knee, however, was a problem: it always was. In 1995, following keyhole surgery, his surgeon suggested to him that he should take up 'a more relaxing game – like golf'. But not yet forty, Eugene was not too impressed. He worked on the weights. He played in the county senior final of 2000. The game was lost, but the year brought a special honour when Eugene was selected as full-back on the Offaly Millennium Team. He played in the junior final of 2002 – that too was lost. The following year the knee was bothering him again. He would be forty-seven in November and knew the knee was on its last legs. He had to quit.

Now in his fifty-third year, as we talk, Eugene is fit, strong and athletic. He still wants to play the game he loves so much. The spirit is willing, but the knee is weak.

Ní bhíonn tréan buan.

Eugene Coughlan.

A hurling selection

Ger Cunningham
(Cork)

Sylvie Linnane   Eugene Coughlan   Pat Fleury
(Galway)   (Offaly)   (Offaly)

Joe Hennessy   Ger Henderson   Ger Coughlan
(Kilkenny)   (Kilkenny)   (Offaly)

John Fenton   Joachim Kelly
(Cork)   (Offaly)

Richie Power   Joe Cooney   Billy Fitzpatrick
(Kilkenny)   (Galway)   (Kilkenny)

Liam Fennelly   Joe McKenna   Joe Dooley
(Kilkenny)   (Limerick)   (Offaly)

A FOOTBALL GAME:

Kerry v Offaly, 1982 All-Ireland final

You'll read in history's pages of great deeds that have been done,
The countless records that are made, the battles lost and won,
But there's one page of glory sets all Offaly's hearts aglow –
'Tis how they shattered Kerry's dream, five titles in a row!

Bernie Robinson, from *In Praise of Heroes: Ballads*
and Poems of the GAA by Jimmy Smyth (Dublin, 2007)

The five-in-a-row remains a dream, although a number of counties have contested five finals in a row. Let us examine them briefly.

Cork hurlers contested the finals of 1901–1905. They lost narrowly to London 1-5 to 0-4 in 1901. It was a closer call in 1904 when they fell to Kilkenny by 1-9 to 1-8. They actually won in 1905 but following a Kilkenny objection and counter-objection by Cork a replay was ordered. The Noresiders won.

Kilkenny had a great team in the 1970s and played in five finals from 1971 to 1975. They lost to Tipperary in 1971 and to Limerick in 1973.

In football, Dublin had powerful units in the 1920s and took part in the five finals of 1920 to 1924. They lost in 1920 to Tipperary by 1-6 to 1-2 and in 1924 to Kerry by 0-4 to 0-3.

Dublin were equally good in the 1970s, contesting all six finals between 1974 and 1979. They won three – 1974 v Galway, 1976 v Kerry, 1977 v Armagh – and lost the other three to Kerry, surprisingly in 1975, sensationally in 1978 and convincingly in 1979.

Kerry came very close in the period 1937–1941. They drew with Cavan in 1937 and won the replay. They drew with Galway in 1938 and lost the replay by 2-4 to 0-7. They won the remaining three All-Ireland titles.

It could be argued that Wexford came closest of all. They played in six successive football finals, 1913–1918. Working backwards they were victorious over Tipperary in 1918, Clare in 1917, Mayo in 1916, Kerry in 1915. It is what happened in 1914 that makes me say they came so close. They drew with Kerry the first day – 2-0 to 1-3 – and lost narrowly in the replay by 2-3 to 0-6.

And so we come to 1982 and the final showdown between Kerry, under the management of Mick O'Dwyer, and Offaly, guided by Eugene by McGee. Offaly had won their third Leinster title in a row by defeating Dublin 1-16 to 1-7. They shaded it in the All-Ireland semi-final against Galway, 1-12 to 1-11, and would now face Kerry for the third year in a row, having lost the semi-final of 1980 by five points and the 1981 final by seven points.

Kerry came through in Munster, following a replay with Cork. They had a good win over Ulster champions Armagh in the semi-final, 3-15 to 1-11.

An All-Ireland final win over Offaly would give Kerry an unprecedented five-in-a-row. Indeed, such a feat might never be replicated.

Scalps to date under Kerry's belt were Dublin (1978 and 1979), Roscommon (1980) and Offaly (1981). The Kerry players were vastly experienced and immensely talented. Twelve of the 1982 lineout had played on the victorious 1978 team. They were honours-laden – as well as All-Ireland medals they had Munster titles, Railway Cups, National Leagues and All-Star awards in abundance – Charlie Nelligan, John O'Keeffe, Paudie Lynch, Páidí Ó Sé, Tim Kennelly, Jack O'Shea, Seán Walsh, Ger Power, Denis

'Ogie' Moran, Mikey Sheehy, John Egan and Eoin Liston.

In victory they would be spoken of by future generations with, perhaps, a greater sense of awe than the mighty immortals of 1929 to 1932 – Joe Barrett, Paul Russell, Con Brosnan, Bob Stack, John Joe Sheehy, the Landers brothers John Joe, Tim and Bill, to name but some.

Confidence was high in Kerry. They were perceived as universal favourites. Ballads were written, T-shirts, scarves and team photos were suitably engraved in advance. Celebrations were in readiness. They had counted the chickens!

Back in Roman times, Caesar was cautioned by a soothsayer to 'beware the Ides of March'. In 1982 there was no soothsayer in Kerry to remind fans to 'beware the presence of the National League cup'. For in 1971, 1972, 1973, 1974 and 1977, when Kerry won the National League they failed in the All-Ireland title race. On the other hand when they won the All-Ireland crown in 1975, 1978, 1979, 1980 and 1981 they were unsuccessful in the National League.

The final was a grand sporting contest, played at punishing pace. Offaly led at half time by a point, and in the course of the game the teams were level nine times. Kerry were finding it difficult to open up a gap in the scoring over a tenacious Offaly.

Then, midway through the second half, Kerry, leading by just a point, were awarded a penalty. Mikey Sheehy was entrusted with the kick. In the Offaly goal was Martin Furlong – veteran of a hundred battles and a man who had won All-Ireland medals in 1971 and 1972. Mikey Sheehy rarely missed. Martin Furlong often saved. Mikey shot to Martin's right. Martin saved. In retrospect it proved decisive. Martin was subsequently honoured as Texaco Footballer of the Year.

Play continued and Kerry appeared to be on their way as they built up a four-point lead with about ten minutes to go. That lead was lost and regained and then cut to two points after Offaly had converted two frees. About two minutes remained. The five-in-a-row was that close.

I close my eyes and can still vividly see those final moments. The referee awarded Offaly a free around midfield. The Offaly men displayed no great urgency. The Offaly psyche was at work – calmness and composure despite the pressure of the moment – a mental resilience that seems innate. Mick Fitzgerald opted for a short free which was gathered by Richie Connor, the team captain. He parted to his full-back Liam O'Connor, who had advanced in support. From the right wing he despatched a high one towards the left of the Kerry goal. Up, up it went. And then down, down, down it came into the outstretched hands of substitute Séamus Darby, who had soared high and caught cleanly. Before Kerry could muster cover he had sent a vicious shot to the top of the net. The green flag waved. Séamus danced a jig. The scoreboard read Offaly 1-15 Kerry 0-17. It all seemed unreal. Kerry efforts to save the day with a draw came to naught. Then it was all over. No-one had said: 'Kerry beware'.

The teams that day were:

Offaly:

Martin Furlong

Mick Lowry   Liam O'Connor   Mick Fitzgerald

Pat Fitzgerald   Seán Lowry   Liam Currams

Tomas O'Connor   Padraig Dunne

John Guinan   Richie Connor   Gerry Carroll

Johnny Mooney   Matt Connor   Brendan Lowry

Stephen Darby and Séamus Darby came on as subs.

Kerry:

Charlie Nelligan

Ger O'Keeffe   John O'Keeffe   Paudie Lynch

Páidí Ó Sé   Tim Kennelly   Tommy Doyle

Jack O'Shea   Seán Walsh

Ger Power   Tom Spillane   Denis 'Ogie' Moran

Mikey Sheehy   Eoin Liston   Johnny Egan

Pat Spillane came on as a sub.

A FOOTBALL PERSONALITY:

Martin Furlong (Offaly)

Martin was one of Offaly's all-time greats. His inter-county career took off in his minor days. He was in goal for Offaly in 1964 when they won the Leinster title with a one-point victory over neighbours Laois, 1-7 to 1-6. They met Cork in the final. Another one-point triumph, 0-15 to 1-11. It was a special victory, the first ever football title, in any grade, won by the Faithful county.

Owen McCann, in his *Greats of Gaelic Games* (1980), says:

> *I still recall vividly the exciting way that [Martin] ensured his county of a famous first back in 1964. Offaly were holding on to a one-point lead against Cork in the minor final with time almost up. Then a last gasp Cork attack was only foiled by a truly majestic save by Furlong.*

Senior ranks beckoned, almost immediately. Martin was called into action for the National League campaign of 1965. Thus began a most illustrious senior career of one of Gaelic football's great goalkeepers.

For twenty years Martin guarded the Offaly net, earning a reputation for brilliant goalkeeping and for saving penalties. He was always cool and calm, displaying an unflappable demeanour. Add to this an intense level of concentration allied to uncanny judgement and swiftness of movement and you had a player who not only excelled but also inspired.

Martin was chosen many times for his province in the Railway Cup. He was captain in 1974, the only time during his footballing days that Leinster won the competition.

A National League title eluded him. Offaly lost the 1968/69 Home final to Kerry and failed again to the Kingdom in the final of 1972/73.

Martin won seven Leinster titles, with Kildare (three times) Dublin (twice) and Laois and Meath all having to yield to Offaly.

Personal awards included four All-Stars, 1972, 1981, 1982 and 1983, and Texaco Footballer of the Year in 1982, breaking a Kerry four-year dominance of the award.

Martin was guarding the net in 1971 when Offaly won its first senior football title, when Galway were defeated 1-14 to 2-8. They put the seal of greatness on Offaly football the next year with a decisive 1-19 to 0-13 win over Kerry, following a drawn final of 1-13 apiece.

Then came *that* day – Sunday 19 September 1982. Midway through the second half Kerry were a point ahead when referee P. J. McGrath of Mayo awarded Kerry a penalty.

Penalties are strange things. A duel, a lottery, a battle of wits. Psychologically it is an uneven contest, because the taker is expected to score; no blame to the goalie if beaten, and hero status when he saves.

All eyes were on Mikey Sheehy and Martin Furlong, each a master of his trade. Then in a flash it was over. Martin had saved – *gaisce arís mar a dhein sé go minic cheana.*

The closing stages of Martin's footballing career beckon. They are ending as they began back in 1964 – doing *gaiscíocht* between the posts.

A football selection

Charlie Nelligan
(Kerry)

Páidí Ó Sé	*Mick Lyons*	*Mick Spillane*
(Kerry)	(Meath)	(Kerry)

Tony Davis	*Tim Kennelly*	*Liam Currams*
(Cork)	(Kerry)	(Offaly)

Jack O'Shea   *Willie Joe Padden*
(Kerry)   (Mayo)

Colm O'Rourke	*Larry Tompkins*	*Eugene McKenna*
(Meath)	(Cork)	(Tyrone)

Mikey Sheehy	*Owen Liston*	*Frank McGuigan*
(Kerry)	(Kerry)	(Tyrone)

The centenary teams, 1884–1984

From the moment I heard the concept of a Team of the Century being mooted I had reservations. I found it difficult to accept that, in 100 years of GAA activity, fifteen players could be placed on a plain apart.

Take the hurling team:

Tony Reddan
(Tipperary)

Bobby Rackard   *Nick O'Donnell*   *John Doyle*
(Wexford)   (Wexford)   (Tipperary)

Jimmy Finn   *John Keane*   *Paddy Phelan*
(Tipperary)   (Waterford)   (Kilkenny)

Lory Meagher   *Jack Lynch*
(Kilkenny)   (Cork)

Christy Ring   *Mick Mackey*   *Jimmy Langton*
(Cork)   (Limerick)   (Kilkenny)

Jimmy Doyle   *Nicky Rackard*   *Eddie Keher*
(Tipperary)   (Wexford)   (Kilkenny)

Great men all – master hurlers. But there were many others just as good.

In honouring fifteen exclusively, it dishonoured (though this was not at all intended), by omission, several others.

A team for each decade would have made much more sense – a total of 150 players at least. Really, there is no such thing as a Team of the Century – rather Teams of the Century.

It is interesting to note that the hurlers on the Team of the Century are chosen, almost exclusively, from the 1930s, 1940s and 1950s. There are no hurlers from the first forty years of the GAA. The earliest honoured player is Lory Meagher, whose career began in the mid 1920s.

There is no player from Kilkenny's golden era of 1904 to 1913 when the county won seven All-Ireland titles and four of its hurling men – Sim Walton, Jack Rochford, Dick Doyle and Dick 'Drug' Walsh – won seven All-Ireland medals.

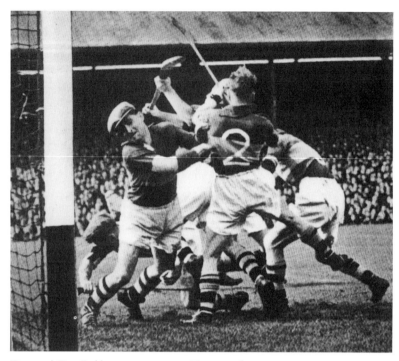

Tipperary's Tony Reddan emerges to save with support from
Mickey Byrne (2) in the 1950 All-Ireland final v Kilkenny.

Nor is there any hurler from the great Cork teams of the 1926–
1931 era – five Munster titles, four All-Ireland crowns, and several
of their players contributed to four Railway Cup wins with Munster – super hurlers, among them Seán Óg Murphy, Dinny Barry-
Murphy, Jim Hurley, Eudi Coughlan, Jim Regan and the Ahern
brothers, Michael 'Gah' and Paddy 'Balty'.

By 1908 Tipperary had won eight All-Ireland crowns. They produced brilliant hurling men such as Mikey Maher, Tom Semple,
Paddy Brolan, Hugh Shelley and Paddy Maher 'Best'. None of them
featured.

The same can be said for great Cork exponents of the game of
those days, including Jim Kelleher, James Ronayne, Willie Mackessy
and the Coughlans – Patrick 'Parson', Denis, Jerh, Dan and Tom.

From Limerick of those pre-1920 days you had Seán Óg Hanly,
John 'Tyler' Mackey, Willie Hough, Paddy McInerney, Bob Mc-
Conkey, Jack Keane and Dinny Lanigan.

The Kilkenny and Limerick teams of the ten-year period 1931–1940 won seven All-Ireland titles, thirteen provincial crowns, six National Leagues, one Oireachtas and seventy-three Railway Cup medals. From that array of stars, Paddy Phelan (Kilkenny), Lory Meagher (Kilkenny) and Mick Mackey (Limerick) were selected on the Team of the Century. So was Jimmy Langton (Kilkenny), but as he arrived on the scene in 1939 he really belonged to the 1940s.

From the remaining Kilkenny and Limerick players of that decade, together with other hurlers of the 1930s, a mighty team could be chosen. One could go on and on about great hurlers.

So just for a little innocent fun, I have picked a team to rival (and defeat!) the Team of the Century. It contains at least one player from each decade of the GAA:

Tommy Daly
(Clare)

Jack Rochford *Seán Óg Murphy* *Billy Rackard*
(Kilkenny) (Cork) (Wexford)

Paddy Molloy *Paddy Clohessy* *Tommy Doyle*
(Offaly) (Limerick) (Tipperary)

Jim Hurley *Timmy Ryan*
(Cork)   (Limerick)

John Mackey *Mikey Maher* *Eudi Coughlan*
(Limerick) (Tipperary) (Cork)

Tony Doran *Martin Kennedy* *Jimmy Smyth*
(Wexford) (Tipperary) (Clare)

The goalkeepers will cancel each other out, even though Tommy Daly's goalkeeping career was twice as long as Tony Reddan's.

On the wind-swept Hill of Tulla,
Where the Claremen place their dead,
Four solemn yews stand sentinel
Above a hurler's head,
 And from the broken North lands
From Burren bleak and bare,

The dirge of Tommy Daly
Goes surging on through Clare.
'Lament for Tommy Daly' by Bryan McMahon

Seán Óg Murphy.

In seven All-Ireland finals, Jack Rochford, we are told, conceded only one goal. Bad news for Eddie Keher – sorry Eddie, you are held scoreless this time by your fellow countyman.

Nicky Rackard may well have to settle for a repeat of the 1954 All-Ireland final when he was confronted by John Lyons. He is now dealing with Seán Óg Murphy, who, according to Martin Kennedy of Tipperary, was 'the best full-back to play the game' and who, according to others, was 'the last of the horrendous full-backs'.

Billy Rackard is selected to contain the immensely talented Jimmy Doyle. That he will do.

My half-back line of Paddy Molloy, Paddy Clohessy and Tommy Doyle are players of sterling qualities. No surrender – Pass of Thermopylae material, a stone wall. They will sweep the sliotar back upfield – in the air, on the ground, first-time pulling. Expect sparks as Ring, Mackey and Langton attempt to assert themselves.

John Mackey of Limerick (centre) watches as Tipperary goalkeeper Jimmy Maher (with cap) is beaten in the 1945 Munster final.

Christy Ring and Tommy Doyle in 1953 following
Monaghan Cup game at Mitchem Stadium, London.

I have chosen two big men at midfield. Timmy Ryan and Jim
Hurley possess boundless energy, physical strength and positional
sense allied to first-time striking on the ground and overhead. They
won't be outplayed.

All six forwards have proven scoring records. Big Mikey Maher at
centre-forward will lead charges and create openings for all those
around him. The wingers, Eudi Coughlan and John Mackey, will
despatch fast accurate ball to the inside men, when not in a position to score themselves.

At full-forward, Martin Kennedy will score goals; grounders from anywhere within 21 yards. His record at finding the net is phenomenal.

Tony Doran, 'The Happy Warrior', as well as picking off vital scores will also ensure that John Doyle makes neither long, raking clearances nor attacking forays upfield.

At 'top of the left' I have chosen Jimmy Smyth – the man from Clare. For ten years he played with Munster in the Railway Cup. I can picture a battle of wits and the most sporting of hurling exchanges between Bobby Rackard and Jimmy Smyth.

So that's it. All good fun. And I have resisted the temptation to pick another team to beat my chosen one.

The following is the football Team of the Century.

Dan O'Keeffe
(Kerry)

Enda Colleran   *Paddy O'Brien*   *Seán Flanagan*
(Galway)   (Meath)   (Mayo)

Seán Murphy   *John Joe O'Reilly*   *Stephen White*
(Kerry)   (Cavan)   (Louth)

Mick O'Connell   *Jack O'Shea*
(Kerry)   (Kerry)

Seán O'Neill   *Seán Purcell*   *Pat Spillane*
(Down)   (Galway)   (Kerry)

Mikey Sheehy   *Tom Langan*   *Kevin Heffernan*
(Kerry)   (Mayo)   (Dublin)

No doubt, readers will select their own football team to rival the official one.

Already I can see some of the great names that will appear – Tom Bourke of Mayo in goal, Joe Barrett of Kerry at full-back, Jack Higgins of Kildare at centre-half-back. At midfield Larry Stanley of Kildare and Con Brosnan of Kerry. Among the forwards will feature Maurice Fitzgerald and Johnny Egan of Kerry, Mick Higgins of Cavan and Bill Delaney of Laois – just some of many.

1991–2000

Teams that participated in the
All-Ireland senior finals

COUNTY	FOOTBALL		HURLING	
	WON	LOST	WON	LOST
Clare			2	
Cork		2	1	1
Derry	1			
Donegal	1			
Down	2			
Dublin	1	2		
Galway	1	1		1
Kerry	2			
Kildare		1		
Kilkenny			3	3
Limerick				2
Mayo		2		
Meath	2	1		
Offaly			2	2
Tipperary			1	1
Tyrone		1		
Wexford			1	

Seventeen counties participated in the senior finals, the largest number in any given decade.

The ten hurling finals involved eight counties, with six of those successful.

The ten football finals involved eleven counties, with seven of those successful.

A HURLING GAME:

Clare v Offaly, 1998 All-Ireland semi-final

Keen hurling followers looked forward with interest to the championship of 1998. And they wondered what unusual combination of clashes it would throw up and what shape the final stages would take.

It had been a good decade for diversity. Between 1994 and 1997, Limerick, Clare and Offaly, each twice, and Wexford and Tipperary each once, had contested the finals.

Following a restructuring of the championship, two teams from Munster, for the first time in the history of the Association, had faced each other in the All-Ireland final of 1997. An exciting contest ended in dramatic fashion with Clare defeating Tipperary by a point.

So what had 1998 in store? Clare and Waterford drew in the Munster final at Thurles, 1-16 to 3-10. The tensions of that game carried over into the replay. At throw-in time, the referee went to the sideline to deal with a matter, leaving the four midfielders waiting for the game to start. It was too much for the pent-up players. Ash swung and sparks flew before the game got under way. Clare won well, 2-16 to 0-10.

In Leinster, Kilkenny, who had not won a provincial title since 1993 (following a draw with Wexford), disposed of their now great rivals Offaly in the final by 3-10 to 1-11. The result had a sequel. Offaly manager Michael 'Babs' Keating from Tipperary expressed public dissatisfaction with his team's performance and departed the scene. He was replaced by Michael Bond, a Galway man.

In Connacht, Galway had no difficulty in dealing with the Roscommon challenge. They won handsomely, 2-27 to 3-13, while up north, Derry pushed Antrim all the way and only lost narrowly by 1-19 to 2-13.

The new structure gave us two quarter-final games at Croke Park on 26 July. Beaten Munster finalists Waterford defeated Galway. In the second game Offaly beat Antrim. Those results paved the way for the two hurling semi-finals of 1998: Offaly v Clare; and Kilkenny v Waterford.

The first of those, Offaly v Clare on 9 August, was the beginning of a three-game saga that had everything. Clare, reigning All-Ireland champions, were almost universal favourites, despite the fact that they were without their dynamic midfielder Colin Lynch, now out of bounds following a controversial suspension. Out of bounds too since the Waterford game was their dauntless full-back Brian Lohan. Offaly, meanwhile, were playing the kind of hurling, when the mood took them, that thrilled and excited traditional followers of the game. It took a late point from James O'Connor to salvage a draw for Clare. The replay was fixed for Saturday 22 August at Croke Park.

We witnessed another fine game of hurling. A game described by journalist Kevin Cashman as 'hurling as we maligned traditionalists know and love it; hard, direct, replete with good ground strokes and magnificent lift and strike.'

Early in the second half, Clare led by ten points and seemed set to coast to victory. But slack defending, so uncharacteristic of the Clare backs, let Offaly through for two goals. With about two minutes of normal time left, Clare were three points to the good, 1-16 to 2-10. They were in possession of the sliotar and launching an attack to the right of the Offaly posts when referee Jimmy Cooney blew the full-time whistle. But it wasn't full time. Jimmy had made a genuine error. He had confused a thirty-five minute half with a thirty-minute half.

Including lost time, there would have been about five minutes left to play when he blew the whistle. One could only have had sympathy for Jimmy. What with all the things a hurling referee has to take care of, it's a miracle something similar had not occurred many times previously.

People still wonder how the authorities failed to get the game restarted by making announcements over the loudspeakers and getting the teams back onto the pitch. It was done in the past. In the 1938 football final replay between Galway and Kerry, the referee's whistle for a free was taken by Galway supporters to be the final whistle, whereupon they rushed onto the pitch to cheer their heroes. Announcements were made. It took some time to clear the pitch, but the game was resumed and the remaining couple of minutes played.

There was a similar occurrence at the Munster final replay of 1940 between Limerick and Cork. The pitch was invaded; bedlam prevailed for a while, but eventually the pitch was cleared and the final minutes played out.

Jimmy Cooney's match report, read in conjunction with the rule book, resulted in a replay being ordered for Semple Stadium on Saturday 29 August. We were now witnessing something unique at All-Ireland hurling semi-final level. It was going to take three contests to decide who would advance to the final.

In Thurles, I was seated close to the sideline, a little to the right of midfield, with the town goal to my right. It was a glorious, sunny afternoon, and the pitch was a hurler's dream. We were treated to a feast of hurling. The exchanges were physical; the pace was furious; the hurling hard and direct, intensely passionate, yet at all times admirably sporting.

Over the seventy minutes, as the game ebbed and flowed, there was much to savour; the resilience and never-say-die spirit of both teams, the impeccable display of Offaly's Joe Dooley, oldest man on the field, who scored five glorious points from play; the brilliant saves by Stephen Byrne when Clare threatened to carry the day with a series of late onslaughts; the heroic play of both defences and in particular the Offaly half-back line of Brian Whelehan, Hubert Rigney, the team captain who gave a capital display, and Kevin Martin.

Offaly led at half time by 0-9 to 0-6. With about a quarter of an hour to go they still held that lead of three points. It had stretched to six with five minutes left on the clock. Clare attacked in waves. They sent over three points. They piled on the pressure for the equalising goal. It didn't come. Spellbinding stuff!

The final whistle saw Clare depart with just a Munster title to show for their fine endeavours. Offaly would return to base and dwell on the benefits of the 'back door' and the vagaries of the fates as they planned the downfall of Kilkenny on All-Ireland final day.

A HURLING PERSONALITY:

Seán McMahon (Clare)

I first started hurling at my home in Roslevan in the late seventies with my father Michael showing me what to do. I spent most weekends and evenings after school hurling with my best friend Felim Collins in the field beside his house. Many an evening was also spent belting balls off the gable end of the house.

I attended Ennis CBS primary school and we played a lot of hurling there. The first time I played in Cusack Park in Ennis was a third class league final where we beat Ennis boys' national school. They got their revenge on us in our final year in primary when they beat us in the county schools final. Teachers there who played a big part in our hurling were Michael Carmody, Brian Fitzgerald, Brother Lynch and Brother Muloughney. Unfortunately we didn't play a lot in secondary school in Rice College, because we had a lot of good players but the interest didn't seem to be there.

I started playing for my club St Joseph's Doora-Barefield at around eight and we won the under-12 B championship in 1982 which was a huge win for us. We had little success despite a lot of effort until we won a minor A title in 1990. We followed this with two under-21 A wins in 1993 and 1994. The players from this group were the basis for the club All-Ireland success in 1999. It was amazing that so many of this group stayed together and it was great to get the reward we did.

Another treasured success was the Fitzgibbon Cup win of 1994 with University of Limerick (UL). We beat UCG, UCC and Waterford IT to win the title. The amazing thing was all three matches ended level and we won all three in extra time. Brian Lohan and Fergal Hartley were on that team as well.

I remember getting called into the Clare panel in the autumn of 1993. I was in UL at the time and there were no mobile phones so my father had to come to Limerick to tell me to be in Ballyline the following night for county training. I was thrilled with the news as I always dreamed of playing for my county at senior level. I remember well feeling out of place the following evening but Anthony Daly, sensing my unease, made me feel welcome and I always appreciated that.

I made my championship debut the following May versus Tipp. This was a massive game for Clare as Tipp had beaten Clare by eighteen points in the previous Munster final. The whole year was spent focusing on this game and victory at the end was very special. Clare beat Kerry in the semi-final and we met Limerick in the final. This was a huge disappointment for Clare and myself as Limerick won by nine points. There were seven points from play scored off myself and that was very disappointing. I learned a lot from that, but still it was a huge let-down at the time.

1995 was obviously a special year for all from Clare. We got well beaten by Kilkenny in the League final, but our win over Cork in the Munster semi-final set us on our way. I was lucky to make the Munster final, as I broke my collarbone against Cork and there was only five weeks to the final. It was a day that no one wanted to miss, as we were very determined to make up for our two previous disappointments. We won by nine points in the end and for me it was my greatest moment in hurling, because we had been beaten so often in Munster finals that to make the breakthrough eventually was unbelievable.

Winning the All-Ireland afterwards was beyond our wildest dreams but it was amazing to be involved and to see what it did for the county.

Winning in 1997 again, and beating Cork, Kilkenny and Tipp twice, was really satisfying as it proved that 1995 was no fluke.

We came close again and had a few near misses and 1998 and 2005 were especially disappointing for different reasons. These were probably my two biggest disappointments – not winning the All-Ireland those years.

Looking back now, I was really very fortunate to have played with the teams and the players that I did, in my club St Joseph's and with Clare. I owe an awful lot to those players in my club and with the county and to all the trainers and coaches who gave their time to improve us as players.

I also feel fortunate to have played against so many great players, such as Declan Ryan, Ken McGrath, Henry Shefflin, Gary Kirby, etc. and to be able to say that I look forward to meeting these bods whenever I do. My family have been a great support from the very start to the end of my playing days.

Finally, I would say that I have enjoyed every minute of my hurling life and feel very fortunate to have been able to play the greatest game in the world. Up the Banner!

Down the decades, Clare produced many wonderful hurlers and some very fine teams. But when it came to honour and glory, the fates were unkind.

Names that come to mind include: Pa 'Fowler' McInerney, Amby Power, Brendan Considine, Tull Considine, Tommy Daly, John Joe 'Goggles' Doyle, Jim Mullane, Larry Blake, Matt Nugent, Jimmy Smyth, Jim Carney, Jimmy Cullinane, Séamus Durack, Johnny Callinan, Ger Loughnane, Seán Stack and Seán Hehir.

Clare won a Munster title in 1889 following a walkover from Kerry. They lost the All-Ireland final to Dublin, 5-1 to 1-6, at a time when no number of points equalled a goal. They had to wait for a quarter of a century until 1914 before taking a second Munster crown with a 3-2 to 3-1 victory over Cork. Well prepared under the guidance of Jim Hehir – father of Micheál of broadcasting fame – Clare defeated Laois in the All-Ireland final.

Almost two decades would pass before Clare would again taste success. That was in 1932. They beat a Cork team, rich in talent, by 5-2 to 4-1 to take the Munster title. Success was assured in the first half of that game when Clare led at the break by 3-2 to 1-0. 'Fowler' McInerney was magnificent at full-back. He was their goalkeeper in 1914.

The All-Ireland final against Kilkenny – a team as rich in talent as Cork – was a close call. Clare failed by 3-3 to 2-3. There were claims that two of Kilkenny's goals came from 'square' balls and that Tull Considine was denied a close-in free in the closing moments, before Kilkenny got their last point.

The years rolled on and Clare gave many gallant displays. They won the League in 1945/46. They played two thrilling Oireachtas finals with Wexford in 1953 and 1954 – winning the latter in a replay. In the championship of 1955 Clare defeated Cork, reigning All-Ireland champions, and Tipperary, league champions. They were favourites – hot favourites – to dispose of Limerick in the Munster final. But in sport there are many twists and turns and surprises. On a sweltering hot summer day at the Gaelic Grounds

– a day when everything seemed to go wrong for Clare – they lost to a young, fast and talented Limerick fifteen, managed by the legendary Mick Mackey, and with that defeat went the prospect of an All-Ireland title.

Clare produced teams of All-Ireland calibre in the 1970s. For three years in a row they contested the League final with Kilkenny. After losing the final of 1976 in a replay they went on to win in 1977 and 1978. One could have wept for Clare following their Munster final defeats of 1977 (when reduced to fourteen men for most of the hour) and 1978 – both to Cork, who on each occasion advanced to All-Ireland glory.

But it is a long road that has no turning. And strangely enough it came against all expectations. Seán McMahon was a spectator at the Munster final of 1993 between Clare and Tipperary at the Gaelic Grounds.

> *It was the worst day I ever put down. I was on the terrace with some friends. Clare were being badly outplayed. Tipp supporters were ragging us – half joking, half serious – saying it was only a training session for Tipp. Coming towards the end my friends wanted to leave, but I wouldn't go – I wouldn't leave a match early ever.*

The final score was a merciless humiliation, 3-27 to 2-12 – a defeat more decisive than the final score might suggest.

Seán was called to the senior panel in the autumn of 1993 and played his first county senior game against Offaly at Birr in the National League. He was born on 27 October 1973 and grew up in a hurling atmosphere.

> *My heroes were Joe Cooney, a fantastic player, Pete Finnerty and Tony Keady – all from Galway. In Clare it was Seán Stack – I only saw him towards the end, but I had heard so much about him.*

And the best of his playing days?

> *D. J. [Carey] was probably the best. Declan Ryan was the one I had the greatest battles with – a brilliant player, so big, a great hurler. I always admired Ken McGrath. The best corner-back, in fifteen years, I saw was Frank Lohan – he had the physique, pace*

and mental strength. His brother Brian was the best full-back.

Seán was centre-half-back when Clare beat Tipperary by 2-11 to 0-13 in the Munster semi-final of 1994. A county's pride was restored. Unfortunately, his hurling world fell apart again when Clare lost the Munster final to Limerick 0-25 to 2-10. Drastic action was needed. And it was taken. In September of that year Ger Loughnane was called in as manager. He had been given his P45 in 1992 after Clare lost the under-21 Munster final to Waterford. A new and fruitful era was about to dawn for Clare hurling. A good League campaign ended with Clare losing the final to Kilkenny by 2-12 to 0-9. Following that result, some said Clare would never win anything. 'But in the dressing room, Ger said there was no one as good as Kilkenny and that we would win the Munster title.'

On Sunday 4 June Clare faced Cork at the Gaelic Grounds. It was a day the gods were favourable.

> *I broke my collarbone as I went to clear a ball – that was in the last fifteen minutes. We had used all our subs so I couldn't go off. I went to corner-forward. I was now a one-handed hurler. Cork were two points up and very little time left when the ball came up to the Cork square. I pressurised the backs and forced them into clearing the ball over the sideline. Fergus Tuohy took the cut and Ollie Baker finished it to the net.*

Clare won by 2-13 to 3-9.

In the other games of the Munster championship, Tipperary hammered Waterford 4-23 to 1-11. Limerick pipped Tipperary 0-16 to 0-15. Now to a Munster final showdown between the Banner and the Shannonsiders – the first since 1981 and the fifth in all, with all finals to date going Limerick's way. But not in 1995. Full-time score: Clare 1-17 Limerick 0-11.

> *My greatest moment in all my hurling years was definitely the Munster final win of 1995. Growing up, my dream was about being in a Munster final – winning a Munster title. Croke Park and an All-Ireland were beyond my dreams. Things couldn't have been more right that day in Thurles. We were lucky with the players – a great blend. We were so determined that day. Davy Fitz came down and got a goal from a penalty – we were a point up at half*

time. I remember we went six points up in the second half. But I was so scared Limerick would get a goal. Damien Quigley had hit the crossbar with a rasper in the first half and kicked a ball just wide of the posts in the second half. That's six points you know. Then we went eight points up. I was still not accepting it. Soon we were nine up. Only then did I accept we would win.

The Clare half-back line that day was Liam Doyle, Seán McMahon and Anthony Daly. It would represent the county for six years, 1995 to 2000 – one of the great half-back lines in the history of hurling.

During those years Seán McMahon grew in stature. He was superb at the heart of the Clare defence and gave displays that made him rank with the great centre-half-backs of the game. So often, he was an inspiration to his colleagues and his points from long distance and far-out frees were McMahon specials.

Success in 1995 opened the door to all kinds of honours for Seán – the first of three Munster titles, the first of two All-Ireland wins, the first of three All-Star awards. His outstanding displays of that year, as Clare accounted for Cork, Limerick, Galway and Offaly, saw him honoured with the Texaco Hurler of the Year award.

In 1996 Railway Cup and Oireachtas medals were won and a few years later county titles and Munster club titles were added to Seán's list of honours. There was much to celebrate at St Joseph's Doora-Barefield – a club that has given to Clare Ollie Baker, Davy Hoey and Jamesie O'Connor – in 1999 when Rathnure were beaten in the All-Ireland club final by 2-14 to 0-8, a game that, up to then, attracted the largest attendance – 40,106 – to a club final.

Clare hurling and its players merited the seal of greatness in 1997, when they accounted for the three superpowers of the game:

v Cork: 1-19 to 0-18 – first round
v Tipperary: 1-18 to 0-18 – Munster final
v Kilkenny: 1-17 to 1-13 – All-Ireland semi-final
v Tipperary: 0-20 to 2-13 – All-Ireland final.

Note the similarity of the scoring, for and against, in all four games of 1997.

That was the year, no question. It was our best combination. We were consistent and very good. If we had a failing it was not killing the opposition off.

Seán looks back on 1998 and 2005 with feelings of regret and disappointment. The three-game saga with Offaly in 1998 makes him wonder what might have been. And 2005 even more so, when Seán was captain.

> *In the semi-final against Cork we had hurled really well – then to get pipped by a point – a killer. I'd have bet the house that we'd have beaten Galway in the All-Ireland final. We lost to Cork by a point but lost an All-Ireland in my eyes that year.*

Seán McMahon, master hurler, prince of defenders, called it a day at county level after losing to Kilkenny 2-21 to 1-16 in the All-Ireland semi-final of 2006.

> *Sár imreoir agus scoth iománaí ab eadh Seán. Is minic, ar fad, na h-amannta gur bhaineas ard-taitneamh agus sásamh an domhain as bheith ag faire ar a ealaíont leis an gcamán. Saineolaí agus cleasaí thar bharr a bhí ann agus é ag tabhairt taispeántas leis an gcamán agus an sliotar i ngach cluiche a d'imir sé.*

Seán McMahon with sons Eoghan (left), Cathal (in his arms) and Darragh in Doora-Barefield jersey.

A HURLING PERSONALITY:

Damien Fitzhenry (Wexford)

I was born into a sporting-mad family of ten boys and five girls at the foot of the Blackstairs Mountains in a village called Kiltealy. It was not so hard for me ever to get anybody to play hurling or football with, as when you looked inside the door, there was a team there waiting. I will attribute this to the reason that I ended up playing in goal. I was the youngest of the fifteen and when a goalkeeper was needed I would have no choice but to go in goal. The games were tough and hard and no prisoners taken. I suppose this stood to all of us in the end during our playing days. I will always remember the two rusty barrels that we used as goalposts.

The next move was to national school in Kiltealy and there we used to join up with the other two schools in the parish, Ballindaggin and Caim, for the famed Nicky Rackard League. I would owe a lot to the teacher called Dónal O'Connor from Ballindaggin, who trained our team and helped us on the skills of the game – something that has stayed with us, and thinking back on it now it was a skill that will remain with us for a lifetime.

Secondary school came next and in the road to FCJ Bunclody I went and followed all my brothers and sisters to the school. Sport was a major part of the school's curriculum around that time and I was very lucky to happen on an excellent teacher during my time there – this was Rory Kinsella. Rory would have represented Wexford in his own career and was an excellent trainer of school teams. Many clubs would have come together for the school teams and Rory would have managed to get them to win many trophies and titles. My fondest school memory was to captain the senior hurling team to Leinster B success in my last year. Rory also went on to be a selector with the 1996 All-Ireland winning team and manager of the 1997 Leinster champions.

It was out into the big world then when we finished school, and shortly after I left at eighteen I got a call from the late Christy Keogh to see would I go for a trial for the Wexford senior team. At this stage I had played under-18 and under-21 for Wexford but I thought I might be that bit young to play senior. I had played for my club Duffry Rovers, in goal, from the time I was fifteen but I thought this might be a step up. Christy got me to go to play Kilkenny in a practice match in Belfield in 1993 and said he would play me for half the match. This happened and I have not been out of the goal from that day – and as they say, the rest is history.

We have had many great days in the Wexford jersey and 1996 will always bring a smile to the faces of Wexford people everywhere. We had a great team and a great management team, especially the charismatic Mr Liam Griffin. Liam left no stone unturned during his reign and through Liam's hard work and the team's hard work we eventually made it to become All-Ireland champions. We had another nice Leinster victory in 1997 and had to wait again until 2004 for our next one. Wexford continue to put in the hard work and soon again we will be back on the winning fields.

I would like to finish off this piece by saying what an honour it is to play for Wexford. Every day I pull on a Wexford jersey, I represent myself, my family who I owe everything to, especially my Mam and Dad, Nancy and Mark, who would have travelled thousands of miles over the years to make sure myself and all my brothers and sisters got to all of the games. My brothers and sisters were always there to tell you that you played well or played badly! My club Duffry Rovers means a lot to me and to see that name on the match programme every day is a real pleasure. And finally, a special word to anyone that helped me along the way, probably too many to mention. Thanks again to everyone.

Damien is the baby of the Fitzhenry household. He arrived on 5 July 1974, the last of fifteen children born to Mark and Nancy (née Fortune). All are hale and hearty and none live more than twenty-five minutes from the home where they grew up. Damien first guarded the net for Wexford in 1993, having had as a model goalkeeper Cork's Ger Cunningham, whom he greatly admired and whose style he observed closely. He has had a long and successful innings, one of the great goalkeepers of modern times – assured, eagle-eyed, inspiring, calm and composed. On Sunday 1 March 2009, Wexford played Antrim in the National League, Damien's 186th game for his native county. He has now overtaken 'The Happy Warrior' Tony Doran's record of 187 games. Regrettably, however, Damien's honours list has not been in proportion to his outstanding performances – one All-Ireland title, three Leinster crowns, two richly deserved All-Stars and captain of the Wexford team in 2007.

Damien admits that he grew up in 'a mad GAA household'. His sister Tina played with Wexford camogie teams for almost a decade, while most of his brothers played at underage level for the county in either hurling or football. John, Paddy and Noel all played senior football; Seánie played both hurling and football; Martin, who was 'a fair hurler', also played for several years with the county. In the Leinster semi-final of 1984 against Kilkenny, Martin scored 2-3 off Nicky Brennan.

One of my abiding memories of Damien centres around the Leinster final of 2004 against Offaly. I was in the Cusack Stand and close to the canal end. In the first half Damien guarded the canal goal. In the opening moments of the game he was peppered with shots from all angles by the Offaly forwards. Undaunted, he blocked every one – brought them down and cleared like Paddy Scanlon in days of yore. He kept Wexford in the game; he was truly magnificent. Offaly put one past him late in the second half but it wasn't enough. Wexford took the Leinster title, 2-12 to 1-11.

There are other memories too, particularly his penalty/close-in free exploits. It was quarter final day at Croke Park in 2001; Wexford and Limerick were serving up some delightful hurling. Time was ticking away and Limerick held a slender lead when Wexford won a 21-yard free in front of goal. Up came Damien. There was a delay as an injured player was attended to. Damien stood and waited, displaying no sense of pressure. Now all was in readiness. In his own mind he had picked his spot. He bent, lifted and struck – and sank the sliotar in the top right-hand corner of the net. Limerick defender Mark Foley threw his hurley to the ground in disgust. Game won, game lost. Wexford 4-10 Limerick 2-15.

Six years later history was to repeat itself – this time in a quarter-final against Tipperary. Wexford won a close-in free to the right of the goal. A Tipperary defender further infringed and the referee moved the ball to the front of the goal. Cue for Damien to advance bearing his pucking-out hurley. The Tipperary citadel fell as Wexford advanced to the All-Ireland semi-final.

In the 1996 championship Damien left his goal on two occasions to despatch the sliotar to the opposition's net. In the Leinster semi-final against Dublin towards the end of the first half he got a vital goal to bring the score to 2-6 to 1-2 in Wexford's favour. Again in the Leinster final against Offaly he was called upon when Wexford were under pressure in the first half. His goal reduced Wexford's deficit to just one point – 1-4 to 1-5.

Wild spirit, which art moving everywhere;
Destroyer and Preserver; hear oh hear!
                                                    Shelley

Damien Fitzhenry.

Not all of Damien's efforts, however, reached the net. In 1992 in his minor days, his penalty hit the crossbar and the rebound was cleared. A late Kilkenny goal gave the Noresiders a 1-9 to 0-11 win. In the quarter final against Waterford in Thurles in 2008, Damien's effort, late in the second half, whizzed just over the crossbar. Waterford survived by one point.

I put a few questions to Damien which he readily answered.

Q: The full-back line of Wexford players he would like to front him?

A: Darragh Ryan, Ger Cushe, Seánie Flood.

Q: The full-back line of non-Wexford players he would like to front him?

A: Ollie Canning (Galway), Noel Hickey (Kilkenny), Willie O'Connor (Kilkenny).

Q: The top forwards he encountered?

A: It would have to be D. J. Carey and Henry Shefflin – nothing to touch either of the two of them.

Q: The stand-out moments of a long career?

A: The Leinster final win over Offaly in 1996 – it was so long coming, coming since 1977. And our performance on the day, maybe our greatest – points going over from all angles. The All-Ireland win over Limerick 1-13 to 0-14 and the lead-up to that in 1996. The Thursday evening after the Leinster final we were in Wexford Park. Liam Griffin called us together. 'Lads', said he, 'if you are happy enough with that Leinster title go out and puck around. How many more All-Ireland semi-finals do you think you are guaranteed to play in?' Liam didn't have to say any more. We all got down to face the challenge that lay ahead. The camaraderie of that panel of players was unbelievable. It has lasted to this day.

It was indeed a very special bond – a spirit of unity and solidarity. It permeated the entire squad, inspired by their manager, Liam Griffin. It won them a Leinster crown and an All-Ireland title – both richly deserved and long overdue.

Myles na gCopaleen used to write about a fictional character called 'The Brother'. What follows here, however, is an account of a real character, a real brother, as seen through the eyes of Martin.

That he would become a top-class inter-county hurler was never really a surprise. What was a surprise, however, is that he would do so as a goalkeeper. Having attended most of the games that he played as a centre-half-back when assisting FCJ Bunclody in the B Colleges championship in his final year in my old alma mater, I was convinced that I was watching the next great Wexford number six in the making. If the late Christy Keogh had not made the bold decision to put an eighteen-year-old in between the sticks in 1993 for the Wexford senior hurling team, who knows how Damien and Wexford's hurling destiny may have turned out.

Damien is the youngest member of a family of ten boys and five girls and Gaelic games were the only pastimes we were really interested in. As the youngest, he was from a very tender age placed between the posts for our 'friendly' games which we played in the half acre behind our house. Despite his age, no favours were given to the baby of the family and in fairness to Damien he wouldn't have wanted it any other way. I remember how he used to be extremely brave in those games and this bravery would stay with him throughout his career. Allied with this bravery was a skill level which was a result of hours and hours of practice, either with some of his brothers or sisters or on his own.

Like most young fellows, Damien joined the local club, Duffry Rovers, where his raw talent was further developed by the many mentors and coaches he would train under at the club. It is fair to say that Damien's sporting ambition was always going to be dictated by what had gone before him in our sporting house. Most of Damien's brothers had played both hurling and football for Wexford at some level – most playing for the senior team at some point, while sister Tina was a very successful camogie player for Wexford senior team, competing in a couple of All-Ireland finals. I had played briefly for the Wexford senior hurling team, making my championship debut in 1984. I was soon joined on the team by my brother Séamus, who had by then played many years for Wexford senior football team and indeed had been honoured by the Leinster selectors in football on several occasions.

Although we have never really spoken about how this might have influenced our young brother, logic would suggest that Damien never really felt that playing for Wexford was anything other than the norm and that his day to wear the purple and gold would arrive in due course. He was selected for both the minor hurling and football teams, having excelled through the ranks with club and school. He made his debut with the Wexford senior hurling team in 1993, having just left the minor ranks, and has been a permanent fixture between the posts since then.

So what makes a great goalkeeper, which is what I believe Damien is? He is, as already stated, brave as a lion, his ability to read the game is second to none, he is a great leader on the field and that he is a top-class shot-stopper goes without saying. In my opinion, however, his greatest asset is his ability to be totally unaffected by the concession of a goal and he continues to man the posts as if nothing has happened. He has always had that coolness under pressure, which in my opinion sets him apart from most of the great goalkeepers of the past twenty years. I almost forgot that he has scored 'one or two' vital goals when the pressure was on, which also sets him apart from his peers.

Although probably coming close to the end of his inter-county career, which in no small way has been extended by his teetotal lifestyle, I look forward again to watching my brother man the posts for Wexford this summer [2009]. He has given his club, and Wexford, and, indeed, the hurling world at large many years of dedicated service and numerous thrilling moments over a long and distinguished career. Thankfully for Damien and Wexford he was part of the 1996 All-Ireland-winning team and with a bit of luck and forward planning our day will come again.

Finally, on a personal note, I would like to thank Damien for the many great memories he has given our family over the past seventeen years playing in goal for Wexford. The journey to Croke Park gives us an extra buzz when you have your brother as the last man standing, when some of the great forwards of our time take him on in a battle of wills. His total honesty and sportsmanship has always made it a pleasure to watch him play. When he finally decides to hang up his boots and his time in goal for Wexford is over he can do so in the knowledge that he has always given his best for the Wexford cause.

No words of mine can do justice to my young brother's contribution to Wexford hurling, but I know he would probably be happy to paraphrase Othello and say: 'I did the county some service, enough of that' and move on to his next great love – horses.

Hurling will miss him.

A hurling selection

Damien Fitzhenry
(Wexford)

Brian Corcoran   Brian Lohan   Willie O'Connor
(Cork)   (Clare)   (Kilkenny)

Brian Whelehan   Seánie McMahon   Anthony Daly
(Offaly)   (Clare)   (Clare)

Johnny Pilkington   Ciarán Carey
(Offaly)   (Limerick)

Martin Storey   Gary Kirby   Jamesie O'Connor
(Wexford)   (Limerick)   (Clare)

Pat Fox   D. J. Carey   Nicky English
(Tipperary)   (Kilkenny)   (Tipperary)

A FOOTBALL GAME:

Donegal v Dublin, 1992 All-Ireland final

My good friend Michael Monagle, a native of the Inishowen peninsula in north Donegal, was, at the time of the 1992 football final, residing in the Marble City. Proof of his citizenship was his membership of O'Loughlin Gaels GAA club and his avid support for the Kilkenny hurling team.

Armed with a stand ticket from the county secretary, the late Ted Carroll, Michael set forth for Croke Park to see his county men do battle for the coveted Sam Maguire Cup.

As he weighed up the prospects of his native Donegal, he saw the manner of their triumph over Derry in the Ulster final as a very definite plus. On the other hand, the semi-final display against Mayo gave him cause for doubt. He was happy that Donegal's opponents were Dublin and not Meath, whose brand of football, he felt, they might have difficulty in coping with.

Michael looked forward to seeing two of Donegal's finest ever footballers in action – Tony Boyle at full-forward and Martin McHugh at centre-half-forward, both of whom he greatly admired.

Tony was one of the best full-forwards of his day – his high fielding, ball-winning ability and distribution to colleagues – a forte of his – made him a joy to watch. A man of strapping physique, he possessed instinctive footballing skills, displaying on a regular basis touches of class and footballing genius. Full-backs struggled to cope with him – so often he was a full-back's nightmare.

Tony was an underage star with his native Dungloe. He played centre-half-forward for Donegal Vocational Schools against Kerry in the All-Ireland final of 1987, only to lose by a point to the Kingdom at Croke Park. He came on the county senior scene in 1990 at the age of nineteen.

Martin, the 5 feet 7 inches footballing genius from Kilcar, was known as the 'Wee Man'. In 1992 he was in the autumn of his footballing days. He was equally effective with both feet – a rare gift, and an attribute that made him a major handful for any opponent. For one never knew whether Martin would veer left or right, or kick with his left or right foot when in possession. At the age of nineteen he won a county senior football title with his parish and scored ten points in the final. Scoring accuracy from frees and from play was his forte. His county senior playing days began with the National League campaign of 1980/81 and in 1982 he was on the Donegal team that brought the first under-21 football title to the county. All-Star and Railway Cup successes followed.

Michael came away from Croke Park basking in the reflected glory of Donegal's victory. His two heroes had excelled – both Tony and Martin had outplayed their opposite numbers. At the final whistle there was a tussle for possession between Martin McHugh and referee Tommy Sugrue of Kerry. The Donegal man won.

Said Michael: 'Kilkenny colleagues in the stand around me were all shaking hands with me. I began to feel as if I had been out there on the pitch playing with Donegal.' Michael looked forward to 1993 and hoped for a two-in-a-row – it would put the seal of greatness on the team. They were moving in that direction until they met Derry in the Ulster final – their fifth provincial final in a row – at Clones in wretched weather conditions, with the pitch resembling a paddy field, and minus their half-back line through injury. Donegal lost by 0-8 to 0-6. It was no consolation to see Derry go on and defeat

Cork by 1-14 to 2-8 in that year's All-Ireland final and take their first All-Ireland crown. These days he relives the victory of 1992 as he peruses the pages of *Sam's for the Hills*, an absorbing account of Donegal's All-Ireland odyssey by Dónal Campbell and Damian Dowds, with a title inspired by, and borrowed from, the final words of Anthony Molloy's speech, to thousands of delirious fans at Croke Park after leading his county to All-Ireland victory.

Donegal featured for the first time in an Ulster final in 1963 when they went under to a then rampant Down by 2-11 to 1-4. Three years later, against the same opposition, they came much closer – losing in the Ulster final by 1-7 to 0-8.

The county won its first Ulster title in 1972, when they were trained by Mick Higgins of Cavan fame in the 1940s. Tyrone were defeated by 2-13 to 1-11. Donegal then faced reigning All-Ireland champions Offaly in the semi-final. They lost by 1-17 to 2-10 and Offaly went on to retain their All-Ireland crown by beating Kerry (after a 1-13 apiece draw) by 1-19 to 0-13.

Three more Ulster titles came Donegal's way in 1974, 1983 and 1990. However, on each occasion they fell at All-Ireland semi-final stage. Then came 1992 and glory under thirty-year-old captain Anthony Molloy from Ardara, who had earlier won Ulster medals in 1983 and 1990. That year the county contested its seventh Ulster title and won its fifth provincial crown.

The Ulster campaign of 1992 began with a first-round game against Cavan at Breffni Park. Donegal were fortunate to secure a draw – a thriller played in glorious sunshine. They won the re-play convincingly at Ballybofey a week later on a Sunday afternoon when the heavens opened.

Next up were Fermanagh at Healy Park, Omagh. Donegal won well and took to serious training for the Ulster final against Derry – the then reigning National League title holders. The game was a test of character; against the wind in the second half and reduced to fourteen men since before the interval, Donegal dug deep and with a dogged performance eked out a deserved two-points win, 0-14 to 1-9 in a game of no frills and considerable controversy.

Donegal were now in the All-Ireland semi-final, where they met Connacht champions Mayo in Croke Park on Sunday 16 August. When the full-time whistle blew, the scoreboard read Donegal 0-13 Mayo 0-9. Although close and exciting, it was far from brilliant. Nothing Donegal had done could have sown seeds of over-confidence.

Watched by the Dublin team, they kicked seventeen wides. Lucky wides, you might say, because when Dublin defeated Clare in the second semi-final a week later, their minds had already been programmed to take not too seriously the Donegal challenge in the final.

Donegal's intensive training continued and the pressure began to build. They would line out in Croke Park for their first ever All-Ireland final on Sunday 20 September. An Ulsterman, Peter Quinn of Fermanagh, was the GAA president. Maybe it was a good omen.

Their opponents in the final were Dublin. Croke Park to them was home territory. To the final they brought the scalps of Kildare from the Leinster final and Clare from the All-Ireland semi-final. More significantly, they also brought a proud tradition. The county had twenty-one All-Ireland titles to its credit.

On final day injury deprived Donegal of stout-hearted defender Martin Shovlin, who was replaced by John Joe Doherty at left-half-back. Their captain, Anthony Molloy, won the toss and decided to play into Hill 16 – an area populated by Dublin supporters. It was a deliberate decision, designed to distance those supporters from the Dublin scores in the opening half. Donegal were slow to settle, and struggled to find a rhythm. Then Charlie Redmond missed a Dublin penalty. Mentally, Donegal began to relax and play the flowing football they were capable of. At half time they led by ten points to seven.

Ten minutes into the second half, Barry Cunningham replaced the injured midfielder Brian Murray – Donegal's only substitution of the day. There he joined his captain, Anthony Molloy, where Donegal continued to hold sway. Entering the closing stages Donegal were three points clear. Then Declan Bonner sent over a point. Final score: Donegal 0-18 Dublin 0-14 – one of those rare All-Ireland final days when the green flag was never once waved. On the stand, GAA president Peter Quinn handed the cup to Anthony Molloy and the Sam Maguire trophy was on its way to Donegal for the first time ever.

Donegal became the third Ulster county to win a senior football title. They joined Cavan and Down, both of whom, at the time, had five and four titles respectively. Since then things have changed for the northern province, as Derry, Armagh and Tyrone have added their names to the Sam Maguire Cup.

Donegal won a fifth Ulster title and a first All-Ireland crown in 1992 – a great year for the footballing men of Ireland's most northwesterly county. Their left-corner-forward, Manus Boyle, was man of the match with nine points to his credit. Seven of the team received All-Star awards – goalkeeper Gary Walsh, full-back Matt Gallagher, centre-half-back Martin Gavigan, midfielder and captain Anthony Molloy, full-forward Tony Boyle and the brothers James and Martin McHugh in the half-forward line. The Texaco Footballer of the Year award went to Martin McHugh. Three of the team – Matt Gallagher, Noel Hegarty and Martin McHugh – assisted Ulster on the following St Patrick's Day at Croke Park in the 1-12 to 0-12 defeat of Leinster in the Railway Cup football final.

Team manager on the great occasion in September 1992 was 49-year-old Brian McEniff – himself a former player, player-manager, National League winner with New York in 1964 and All-Star in 1972. Attention to detail was one of Brian's fortes. He even had an observer in the grounds at the Dublin training sessions.

A FOOTBALL PERSONALITY:

Maurice Fitzgerald (Kerry)

It has always been my great privilege to have played football and, ever since a young boy growing up in Cahersiveen, football was my first love. Living just a stone's throw from the pitch, never was a ball kicked but I was in the middle of it – staying down at the pitch till long after dark and being called eventually by my mother to get organised for the following day.

Football was a great passion in the house. My father Ned played with the local St Mary's, south Kerry, and trained and played also with Kerry back in the 1950s and his great claim of having captained Kerry to defeat in the first round of the Munster championship is something we still make fun of. It is often said in my

house that I have my 'mother's legs' – she also hailed from a great
footballing family, the O'Connors, and her three brothers Francey,
Bernie and Séamus, God rest them, were famous in south Kerry
for their footballing ability in the 1950s and 1960s. So you could
say football was in the blood and here in Cahersiveen growing up
in the 1970s and early 1980s we got the best of encouragement
from the local mentors.

They were numerous at a young age – people like Junior Murphy
and Paddy Reidy gave us great time and we were always taught to
kick with the left and right leg. Later, Christy Connell and Kieran
McCarthy were great influences. All these men were a great influ-
ence. Then on into CBS secondary school, where we were given a
great education and of course football played a major role. Here we
had great mentors. Those that were special included Joe O'Connor
(RIP), Donie Riney (RIP), John Costello (RIP) and Joe Mahoney
(RIP). These men gave everything in pursuit of our education and
in developing our football ability and of course our character. We
owe them a debt that can never be repaid. Growing up and being
fed on stories of some great footballers, and my Dad's great friend
Mick O'Connell, of course was a great influence, and listening to
him recalling his footballing days always excited me.

It was for me a great pleasure to have played so much football
with so many great friends that this, was for me, the real victory.
Travelling the country, meeting so many like-minded people who
just loved the game, was indeed a wonderful thing. I loved watching
the game, and still do. Jacko [Shea] was a neighbour just across the
road, and boy did I love to see him going for a kick at Con Keating
Park!

The great man, who played his club football with St Mary's, Cahersiveen, and with which he won three county titles, made his county
senior championship debut in 1988 at the age of eighteen. In the
Munster final of that year, in a fractious game with Cork, Maurice
gave evidence of his potential. He kicked with both feet with equal
proficiency. He scored ten of Kerry's sixteen points – seven from
frees – in his team's one-point defeat of 1-14 to 0-16. He called it a
day after the championship of 2001. In 1988 and 1996 he was the
only Kerryman to receive an All-Star award. He got a third in 1997
(a year when he was top scorer in the championship), was chosen
as Texaco Footballer of the Year and was also chosen as Guinness

GAA Writers' Footballer of the Year. Maurice's father, Ned, had a relatively short innings with the Kerry team in the 1950s. No glory came his way.

What follows is a contribution, by my son Brendan, on a very talented footballer he greatly admired.

One day not so long ago, I was in the local butcher's shop. Myself and Eddie the butcher, as we often do, got talking about sport. Now, Eddie runs marathons, cycles, plays soccer, supports his county [Waterford] in hurling, and will watch a good game of Gaelic football. Like many Irishmen, Eddie loves his sport – all sport – and in talking about it, his opinions are at all times considered and balanced. You'd enjoy doing your business there and having a few words, be it about Lance Armstrong, Steven Gerrard, the Irish cricket team or Dan Shanahan.

Anyway, on this particular day Eddie asks me to pick my 'standout' sports figure from any code and from any era. I paused briefly. They say a dying man sees his whole life flash before him. Well, I think I know what they mean. In those couple of seconds I watched fifty football and hurling All-Ireland campaigns, nine soccer world cup finals, I considered all the other great figures in so many other sports and then having completed my daunting task I blurted out – Maurice Fitzgerald. Eddie looked at me for a second. He half smiled as he nodded slowly and then quietly said, 'That's a good choice.'

To reiterate, this conversation took place in Waterford city and not in the local shop in Cahersiveen, three doors down from Maurice's granny's house, where you might be compromised in your answer, lest word got back that you said the wrong thing.

In my lifetime, I have been fortunate enough to see Maradona, Platini (who, contrary to Éamon Dunphy's opinion, was a world-class player – I think even Éamon smiles about that one now), Muhammad Ali, Tiger Woods, John McEnroe, Mikey Sheehy, D. J. Carey, Seán Kelly, Johann Cruyff (the total football of that Dutch team on which he played in 1974 was the first thing to fire this young boy's imagination), Tony Ward, Daley Thompson, Sebastian Coe – you could keep going and going. I reflect on that array of talent and remain happy with my choice of Maurice Fitzgerald.

At this point I had better state my credentials. It might help to explain things better. I was born in Wexford in 1965. In 1967 we moved to Kerry. I didn't have much say in the matter. I was aged two and my opinion was not sought. My dad was in the bank and in those days a nomadic-type lifestyle went with the job. After four years in Tralee, we packed up our tent and moved to Killorglin. By this stage I was beginning to get indoctrinated in Kerry's footballing tradition. There were no PlayStations or satellite TV channels to divert my attention. Football was the thing. I just about knew what a hurley was and there were rumours that you could see one if you crossed the border into Cork or Limerick.

As so often happens, things don't travel in straight lines. My dad, who is a hurling man if ever there was one, had a son who developed into a football fan. He was absolutely OK with this. When in Rome do what the Romans do and we were in Kerry now. Anyway, like many enlightened dads, he believes all sport is good and that whatever expression becomes manifest is not really that important.

So football it was. We had a fantastic garden in Killorglin with the wall of a large storage shed backing onto it. I recall going outside for hours on end, and kicking the ball against the wall. The time spent by a child in such manner can often seem trivial and inconsequential, but in those hours skills are honed and lessons learned. I kicked and fielded that ball countless times as it bounced back to me from the wall. The wall didn't tackle me, so you didn't have the intensity of man-to-man interaction in the garden. But you had almost everything else and the school yard and training sessions provided the opportunity to test your progress and development.

My Killorglin football career climaxed when in 1974 my team reached the under-10 local final. We had a good team. I was midfield with the legendary Mick O'Connell's nephew, John O'Connell (now, sad to say, deceased). Frank Foley was the local pharmacist's son. He used to give us dextrose (sugar) sweets before each match for energy and we were convinced it enhanced our performance. As a pharmacist now myself I smile at this memory and appreciate the power of the placebo effect.

Anyway, we lost the final to Caragh Lake. I was gutted. Perhaps this was karmic justice for us taking a performance-enhancing product!

Soon after this we were on the move again to live in Wexford. As I look back on my time in Kerry you get a sense of how a tradition develops and perpetuates itself. Football was what people talked about. Football was what mattered. Virtually every boy in Killorglin and its environs was playing in the local league. Nobody slipped through the net. In other counties, how many talents go unspotted, unnurtured, and as a consequence potential never realised. This doesn't happen in Kerry. Anyway, I was lost to the system. It's a long way from Killorglin under-10s to the Kerry senior team and I'd never claim I'd have realised that boyhood dream. Even if I had, I'd have been playing during a barren time – 1986–1997 – the era of the great Kerry football famine.

When I was leaving Killorglin there was, unknown to me, a boy a few years my junior twenty-five miles down the road in Cahersiveen. He was probably learning to kick a football. He was unusual in that he was kicking with both his feet. This boy didn't know it then, that as a man he was going to have the task of leading his county, Moses-like, out of the desert. This boy was Maurice Fitzgerald.

So 1974 saw us leaving Kerry and going back to live in Wexford. However, a substantial amount of my boyhood heart (and my parents' and four sisters') belonged in Kerry. We satisfied this by coming back for a month every summer to Killorglin for our holidays until we finished secondary school. Kerry were entering a golden era in football. We all know they won eight titles between 1975 and 1986. This was a magnificent achievement by a fantastic team (and coach) and my family revelled in it. When that Kerry team had a few titles in the bag, my Dad starting making sounds on All-Ireland Sunday about the merits of others having their day in the sun, and seeing things go around a bit. So part of him, at least, wished for Roscommon or Offaly or Tyrone to get a title. Of course the young don't have the perspective, the broadmindedness, the compassion and the maturity to wish for such things. We all shouted for Kerry every time. But nothing is lost or unnoticed and I find myself now wishing, for example, that Mayo had won one of the finals they lost to Kerry in recent years. In my boyhood, I supported Kerry and Liverpool. The 1970s and 1980s was a golden era for both teams, and as a boy you'd think that this will go on for ever. Of course it doesn't. The barren spells for both teams sort of coincided, too. As with life, the good times when they come are fantastic, but it is during the tough times that you really learn. If all there was was success and glory, we would stay self-centred and egotistical. But don't tell that to a child. Success is very glamorous and alluring. Not too many children support Middlesbrough or West Ham. But even empires like Man Utd or Liverpool or Kerry do not dominate continuously.

So after 1986 the well ran dry in Kerry. You could kind of see it coming. Kerry were lucky in some ways to beat Tyrone that year and Cork were starting to get a serious-looking team together. They had great underage talent coming through. Meanwhile in Kerry the production line seemed to be grinding to a halt. That Cork team lost two finals before they won two, and really in my opinion they were good enough for four in a row.

Now we were entering the 1990s. The world seemed to be changing. The Ulster champions, who used to come to Croke Park to get pummelled in the semi-final by Kerry or whoever else, now emerged as serious contenders. Down twice, and Donegal and Derry made it four-in-a-row for Ulster. This was fantastic, but where were Kerry? Well, they were stuck in Munster, emerging only once from the province in the years 1987 to 1995 and when they did come through in 1991 Down did a demolition job on them in the All-Ireland semi-final. These were, indeed, sobering times for all Kerry fans.

During this time a new forward named Maurice Fitzgerald emerged. I could see straight away that he was a special talent. He was tall, elegant in movement, graceful, stylish, and kicked equally well with both feet. He took place kicking to an exceptional standard. He could run with the ball, take on a man and beat him, sell a dummy, and kick points from play. He had foresight and vision. He could pick out and execute the best pass option. We wondered each year would Maurice beat Cork. I believe that Maurice would have stood out in any team, in any era, but at this time he had become the focal point, for all Kerry fans, of a breakthrough.

Now, I need to develop further my case for Maurice. The case thus far would make him a 'stand-out' talent of his particular era, but I am making a greater case for him. The case I am making is that he is a 'stand-out' talent that belongs in the pantheon of greats from all codes, from all eras. Then from that vaunted group, I am choosing him as my own 'stand-out' sportsman.

Maurice, I believe, belongs to a rare group of sports people who actually transcend their chosen sport. I had better explain this. I refer to a book called *Zen and the Art of Archery* which describes the path a particular sportsman took to achieve mastery of his particular sport – in this case archery.

Initially, you have to become technically proficient at your chosen sport. This comes from the endless hours put into learning the skills of your sport so that they become second nature to you.

The next stage is cultivation of mental strength and stability. This is important so that in times of pressure the sportsman is able to make his technical skill count. Matches can be cauldrons of intensity, and certain matches, and certain times in matches, can be very pressurising. If the sportsman has not got mental strength and stability, the countless hours spent gaining technical proficiency may be for naught.

The next level is very subtle. Having gained technical excellence, and strengthened the mind, the next step is to actually lose the mind.

The sports psychologists encourage positive thinking and the visualisation of positive outcomes. This is indeed very useful. It is far better to think and visualise positively than to think and see negatively. However, it is vastly superior again to not think at all. Thinking actually gets in the way. Sport played at the highest level is actually like a meditation. And thus it was with Maurice.

At this level, the player's self-awareness drops away. His mind is calm, still, open, yet fully alert, and aware and pregnant with possibility. There is intuitive knowledge of exactly what to do and the ability to execute it. What emerges is inspirational, simple, beautiful.

Exceptional sportsmen do not exist in this space all the time, but some, by virtue of good fortune of birth or genetic inheritance or life influences or personal endeavour (or a combination of some or all of these factors) arrive at being able to exist in this state, at least some of the time, in the most extraordinary of circumstances – in the very heat of battle. I watch sport to witness this, to see those beautiful moments, those creative inspired moments. It is the sportsmen who have been able to create those moments who are my inspiration. So back to Maurice and some moments of magic from him, etched indelibly on my mind.

It is September 1997 and Kerry are in their first All-Ireland final for eleven years and playing against Mayo. I have forgotten much of the game. What I haven't forgotten is the display of Maurice Fitzgerald. He was on fire. He beat Mayo that day. He won the title for Kerry. In what was a truly phenomenal performance, he scored nine of Kerry's thirteen points – four from play – in their 0-13 to 1-7 win. Maurice scored from frees and from play. He scored with the left foot. He scored with the right foot – angles and distances mattered not. As the clock ticked to the sixtieth minute the score stood at Kerry 0-11 Mayo 1-7. Then Maurice Fitzgerald pointed.

It eased the pressure somewhat. It didn't remove the danger. I can still see him in the closing stages with Kerry holding on grimly to their two-point lead. He is standing on the sideline at the Cusack Stand side about fifty-five yards out from goal, ready to take a line ball. He uses the right foot. Away goes the ball and, radar-like, it travels over the crossbar for a remarkable score.

In the next day's *Irish Times*, Tom Humphries had this to say:

> *The elegance and grace of Maurice Fitzgerald from Caherciveen was the difference ... His genius illuminated the match ... It was Maurice Fitzgerald who made space to provide the moments of ecstatic beauty ... Fitzgerald is a throw back to a different era when skill counted for as much as endless endurance training.*

In 2000 Kerry came up against an emerging Armagh side in the All-Ireland semi-final. Armagh were tough as hell, good footballers, and had a tactical game plan, which closed opposition teams down, making it very hard for them to play. Maurice scored the goal of goals that day. He came on as a sub early in the second half and after about twenty minutes got possession on the Cusack Stand side. In he came by Hill 16 on a solo run – toe to hand, toe to hand using the right foot, all the time shadowed by an Armagh defender. Maurice now had the ball in his hand from the right foot and suddenly a left-footed shot shook the rigging. It was a move of pure beauty, sheer inspiration, a display of mastery of some of the game's many skills – 'a goal of typically languid beauty', wrote Keith Duggan in *The Irish Times*.

Four minutes into injury time, with Armagh one point ahead, Kerry got a free about 45 yards out. Up steps Maurice; Kerry live to fight another day. In response to a query from Keith Duggan on the thoughts cascading through his mind at that moment, Maurice replied: 'Well, to be honest no, nothing ... you try and keep your mind clear and go through the motions of the kick without thinking of the actual result.'

The replay, another epic contest, ended in a draw and went to extra time. In that contest Maurice came on as a sub early in the second half. The clock had ticked past the hour when Maurice got possession near midfield. He had only one teammate to aim at, such was the defence effort of Kerry to keep Armagh at bay. He executed a perfect fifty-yard diagonal pass to the hands of Mike

Frank Russell from Killorglin by the Laune. Bang, goal – Kerry in the lead, 1-10 to 1-9, for the first time in the second half. I have always felt that that perfect pass and grand goal saved the day for Kerry. The game ended 1-11 apiece and after a half hour of extra time the scoreboard read Kerry 2-15 Armagh 1-15.

And finally, there was that quarter-final day in Thurles against Dublin on Saturday 4 August 2001. Kerry, seemingly on the road to victory – eight points up with twelve minutes to go – were hit by a Dublin onslaught that yielded 2-3. Now the Kingdom were one point behind with about a minute left. They won a sideline kick – fifty yards or so from goal, and Kerry's fate was in the hands – and feet – of Maurice Fitzgerald. He had to cope with not only the mighty pressure of the moment, but also the roar of the crowd, the vagaries of the elements and the unwanted close attention of the Dublin manager, Tommy Carr.

Maurice let fly with the foot. Away went the leather – away on a trip of destiny – up, up, up. I watched and wondered. And then it fell, dead on target – radar-guided, Fitzgerald-style. Maurice, in the circumstances, had delivered, arguably, the greatest point ever scored in Gaelic football – a master lost in his own world of meditation.

Maurice was in many ways, at one and the same time, both blessed and cursed. He was blessed with his talent. He was blessed to be a Kerryman where his talent got nurtured, found expression and had its potential realised at the highest level.

He was cursed to have played a large part of his career in a most barren time for Kerry football. He was cursed that his county career ended when there was still more glory in the days ahead.

Maurice has left me with some outstanding inspirational moments that have a special place in my memory beside moments from other magnificent sports people.

And in the next lifetime on planet earth (if there is one), my father will not work in the bank. So we won't get moved from place to place. He will be a schoolteacher in Beaufort and myself and Maurice Fitzgerald will play in the famous to be 'Kerry five-in-a-row' team. I'll dream on.

Maurice Fitzgerald. In the photograph beside him, his father, Ned – a member
of the 1955 Kerry panel – is 1st on left, 2nd row from back.

A football selection

John O'Leary
(Dublin)

Kenneth Mortimer	*Darren Fay*	*Tony Scullion*
(Mayo)	(Meath)	(Derry)

Séamus Moynihan   *D. J. Kane*   *Anthony Rainbow*
(Kerry)   (Down)   (Kildare)

Anthony Tohill   *Gerry McEntee*
(Derry)   (Meath)

Maurice Fitzgerald *Martin McHugh* *Michael Donnellan*
(Kerry)   (Donegal)   (Galway)

Padraig Joyce   *Charlie Redmond*   *James McCartan*
(Galway)   (Dublin)   (Down)

2001–2008

Teams that participated in the
All-Ireland senior finals

COUNTY	FOOTBALL		HURLING	
	WON	LOST	WON	LOST
Armagh	1	1		
Clare				1
Cork		1	2	2
Galway	1			2
Kerry	3	3		
Kilkenny			5	1
Limerick				1
Mayo		2		
Meath		1		
Tipperary			1	
Tyrone	3			
Waterford				1

In the decade to date twelve counties participated in the senior finals.

The eight hurling finals involved seven counties with three of those successful.

The eight football finals involved seven counties with four of those successful.

A HURLING OCCASION:

Waterford v Wexford and Clare v Cork, 2008 All-Ireland quarter-finals

It was Sunday 27 July 2008, quarter-final day in Thurles. We were treated to a feast of hurling, two great games.

Was it the best double-billing ever? We had witnessed two spell-binding contests – hurling in all its stern, naked grandeur before an attendance of 37,812. Games to set the heart throbbing and the blood pulsating, games that might have gone either way.

In literary terms we had seen classic prose and beautiful poetry, some poetic licence and, *mirabile dictu*, not a sign of a card in the Cork v Clare contest – a tribute to both sets of players and to referee Dickie Murphy of Wexford.

On a sunny afternoon in Thurles, the final scores in both games were remarkably similar: Waterford 2-19 Wexford 3-15; Cork 2-19 Clare 2-17.

The paths of the four teams that brought them to the quarter final stage at Semple Stadium were:

Waterford:
v Clare: 0-23 to 2-26 (lost)
v Antrim: 6-18 to 0-15
v Offaly: 2-18 to 0-18
Wexford:
v Dublin: 2-13 to 0-19 (draw)
v Dublin: 2-15 to 1-15 (replay)
v Kilkenny: 0-17 to 5-21 (lost)
Cork:
v Tipperary: 1-13 to 1-19 (lost)
v Dublin: 1-17 to 0-15
v Galway: 0-23 to 2-15
Clare:
v Waterford: 2-26 to 0-23
v Limerick: 4-12 to 1-16
v Tipperary: 0-19 to 2-21 (lost)

The curtain-raiser was between Waterford, under the management of former Clare goalkeeper Davy Fitzgerald, and Wexford under the guiding hand of John Meyler.

Wexford gave their best seventy-minute display for quite some time. And they might well have stolen the game in the closing stages. They were awarded a penalty. Their goalkeeper, and 'penalty king', Damien Fitzhenry, headed downfield. For once his effort for a goal whizzed over the crossbar. There was a moment of levity as Damien thundered back to man his goal line. The Waterford puck out broke into his path. He quickly gathered and despatched the sliotar downfield and then continued quickly on his way.

The game opened briskly and after six minutes Rory Jacob sent an inch-perfect pass to Stephen Doyle, who lifted Wexford's team and fans with a smashing goal.

Approaching half time, Waterford were awarded a 21-yard free. Up stepped Eoin Kelly. His approach revealed his intent, and he sent the sliotar crashing to the top right-hand corner of the net between the hurleys of two defenders. Half time: Waterford 1-10 Wexford 1-6.

Early in the second half the green flag was raised three times in quick succession. First, a high ball into the Waterford goalmouth was contested by a back and a forward, only to whiz past goalkeeper Clinton Hennessy. Then Stephen Doyle, an accomplished performer, received a pass, side-stepped his marker and scored his second goal of the afternoon. Waterford's response was prompt. John Mullane, who was having a fine game, sent a high pass that was grabbed by big Dan (Shanahan). His shot shook the rigging. Dan wasn't back to his 2007 form, but he was causing problems for the Wexford defence. John Mullane was on fire – he scored three fine points. Eoin Kelly finished with 1-8 to his credit – 'performing on another planet to most fellas', observed Nicky English. Tony Browne at centre-half-back gave a performance that belied his years. In the end Waterford prevailed, but only just.

Two vastly experienced hurling men were in command of the contestants of the second game of the afternoon – Gerald McCarthy with Cork, Mike McNamara with Clare. Right from the throw-in Clare set about their task in a game played at high intensity; Colin Lynch operated like a teenager rather than a man in his mid-thirties. On the Cork side Ben O'Connor traversed the pitch like an Olympic sprinter.

Clare were physical and passionate, rampant throughout the pitch. They goaled on the half hour following a free by Gerry Quinn and a deft one-handed flick by Barry Nugent that directed the sliotar out of the reach of Donal Óg Cusack.

Leading by nine points at one stage in the first half and by eight at half time, despite some bad wides, Clare appeared to have Cork on the rack. However, within moments of the restart, substitute Timmy McCarthy had a goal, and further Cork scores cut the Clare lead to three points. But the Banner men responded, and about midway through the half Diarmuid McMahon contested a ball with a defender. Donal Óg advanced only to see the ball roll between his legs and just over the goal line. Clare again seemed set for victory.

Then a few things happened that had a key bearing on the result. Cork took off the 'Rock', Diarmuid O'Sullivan. They made switches and substitutions and tightened up their defence. I was sorry to see Diarmuid going off. It seemed to many of us that we were witnessing the sunset of a very fine career. I always liked the 'Rock'. He took hard knocks and gave them and got on with the game without rancour. As he left the pitch an image from the past flashed through my mind. It was a championship game between Limerick and Cork at Páirc Uí Caoimh. In the opening minutes of the second half the 'Rock' advanced to an incoming ball. He grabbed it in mid air, made a few yards, and then, aided by what breeze there was, despatched a mighty drive that travelled over the bar at the Blackrock end of the pitch for an inspirational point. It was the stuff of Fianna folklore.

In a game that ended in a two-point victory, that had at least two Lazarus-like comebacks by Cork, it could be hard to pick a turning point. And yet in this game there was one that, even at the time, I felt was crucial.

The 'Rock' was not long gone from the pitch when Clare were awarded a sideline ball not far from their own goal. It did not rise and from the ensuing tussle went over for a lineball to Cork. Somehow, one sensed danger. The ball was beautifully struck and floated towards the goalmouth where Kieran Murphy, just two minutes on the pitch, having indirectly replaced the 'Rock', was on hand to finish the ball to the net. Clare's lead cut to two points – fifteen minutes to go – the momentum now with Cork, but only just.

Clare will feel they let the game slip. Cork will savour a famous victory. A game to tell the grandchildren about – by which time, of course, the story will have gathered moss and much added value.

The atmosphere generated by this contest was summed up succinctly by Tom Humphries in *The Irish Times* the following day:

> *Another Monday morning. The heartbeat settles back to medically prescribed levels, the slight whiplash from being on a roller-coaster watching end-to-end genius subsides and the real world hoves slowly back into view … This was the stuff of high summer, the fodder of myth, Hemingway's bullring, Setanta's hound, di Maggio's streak.*

We looked forward with relish to the semi-final clashes of Kilkenny v Cork and Waterford v Tipperary.

A HURLING PERSONALITY:

Brendan Cummins (Tipperary)

> *Oh! Where is the spot on the face of the earth*
> *To which I can ever compare thee?*
> *Fair queen of my dreams, happy home of my birth,*
> *Magnificent, sweet Tipperary.*
> *From smooth gliding Shannon, to silver-streaked Suir,*
> *Softest smiles thy bright face are adorning,*
> *As tender as first breath of dawn, and as pure*
> *As the rose, in the dew of the morning.*
> Thomas Keating

> *I would like to reflect on 2001 as it was the year of my biggest achievements, to win League, All-Ireland, All-Star and be part of a squad that were undefeated in every game played that year.*

In 1999 Nicky English took over as manager. He had Ken Hogan and Jack Bergin as selectors with him. The training started in November that year and was totally physical, all running – getting up at 6 a.m. and heading to the Devil's Bit outside Templemore more times than I care to remember. We won the League that year but Clare beat us in the first round of the championship so that was the end of our year.

We met again in November 2000 to start the process again. The training changed slightly as it was decided that there was no game played on the side of a mountain and so we would have to change our style to win. The training changed to more speed work with shorter runs and the intensity had increased. The game was changing so we had to adapt. We were beaten in the Munster final 2000 by Cork, and Galway three weeks later beat us in the quarter-final in Croker by three points. This was one of the lowest points in my career. So much effort for no reward. We formed a circle in the dressing room after the game and made the promise to each other that the following year 'Liam' would be in the middle. A meeting was held in Thurles in December that year to plan for 2001. We all had gained enough experience over the previous year – it was now time to win something. The training was a mix of the previous two years. I can remember thinking that I had never trained so hard and made as many sacrifices – the team all felt the same.

We played the usual challenges prior to the League, winning all the initial ones easily against college teams. The real day we knew something was going to happen was against Limerick in Nenagh. We came from behind to draw. This signalled a maturity and a determination not to be beaten, which stayed with us all year. The League went well again, winning all the close games. We beat Clare in the final in Limerick. Things went well for me on the day, always great to contribute to a win, especially a final. The cup was put to one side; there was a bigger prize.

We went back down to Cork to play Clare. This time we won by one point. Players collapsed after the game – the heat and the relief that we had gotten over the hump. Clare were going well – we had beaten them. In the Munster final we beat Limerick – hottest day of the summer – two-point win this time. When the whistle blew the sense of achievement was great but we all knew this was still only a stepping stone to the bigger prize.

We had six weeks off before Wexford and this was nearly our undoing. When we arrived in Croker for the semi we were nearly caught. This was the worst I have ever felt in the goals. I was very nervous on the day. Wexford got three goals and we escaped with a draw.

The replay the following Saturday we won easily in the end. We had gotten our wake-up call. I felt like myself again in goal.

The final was a huge occasion. We headed to Dublin the day before with a band at the train station. I had played in the 1997 final but was too young to appreciate the importance of it all. This could be the last final I would ever play in. It was to be enjoyed but had to be won. The feeling leaving the dressing room heading for the tunnel and the wall of noise hitting the field was like nothing I had ever experienced. All work had been done since 1999 – we were ready. The parade and meeting the president was to be enjoyed but I was looking forward to getting the game going.

Jack Bergin used to tell us the national anthem was like the minutes before you turn over an exam paper. If you haven't the work done it seems to go on forever but if you are ready it flies. We got off to a good start, which helped, and even now when I close my eyes I can feel the heave of the crowd during the game. The end came when we were three points up and Pat O'Connor signalled to me I had the last puck out. I can remember delaying it. I wanted that moment to last forever. One more hit and the job was done.

In the dressing room after the game we formed the circle and 'Liam' was in the middle.

I want to recognise the contribution my family has made to that day and my hurling career. My wife, Pamela, who has always been very understanding – there are new beginnings now with the arrival of my son Paul on 17 January (2008). I have a few years left in the game – hopefully more highs to come.

Brendan, an only child, was born to John and Ann (née O'Donoghue) on 11 May 1975. He grew up in football territory in south Tipperary and until his minor days football would have been his number one game. This, no doubt, was influenced by the fact that his father had played at county level for Tipperary and was chosen in the 1960s to play for Munster in the Railway Cup. That Munster jersey was a prized possession until it disappeared one evening from his bag while he was training – never to be seen again.

When Brendan played hurling and football, his proficiency took him to the highest level in both games. He played in goal for the county senior hurling team and at centre-half-forward for the senior football team. As a dual player he was following in the footsteps of fellow-parishioner Michael 'Babs' Keating. Indeed, Brendan and 'Babs' are the only two sons of the parish to have won All-Ireland senior hurling medals. In 1993 Brendan played in all grades of hurling and football for his native Tipperary – not yet fully established, still only eighteen.

As I travelled to meet Brendan, I couldn't help reflecting on some of the many great net minders Tipperary had produced in bygone days. In the early years of the last century there was Jim 'Hawk' O'Brien of Thurles, followed by Jack 'Skinny' O'Meara of Toomevara. 'Skinny's' brother Tom also kept goal for Tipperary, and his incredible display in the Munster final of 1930 was a major factor in the defeat of a fine Clare team. Little Jimmy Maher of Boherlahan was 'stopping hailstones' in 1945 when he defied

Brendan Cummins.

Kilkenny's greatest efforts in the All-Ireland final that year. After that came the legendary Tony Reddan and in more recent times Brendan's predecessor, Ken Hogan.

Brendan, who grips the ash right-hand under, played his first county senior game at Cappoquin in a National League match against Waterford in 1993. His first championship game was against the same county at Pairc Uí Chaoimh in 1995.

A certain affinity exists among goalkeepers. They know that on the goal line you can be the hero or the fall guy. So they wish each other well. Brendan recalls the pre-match parade of the 1996 Munster final. Joe Quaid, the Limerick goalie, looked across and said: 'Have a good game, young fella', to which Brendan replied: 'Thank you.'

It reminded me of a similar gesture by Jackie Kyle, many decades ago. As the Ireland and Wales teams ran onto the rugby pitch, Jackie, one of Ireland's greatest in that field of sport, turned to Cliff Morgan in his first year at international level and said, 'Have a good game.' Cliff never forgot it.

'Often in the parade,' said Brendan, 'I wink across at the other goalkeeper and he winks back. I have the greatest sympathy for any goalkeeper who is beaten for a "soft" goal – think about it, maybe over 80,000 people watching.'

Supporters tend to remember the 'soft' ones that go in. I recalled for Brendan the succession of marvellous saves he made in the All-Ireland semi-final of 2003 against Kilkenny. He remembered that a rampant Kilkenny had put two past him as the game pro-gressed. Coming to the final stages, Henry Shefflin was close at hand. 'You're looking for one,' said Brendan. 'Yes,' said Henry. 'No way,' said Brendan in his own mind. And? 'Yes, he sneaked one in before the end. We talked about it together as we walked off the pitch.'

Martin Breheny reported on the game for the *Irish Independent*:

> *The winning margin (3-18 to 0-15) would have been far higher were it not for the remarkable defiance of Cummins, who pro-duced at least six truly amazing saves ... Cummins' heroic defence kept Tipperary in front until the forty-fifth minute.*

And then there were the two that he did not see at all.

... a penalty by D. J. Carey in a Saturday evening League game at Semple Stadium in 1998. It flew in between Paul Shelly and the post ... The second was a goal by Ben O'Connor from close range in the Munster final of 2006 ... Those shots were probably travelling at a hundred miles an hour.

Little wonder then that folklore has it that Tony Reddan used say he only saw half the shots he saved – the other half were pure instinct.

Growing up, Brendan's heroes were Ger Cunningham, who for close on twenty years was brilliant between the posts for his native Cork; Ken Hogan, so reliable for Tipperary in the same position, and Nicky English, 'whose hurling class was something special'.

Brendan has given wonderful service to his county since he became its established senior custodian in 1995. Between the posts – agile, ever-alert, composed and athletic – he is at all times in tune with his defenders. 'I live with my backs – we set out a plan and stick to it.'

He talks about the level to which the game has evolved, even during his own playing days.

It has become a science. It was all about natural skill before – now the mental aspect is large. You have all kinds of coaches, one for nearly every position on the field. The placing of the puck-out has become vital. It's part of the game plan. The team has to function mentally as a unit – possession well used – find a colleague – you are expected to be reading each other's mind. And then there is the training schedule – we can thank Clare for that – they started it in 1995.

In time, Brendan can see teams being reduced to fourteen or perhaps even thirteen.

Measured against Tipperary's proud success record since the foundation of the GAA, Brendan's years of activity have reaped rather small harvests. Now in his thirty-fifth year (summer 2009), the sands of time are running out as regards opportunities to add more major honours to his existing achievements.

'I played in twelve Munster senior finals, including replays, in hurling and football and won only one.' Hard to believe! So close so often – so little return.

In 1995 an under-21 hurling title was won. Brendan's only senior medal, so far, came in 2001. It was a nail-biting campaign – a two-point win over Limerick in the Munster final; a draw and a replay with Wexford in the All-Ireland semi-final; just three points to spare over Galway in a great final. The same year Brendan won a National League medal. He played for his province in the Railway Cup and was successful on three occasions. On a personal level, Brendan has had the distinction of receiving three All-Star Awards, 2000, 2001 and 2003 – all richly deserved and reflecting his status as a brilliant net minder and true sportsman.

Since meeting Brendan in the early days of spring 2008 he has added a National League and Munster medal to his list of honours, and also a fourth All-Star.

A HURLING PERSONALITY:

Seán Óg Ó hAilpín (Cork)

His father's from Fermanagh, his mother's from Fiji, neither a hurling stronghold.
                Micheál Ó Muircheartaigh

I only started playing this great game of hurling from eleven years of age. I was born on my mother's island of Rotuma in the Pacific Ocean and grew up in the southwest suburbs of Sydney, Australia, where I spent the early years of my childhood. Having an Irish father, I would have heard of hurling and Gaelic football, but growing up in Sydney, where I didn't see or hear much of it, I thought hurling was another piseog, like the leprechaun!

When it was announced in 1987 that the family were moving to Cork, Ireland, I didn't believe such a place existed but reality hit me when I left Sydney Airport in October 1987 to embark on an amazing journey and new chapter in my life.

Tosnaíonn turas fada le coischéim amháin. *I remember land-
ing into Cork on a miserable February day in 1988, having spent
the Christmas in Rotuma when Mum said her final goodbyes
to her family. That was a tough day for her and her emotions
showed it too. After the initial few weeks and shock of settling
into our new life in Cork, hurling came to my rescue. I joined the
nearest hurling club from our house in Fair Hill, Na Piarsaigh
H & F club, and never looked back. I became part of a community and the Northside people accepted their new adopted son.
I started to make friends but there was one more obstacle I still
had to overcome – I had to master this beautiful ancient game
of hurling. Having played rugby league for most of my childhood
years in Sydney, I wasn't exposed to the game and experienced
early years of frustration and embarrassment when starting off.
That's why I have the Na Piarsaigh club and my school, North
Monastery CBS, to thank, for without their endless help, support and encouragement I wouldn't have fulfilled my dreams
of making it to the top level. I want to thank the early influence
of Abie Allen, Tony Hegarty, Billy Clifford and Christy Kidney
of Na Piarsaigh H & F club. They laid a strong foundation to
my hurling career which was built on further at the North Mon
CBS. I enjoyed my five years immensely at 'The Mon', home to
Jack Lynch and many more Cork stars previously, and it was
due to the work of Nicky Barry, Gerry Kelly and Dónal O'Grady
that my hurling career progressed to another level. Having been
part of the 1994 victorious Harty Cup team with 'The Mon', this
gave me huge confidence in taking my hurling to the ultimate
level – inter-county. I played two years minor for Cork where
I won an All-Ireland in 1995 under the guidance of the former
Cork great Jimmy Barry-Murphy. Another stepping stone. Next
up was the three years I played for the Cork under-21s where we
landed two All-Irelands in 1997 and 1998. Great achievements
but you soon realise after spending years in Cork that it's about
winning senior All-Ireland medals. My first break came in 1996
when I was called into the Cork senior hurling squad by the then
manager, Jimmy Barry-Murphy after guiding the Cork minors
to All-Ireland glory the year before. A dream was realised when
I made my debut in senior championship hurling for Cork when
I came on as a sub against Limerick that year.*

Now Cork is bet, the hay is saved!
The thousands wildly sing
They speak too soon, my sweet garsun
For here comes Christy Ring!

My dream of playing for Cork started when the 'Liam McCarthy'
was brought to the school in 1990 when Cork beat Galway in that
year's final. I looked up to the 1990 team when growing up and
they were my idols. I followed Cork teams everywhere and looked
forward every year to see them in action. By following my heroes I
started to discover the best in myself and one of the main reasons
for fuelling my new-found ambition of playing for Cork some day.
I couldn't wait every summer to travel to Páirc Uí Chaoimh or the
Mecca of hurling in Semple Stadium Thurles to see Cork in action.
My vivid teenage memories were the ones we spent in the back of
our house, replicating what Tony O'Sullivan, Ger Cunningham,
Kevin Hennessy and Co. did earlier that day at a championship
game, before darkness spoiled our party. Great years and great
memories being an adopted Corkonian. I soon realised after rep-
resenting Cork that it's more than a game of hurling. It's a way of
life and a tradition that dates back decades. And the reason why
every child aspires to play for Cork is two words – Christy Ring. One
can't go anywhere in Cork without Christy Ring being mentioned
and he has laid the path for future players to follow.

Hurling came at a time in my life when my morale was low
after leaving Australia. I was heartbroken leaving Sydney. Hurl-
ing and its demands have developed me from a boy to a man.
Without the game I would definitely have not turned out to be
the rounded, groomed person that I am today. I thank the game
for that. I thank the sport for introducing me to values such as
determination, commitment, honesty, will to win, dedication and
respect – values that I have brought to other aspects of my life.
But most of all I thank the game for the endless friends, players
and people that I have met. Hurling community is unique. Mar
a deireann an seanfhocal – An rud is annamh, is iontach.

In the Pacific Ocean, on a line of east longitude close to the International Date Line and about 12 degrees south of the equator, lies
a Fijian island called Rotuma. It was there that Seán Óg, the eldest
of a family of four boys – Seán Óg, Setanta, Aisake and Teu – and

two girls – Sarote and Etaoin – was born on 22 May 1977. The social structure on the island, under seven chiefs, was tribal.

Seán Óg's mother, Emeli, is Fijian – her ancestors were Polynesian – sea-faring people, warriors of tremendous strength and physical endurance. Emeli was taught at school by two Irish missionary priests, Fr Maguire, now enjoying his eternal reward, and Fr Johnson, both members of the Marist order.

His father, Seán, hailed from Rosslea, in County Fermanagh. In the early 1970s he headed for Scotland in search of work and from there to Australia. While there, he and a few friends decided to take a holiday in Fiji. The receptionist in the hotel where they stayed was Emeli. The rest is a little piece of history.

Seán Óg, who was often, in later years, told by the two priests that they could recognise in him the features of his uncles, was only two when the family moved to Sydney on the east coast of Australia. He remembers getting up with his father at midnight to listen to the All-Ireland final broadcasts. Jimmy Barry-Murphy became a hero – the name appealed to him. Little did he realise how closely their future would be linked. He took to his young heart the Kerry footballers, influenced by the fact that his grandmother, Peggy O'Sullivan, came from Kilgarvan. At the age of eleven, in 1988, he moved with his family to Ireland and settled in Cork city – the north side of the city, close to Na Piarsaigh GAA club and the North Mon.

From his early youth Seán Óg had a passion for sport and joined Na Piarsaigh. As a student at North Mon he excelled at hurling and football. It was not long until he made his mark at county level, winning an All-Ireland minor hurling final in 1995 at centre-half-back and All-Ireland under-21 hurling titles in 1997 and 1998, playing in what was to become his favourite position – left-half-back.

He was in senior ranks in 1996 – a protégé of Jimmy Barry-Murphy's. He remembers well his first day in the dressing room. Looking around, he saw the stars of many a hurling epic and wondered if he should be in their company at all. Then Brian Corcoran came over to him and said 'Welcome to the squad'. 'It made me feel better. I have never forgotten Brian for that. It meant so much to me – it put me at ease.'

For two years Seán Óg played in the full-back-line in front of goalkeeper Ger Cunningham and he likes to recall the support and encouragement he got from Ger.

Success came Seán Óg's way quickly – a National League medal in 1998, followed by All-Ireland titles in 1999, 2004 and 2005. As a dual player Seán Óg lined out at full-back for Cork in the 1999 football championship. The team was successful in Munster but lost to Meath in the All-Ireland final by 1-11 to 1-8. Earlier that year he won a National League medal with a win over Dublin and a Railway Cup medal following victory over Connacht.

The demands of the modern day game on a dual player can be immense, so Seán Óg decided to concentrate on one game and opted for hurling. That career almost came to an abrupt end following a car crash in 2001 that left him with a severed knee. However, he recovered and returned to action on the hurling field.

Seán Óg has collected three All-Star awards. In 2004 there was no doubting the outstanding hurling man of the season. He received the Hurler of the Year award from three sources – Texaco, Vodafone and GPA. He was also named as RTÉ Sports Person of the Year.

His versatility was in evidence in 2004 and 2005 when he was selected to play against Australia in the Compromise Rules football games.

There were joyful celebrations in the Ó hAilpín household in 2004 after Seán Óg, Setanta and Aisake – three giants of 6 feet 2 inches, 6 feet 5 inches and 6 feet 6 inches respectively – had won the Cork county senior hurling title with Na Piarsaigh.

Seán Óg Ó hAilpín (r) being presented with his All-Star award in 2003 by then GAA president, Seán Kelly.

Seán Óg has been a wonderful ambassador for our games. His sportsmanship on the pitch has been impeccable, his commitment total – a truly superb role model for youth.

The man is physically very strong and fiercely committed. He won't be shouldered off his feet. There is tremendous strength in his body and hips – the kind of strength we associate with rugby players from the part of the world where he was born – the strength of the warriors that were his mother's ancestors.

Seán Óg is more than an ambassador for our games. He makes one feel proud as he speaks in our native language – one of three languages spoken in the Ó hAilpín household. I have particularly in mind his speech in Semple Stadium in 2005 after he had captained Cork to a Munster crown – a speech for which he thanks Brother Jack Beausang, his Irish teacher at North Mon.

Our very pleasant meeting drew to a close and we prepared to go our separate ways. *'Go mbeirimid beo ar an am seo arís,' arsa Seán Óg, agus sinn ag fágaint slán le céile. Maith thú a Sheáin.*

A HURLING PERSONALITY:

Ken McGrath (Waterford)

My earliest hurling memories are chasing my father around Mount Sion's pitch – I'd say I was around four or five. My father played for Waterford and Mount Sion for most of the 1970s and 1980s and myself and my older brother Roy would watch him train any chance we could. We only lived down the road from the pitch, so we were always there. And we would be up there nearly every night for the next ten years, especially in the sum- mer months. Mount Sion is a great club with a lot of tradition so it was a great place to learn the game.

To us in the house my father was our hero. He had played for Waterford for years without much success but he was still talked about as a great player in hurling circles. Mount Sion offered more hope and he won seven county medals and a Munster club medal.

We all started off playing for Mount Sion – myself and my three brothers, Roy, Eoin and Pat. At underage we always had a good team and we won county medals at all ages. I was playing well enough and I was asked up to the senior Waterford team the day after an under-21 county final in November 1995. I had a few pints after the county final so my preparation wasn't great for my big break but I was only seventeen. I didn't get a start but my full debut was in February 1996 against Offaly. I was marking Brian Whelehan so it was a tough introduction.

With Waterford our first real breakthrough came in 1998 under Gerald McCarthy. We reached the first of our semi-finals which for the next ten years would cause unreal heartbreak for myself and Waterford. Kilkenny beat us by a point in a poor game. We didn't play great but the buzz in Waterford hurling was back and we felt we were going in the right direction. It wasn't until 2002 that we really won something. Under Justin McCarthy our hurling improved immensely and we reached a Munster final against Tipperary who were raging favourites. It was a great match. We hurled with great confidence and beat Tipp by eight points to win our first Munster title in thirty-nine years. I scored seven points from play and got Man of the Match. The county went crazy. But we deserved to celebrate – we were down for so long it was great to be up with the big boys of hurling. Clare beat us by a goal in the [All-Ireland] semi-final – a game we started great in, but faded badly – another heartbreaking defeat.

The Munster final of 2004 was the greatest match I had ever played in. We have had some brilliant battles with Cork over the last ten years but that game had everything. With a man down we hung on and beat them by a point. The crowd invaded the pitch. Everyone knew it was special to beat a Cork team in Thurles. I was captain so it was extra special and with Eoin also playing a major part in the win, it was a special day for the family.

Under Justin, we had some great days – three Munster titles, a National League, things we never dreamed of twenty years ago. But as a group we wanted more, so the five All-Ireland semi-final defeats were very hard to take, with probably the 2007 loss to Limerick the hardest. They fully deserved it but we were sick for months after that one. But to come back in '08, and beat Tipp.

with Davy Fitz as our manager took a lot of courage. When the final whistle went that day the feeling was unreal. The county went mad. But three weeks later our dream was crushed – won't go into that day but it is the hardest sporting thing we ever had to get over. But we will, and we will bounce back stronger than ever, both as a team and personally. 2009 brings fresh hope and the feeling is we can achieve something under Davy.

Finally, one of my fondest memories is when the four brothers – myself, Roy, Eoin and Pat – played together in a winning county final team against Ballygunner in 2006. It was a special thing to play with all the lads on the one team and hopefully we will do it again soon.

Hurling flows in Ken McGrath's blood. His father excelled for club and county. He was chosen on the Munster Railway Cup teams and won medals in 1976 and 1978. He was in good company. The Munster half-back line of 1978 read:

Ger Loughnane	*Pat Hartigan*	*Pat McGrath*
(Clare)	(Limerick)	(Waterford)

Ken was born on 20 February 1978 and grew up in the hurling atmosphere of his home and club Mount Sion. He made his county senior championship debut against Tipperary in 1996. In fact, he played in all three grades for Waterford that year – senior, under-21 and minor.

In his years wearing the Waterford jersey, Ken has known success and heartbreak. A National League, two Railway Cup wins, three Munster titles and three All-Star awards add up to a level of achievements that many Waterford hurlers of former days could only dream of. And add to that six county titles and a Munster club title.

Over a period of ten years, an All-Ireland title – in teams of All-Ireland potential – has proved to be elusive. Ken has known that crushing and disconsolate feeling that accompanies defeat. Five All-Ireland semi-finals have been lost:

1998 v Kilkenny, 1-11 to 1-10
2002 v Clare, 1-16 to 1-13
2004 v Kilkenny, 3-12 to 0-18
2006 v Cork, 1-16 to 1-15
2007 v Limerick, 5-11 to 2-15

While many would have seen the capital displays of Waterford in 2004 and 2006 deserving of victory, Ken himself, strangely enough, found the losses of 2002 and 2007 more galling.

As I awaited my meeting with Ken, I reflected on the many great names his club Mount Sion has given to hurling – among them Andy Fleming, who played many times for Munster in the 1940s and won an All-Ireland in 1948; Phil Grimes, who captained the 1957 team to a Munster title and whom I saw give a majestic display at centre-half-back in the final of 1959 against Cork in Thurles; Séamus Power, who scored the equalising goal in the dying moments against Kilkenny in the All-Ireland final of 1959; Frankie Walsh, who at wing-forward captained Waterford to All-Ireland victory in the replay against Kilkenny in 1959; Tony Browne, a present-day teammate of Ken's and one of the outstanding wing-backs of the game; and finally that most versatile of hurlers, John Keane, a master of the game in the loftiest of company.

Ken McGrath.

The Munster half-back line of 1942 read:

Johnny Ryan	*John Keane*	*Peter Cregan*
(Tipperary)	(Waterford)	(Limerick)

The Munster full-back line of 1947 read:

Willie Murphy	*John Keane*	*Peter Cregan*
(Cork)	(Waterford)	(Limerick)

Waterford's half-forward line in the All-Ireland final of 1948 read:

Kevin O'Connor	*John Keane*	*Christy Moylan*

The Munster half-forward line of 1949 read:

Christy Ring	*John Keane*	*Seán Herbert*
(Cork)	(Waterford)	(Limerick)

Ken has followed in the masters' footsteps. He too is a most versatile performer. Apart from goal, he has played in every line on the field – always excelling but particularly so in the positions where John Keane shone – full-back, centre-half-forward and centre-half-back.

Watching Ken in full flow, at centre-half-back, playing the hurling of a free spirit, is a sheer delight. He has a great pair of hands, excellent under the dropping ball, so often an inspirational figure. Little wonder that that great Tipperary hurler Nicky English once described Ken as 'my favourite all-round player'.

Tá clú agus cáil bainte amach ag Ken le linn a ré agus beidh cuimhne air le fada an lá. Ba dheacair a shárú a fháil. Tá sé mar eisiompláir dúinn go léir mar fear spóirt speisialta. Go mairidh tú céad, a Ken.

A HURLING PERSONALITY:

Henry Shefflin (Kilkenny)

My earliest memory of hurling would be of myself and my younger brother Paul getting two squash rackets and a tennis ball and heading out to the squash court behind my father's public house in Ballyhale. There we would play a hurling match between us until one of us started crying and went running in to my mother. (I must say this was normally Paul!) This is where I learned so much, as we just practised and practised playing hurling in that court. I must say that it was brilliant to learn the skills of our game. Nothing only four big walls and me. These are memories I will always have.

In those early days I was in the heartland of hurling. My club Ballyhale Shamrocks was contesting county titles each year and were the most successful club around at that time. I, as mentioned, was living in the family pub in Main Street, Ballyhale. Everything that went on went on here and it was hurling 24/7. This is where I developed the love for the game.

From the mad world of the pub I moved up the 100 yards to my local national school. This is where I came across Joe Dunphy, who developed so many hurlers for Ballyhale and Kilkenny. This to me is what hurling/sport is all about – people giving of their free time to teach young players. I am grateful to Joe Dunphy.

From there to the other heartland of hurling in Kilkenny – St Kieran's College. Both my older brothers had gone there so I kept up the tradition. I must add that I suffered a bit here as I was not up to the standard of a lot of the other kids and was well down the pecking order in hurling teams. But it did teach me to work hard and by the time I had left Kieran's, I felt I had done this – with an All-Ireland Colleges medal to boot.

Staying close to home was a big thing for me, hence my choice of WIT [Waterford Institute of Technology] as my college. A lot older, and now realising the effort that must be put in to achieve, I think WIT helped me with this. I found out here the harder you train the better you get. As can be seen from my school days, there is not much mention of schooling but I did end up with a degree from WIT!

I have been very lucky to come (a) from a club like Ballyhale and (b) from a county like Kilkenny. Yes, I have had success to date but what I take more pleasure out of is the friends and enjoyment I have got out of all those years. People often ask me: 'What was your best achievement?' Winning my first club county final, 2006. Full stop.

I would like to say special words of thanks to all who have helped me in the numerous ways over the years in my hurling endeavours. Special word to Joe Dunphy, Brian Cody (greatest manager ever), the Shefflin family and my wife Deirdre O'Sullivan and her family. There are a lot more people but too many to name.

I write this piece on Wednesday 11 February 2009 at 5 p.m. We as a country are in the middle of a major recession. Ireland beat France in a rugby game in Croke Park last Saturday evening and I noticed, Monday, everybody in good form talking about the excellent match that had taken place.

That has told me everything I need to know – above all else, sport is about enjoyment for you, me and all. It is a great honour for me to be part of that enjoyment.

The name Shefflin intrigued me. I had never come across it in GAA lore or, indeed, anywhere else for that matter. I wondered if it was of Norman origin, given Kilkenny's strong Norman links. I probed and discovered that Henry's great grandfather emigrated from Carrickmacross, County Monaghan towards the end of the nineteenth century. He left Ireland as Shevlin. He returned as Shefflin.

Henry is one of a family of seven, four boys and three girls, born to Henry and May (née Fitzgerald) on 11 January 1979. Henry senior spent a few years in England and played with Warwickshire in the All-Ireland junior hurling final of 1965 against Roscommon at Dr Hyde Park. They lost by two points, 3-10 to 2-11. On the Roscommon team was Gerry O'Malley of football fame. The Warwickshire team was trained by Paddy Phelan, a Kilkenny man, one of the great wing-backs of hurling, who excelled for Kilkenny in the 1930s. Henry was home to stay in 1965. He played with the local club – no honours came his way. However, his brother Denis captained Ballyhale Shamrocks to their first county title in 1978.

On the Fitzgerald side (definitely Norman) Henry's uncle, the late Monsignor Paul, played minor for Kilkenny, while a cousin, also Paul, played at senior level and also played for Leinster in the Railway Cup. So there was hurling in the blood. Henry's three brothers, John, Tommy and Paul all wore the county jersey at under-21 level. Tommy won an under-21 All-Ireland medal in 1990 and John won a minor title the same year.

Talent and artistry are manifested in a variety of ways. In the case of Henry Shefflin this was done through the medium of hurling. He has proved to be one of the great exponents of the game and when he retires his name will reside in the company of the all-time greats.

If Henry had been born at a time that saw him make his debut with Kilkenny in 1914, he would have just missed the golden era that brought Kilkenny seven All-Ireland crowns in the space of ten years and he would, during a career lasting fifteen years, have won one All-Ireland (1922), five Leinster titles and more than likely the first Railway Cup in 1927. But of course things did not happen that way. Henry made his county senior debut in 1999 just as the door opened on another golden era that has rivalled, and may yet surpass, that of the early days of the twentieth century.

Henry has played a major role in the glorious days that began following a one-point defeat by Cork, 0-13 to 0-12, in the All-Ireland final of 1999. Throughout his career he has been a prolific scorer, a consistently high performer, an inspirational colleague. Just picture him on the pitch – tall, slim and athletic, 6 feet 2 inches and just under 14 stone; full of speed, stamina, and skill; possessed of a huge work rate and driven by a never-say-die spirit.

Nicky English said he 'adds perspiration to inspiration and raises the team's tempo', while Brian Cody has described him as 'the best I've seen'. Kevin Cashman, who only uses words of praise when they are well earned and hard won, chose the word 'supernal' to describe Henry Shefflin.

Henry has won every honour in the game, beginning with the All-Ireland Colleges title with St Kieran's in 1996. The same year, and again the following year, he won Leinster minor medals. At WIT he won a Fitzgibbon Cup title in 1998/99 and followed on with an under-21 All-Ireland victory. His first of six senior All-Ireland successes came in 2000 and in the same year his first of eight All-Star awards and nine provincial titles. In 2002 he collected his first of four National League medals.

He was nominated Hurler of the Year in 2002 and again in 2006. The first of three successive county titles with his club Ballyhale Shamrocks was won in 2006 and that first win led to an All-Ireland club victory over Loughrea in 2007. The ultimate personal accolade came in September of that year when he captained Kilkenny to All-Ireland victory over Limerick.

During his playing days to date, Henry has reaped harvest after harvest – each high in yield and rich in quality. Henry knows he has been fortunate and privileged to have come on the hurling scene at a time when his club and county reigned supreme.

So, with all those trophies, medals and awards to his name, was there ever a disappointing moment? 'Yes there was. It was the 2005 county final against James Stephens. I played very poorly. I missed chances. We lost. I got a lot of the blame. It hurt a lot, especially as part of the club. I had never won a county final – I began to feel can we ever win one. I felt bad.'

Homer had nodded. But not for long. Henry was back with a vengeance in 2006 to play a great championship and score ten points against O'Loughlin Gaels in the county final.

Henry Shefflin.

A hurling selection (Kilkenny only)

This all-Kilkenny selection is a tribute to the performances of its hurlers and the remarkable success rate of the county in both the League and championship.

James McGarry
(Bennetsbridge)

Michael Kavanagh   *Noel Hickey*   *Jackie Tyrrell*
(St Lachtain's)   (Dunnamaggin)   (James Stephens)

Tommy Walsh   *Peter Barry*   *J. J. Delaney*
(Tullaroan)   (James Stephens)   (Fenians)

Derek Lyng   *James 'Cha' Fitzpatrick*
(Emeralds)   (Ballyhale Shamrocks)

Owen Larkin   *Henry Shefflin*   *D. J. Carey*
(James Stephens) (Ballyhale Shamrocks) (Young Irelands)

Eddie Brennan   *Martin Comerford*   *Charlie Carter*
(Graig Ballycallan)   (O'Loughlin Gaels)   (Young Irelands)

A hurling selection (excluding Kilkenny)

And now for a selection excluding Kilkenny ...

Brendan Cummins
(Tipperary)

Darragh Ryan *Diarmuid O'Sullivan* *Frank Lohan*
(Wexford)   (Cork)   (Clare)

Tony Browne   *Ken McGrath*   *Seán Óg Ó hAilpín*
(Waterford)   (Waterford)   (Cork)

Colin Lynch   *Michael Walsh*
(Clare)   (Waterford)

Ben O'Connor   *Ollie Moran*   *John Mullane*
(Cork)   (Limerick)   (Waterford)

Eoin Kelly   *Joe Canning*   *Eoin Kelly*
(Tipperary)   (Galway)   (Waterford)

CAMOGIE PERSONALITIES:

Mary and Úna Leacy (Wexford)

I first saw Mary and Úna, then aged ten and eight respectively, swinging ash when I visited their mother Margaret of camogie fame in the spring of 1996. Little did I realise then that I was looking at two stars of the future.

Both, no doubt, have been greatly influenced by their mother's passion for the game – a passion that goes back to her childhood. That, coupled with dedication, commitment, fervour and enthusiasm, made Margaret one of the great centre-half-backs of camogie. She has honours galore to her name – three All-Ireland crowns (1968, 1969 and 1975), six All-Ireland club titles, eight county successes and inter-provincial honours on six occasions. Even to the present day Margaret continues to coach, develop, guide and inspire the underage players entrusted to her.

During my years in Kerry, I knew an elderly lady who, when she saw football talent breaking out in the young generation, would say: 'It's the *dúchas*, it's the *dúchas ag briseadh amach*.' So where Mary and Úna are concerned it's the *dúchas*. *Ba dúchas díobh bheith 'na camógaidhe.*

Úna plays in the forwards. Mary follows in her mother's footsteps and lines out at centre-half-back. She is also a fine footballer and was on the Wexford intermediate team beaten by Leitrim in the All-Ireland final of 2007.

All-Ireland camogie honours came to Mary and Úna when Cork were defeated in the final of 2007, two first half goals by Úna paving the way to victory. Celebrations were widespread, both at home and further afield. The Ballycastle club in north Antrim invited mother and daughters to a social where all three were honoured and feted. A man from Armagh phoned to offer his congratulations. The medals were presented in January 2008 at a special occasion in Enniscorthy. In attendance was Brian Cody, who in the course of the evening spoke to a captive audience.

The 2007 camogie victory, Wexford's fourth, gave us for the first time in the world of Gaelic games a household in which mother and daughters were winners of senior All-Ireland medals.

We already have, from Kilkenny, father and daughters – Shem Downey (1947) and twins Angela and Ann, with eleven titles each.

In Cork we have a household with brother and sister. I refer of course to Mary O'Leary (four titles) and Seánie (four titles). Interestingly, in 1978, both Mary and Seánie won All-Ireland honours. That too is unique.

We also have households where husband and wife have All-Ireland medals – Brian Cody of Kilkenny and his Wexford-born wife, Elsie Walsh. Also, Jimmy Cooney of Tipperary and his wife, Angela Egan from Dublin.

There are, of course, households of brothers in both hurling and football, too numerous to mention.

The 2007 All-Ireland Wexford team lined out as:

Margaret D'Arcy

Noeleen Lambert   *Catherine O'Loughlin*   *Avis Nolan*

Aine Codd   *Mary Leacy*   *Deirdre Codd*

Caroline Murphy   *Brona Furlong*

Michelle O'Leary   *Rosemary Breen*   *Kate Kelly*

Ursula Jacob   *Michelle Hearn*   *Una Leacy*

a, Margaret and Mary Leacy.

What follows from Mary and Úna is, in each case, in the words of an t-Athair Peadar Ó Laoghaire, 'Mo Scéal Féin'.

Mary:
One of my earliest memories of playing camogie is at my home place in Oulart, spending hours upon hours trying to roll-lift the ball and every time I thought I successfully had managed it, I used to run in to my house and drag Mam and Dad out to see me do it. My Mam has been a major influence on my camogie career since I first started to play. I could honestly say she has been at 99 per cent of my matches.

When I was younger, me and my sister Úna would be up at the hurling pitch with Mam while she trained, or trained the underage – always of course with a hurley in our hands. In primary school, Breda Flood was a major influence. She had us outside at lunch with a hurley in our hands and also introduced us to indoor hurling. The fun we had, girls playing against the boys!

Ann Kirwan, the late Dave Sinnott, Aidan Moran, Pat Ryan and my mother were over us in underage and have influenced me greatly, each with their own unique approach and input. My first memory of playing competitive camogie was an under-10 camogie tournament in Oulart, which was organised by Mam and Ann. We ended up in the final against Blackwater. We did win that match, but I especially remember this final as I fractured my finger in two places in the first half (my first real injury due to camogie), but because I was so determined to win my first trophy, I continued on. Another key memory was our first Rackard League final 1996 – very exciting, my first time playing in Wexford Park. Also it was our first big win over our rivals, Rathnure.

In 1997, as well as playing and winning the under-12 camogie championship, I also played with the under-12 Oulart boys. At first playing with the boys was a bit awkward, but Mick Jacob, the manager at the time, settled me into the team and by the time we got to the Premiership final I was part of the gang. This final really sticks out in my memory. We were losing by two points with one minute left. The referee blew for a free to us but, for whatever reason, Bunclody, the team we were playing, thought it was the final whistle and invaded the pitch and were celebrating. After five minutes the referee finally cleared the pitch and we got the free that was awarded to us. From this free, the ball somehow ended up in the net, so this left us leading by a point. In the end we won by a point, one of the most exciting endings to a match I have been involved in.

Féile na nGael 1998 – the first of five Féiles our club won, was also one of the most exciting matches I have played in – the lead changed hands on several occasions. We looked to be in big trouble early in the second half when we fell in arrears by six points. But due to heart and determination we never gave up and eventually won by a point. There were joyous scenes when Caroline our captain lifted the cup, and major celebrations followed. The weekend itself was brilliant, hosting other clubs; Féile na nGael was truly a marvellous experience.

The 1999 Féile was very special to me as I was captain. I remember the morning of the final. I was at Mass in Oulart and Fr Jordan was wishing us all the best and said from the altar: 'If Mary is able to hold number eleven from Milford scoreless we will win.' Talk about pressure! We won by 2-3 to 0-0.

That year – 1999 – was a very special year for camogie as it was the first year of fifteen-a-side, which I think has contributed enormously to camogie. In 2000 at the age of fourteen I made my senior county debut at wing-back. This was against Dublin in the first round of the All-Ireland championship. I was so thrilled. It's funny – of all the matches I have played, I still remember this one like yesterday. I remember Dan Quigley, our manager at the time, telling me not to let any of the Dublin players bully me on the pitch, as they would know I was only a young one.

I was very lucky to be part of the Coláiste Bríde junior (2001) and senior (2003 and 2004) All-Ireland-winning teams. These school years, because of camogie, were unbelievable. The team atmosphere and the friendships formed will be remembered for many years – thanks Mrs Moriarty, Mr Guinan, Martin Storey and Fran Fitzhenry for those years. They'll never be forgotten.

2002 was an unbelievable year – our first senior club title. We had been knocking on the door for about five or six years, losing county final after county final by the narrowest scorelines. I remember in the dressing room before we went out, Fiona Dunne got us all to hold hands and to look each other in the eyes – we promised each other we were going to give it everything and this is what we did. This was one of the joyous occasions of winning at club level. After winning the first one we completed five in a row and hopefully some day we will get a chance to win the All-Ireland club title.

2007, what a year – the most memorable camogie experience of my life. Being captain of the Wexford camogie team on All-Ireland day was a huge honour and a very special memory. When the final whistle went the feeling was unbelievable. Every camogie player's dream is to play in Croke Park and win an All-Ireland – to see the sea of purple and gold across Croke Park is a vision I'll never forget. And lifting the O'Duffy Cup was the most exciting feeling ever. It meant so much – words can't describe how much.

The homecoming to Wexford was brilliant. We didn't expect so many people to turn out – that's why it was so special to me and all the girls. I think one thing evident from this panel of girls was that we were not just team players – we were all friends. I think the friendships formed during 2007 significantly contributed to our success.

Another fond memory of the All-Ireland day was seeing my granny – Margaret O'Leary – with the biggest Wexford hat on her, standing close to where I was lifting the O'Duffy Cup. At the age of eighty-seven this was no mean achievement.

Just to conclude, I would like to sincerely thank all my trainers, managers and selectors over the years and hopefully I will continue to play for many more years. A special thanks to my Dad and Mam and family, who have supported me throughout my life so far.

Úna:

My first camogie memories would be as a kid going to Josie's pitch in Oulart with my Mam, the biggest influence on my camogie . career. There, Mam trained the underage or trained herself with the adult teams. There were plenty of evenings of the week that hours were spent on the pitch.

At school, there was a skills competition I will never forget, where the boys and girls competed against each other. I remember one particular year I really wanted to win, so I practised so much I had to win. I had my roll-lifts and frees over the bar down to a tee.

Breda Flood, our principal at the time, was very influential. She had us entered in any camogie competition there was. Also she gave us cereal before any match we played.

Mam was a selector with the county camogie team in the early 1990s. I remember, being at a very young age, going to county training with her, particularly one day in Wexford Park – myself and Mary were behind the goal when I got a smack of a ball in the eye.

Underage was always very special in the club. My Mam, Ann Kirwan, Aidan Moran, the late Dave Sinnott and Pat Ryan were involved for years coaching us the best they could. It was all their hard work and effort that made Oulart the Ballagh the club it is today. The club won numerous underage titles before the most prolific success – the five Féile na nGael successes in a row. I will never forget the Féile. It was the most fun-filled weekend of any camogie girl's career. Our first two years of success was had in County Wexford in 1998 and 1999 where we hosted a club from Galway (Clarinbridge) and a club from Tipperary (Templemore). It was lovely to win it while it was being held in Wexford and especially with the victories, in both finals, being very marginal.

In 2001 we won our fourth Féile – particularly special for Oulart the Ballagh, as we won the top grade in both camogie and hurling and the celebrations definitely went on for weeks.

2002 was my last year under-14 – Féile was held in the North of

Ireland for the second time. We stayed in Dungiven, County Derry, where we had a brilliant experience. We made great friendships and had a fun-packed weekend, with the focus still on winning. I will never forget the final that year in Casement Park. It was such a special and honourable moment for me as it was my fifth title won and I was captain of this great team.

The schools I attended were hugely part of the camogie tradition. Coláiste Bríde, under the influence of Elva Moriarty, Jimmy Guinan, Martin Storey and Fran Fritzhenry, where we enjoyed many All-Ireland junior and senior successes. The craic with this team was mighty and the friendships still remain to this present day.

Another key memory was making my senior club debut in which we lost a county final to St Ibar's – played up in Ferns in 2000. Fiona Dunne, one of the best camogie players in Oulart, broke her ankle and I was the player to replace her.

Senior success eventually came to the club in 2002. We had been knocking on the door for years before we made the breakthrough – very special year for the club, particularly winning the fifth Féile na nGael and then our first senior county title. Our first senior win will never be forgotten, with Butch O'Connor, Mick Redmond and Pat Ryan, who got us on the road to senior success. Martin Storey also helped in training the team that year, giving motivating speeches. Martin has been very influential over the years with training in Coláiste Bríde and eventually he became manager of Oulart the Ballagh alongside two other sporting legends in the club – Martin Dempsey and Seán Dunne.

Over the years I have played camogie with so many different teams, ranging from under-12 hurling with the boys in Oulart to Coláiste Bríde, UCD, Leinster inter-provincials and with the county teams.

Playing camogie is an important part of my life. From the day I could walk I could imagine my mother placing a hurl in my hand. My older sister Ramona had twin girls, Rachel and Catherine, who are two years old and what would you think Mam gave them for Christmas – two little hurleys. They have no getting away from it – give them another year or two and she will have them at the pitch training.

The most memorable camogie experience was definitely in 2007 when we won the senior All-Ireland, beating Cork in the final. To play an All-Ireland final in Croke Park really was a dream come true and for me to score two goals was the best feeling in the world. When the final whistle eventually came, all I can remember is jumping around with Aoife O'Connor as people knocked us to the ground with such happiness. The crowd got out to us so quick – there was no holding back by the stewards. Ciara Storey in particular must have been out before the final whistle because she was hugging me within seconds of the whistle.

We will never forget my granny, Margaret O'Leary. She was with us everywhere we went, as proud as punch. I remember the homecoming. We stopped in every town en route to Wexford with granny being there each step of the way. We reached the Ferrycarrig Hotel about midnight and who was there only my wonderful granny.

Throughout my camogie career I have made so many good friends in Coláiste Bríde, UCD, the county teams and – most importantly – my brilliant club team. I am sure these friendships will last for ever.

Every match that I have played, once I get home, I get the match analysis of my Dad and Mam. If we lose, we are told what we did wrong – also if we win, we are told what we could do better. Thanks Daddy and Mammy.

My main aim will be to be like my mother and to play for as long as I am able and to hopefully, at some point, win a club All-Ireland with Oulart the Ballagh – the only title we have yet to achieve.

Five Féile captains: (l-r) Emma Moran, 2001; Mary Leacy, 1999; Úna Leacy, 2002; Caroline Murphy, 1998; Claire Sinnott 2000.

A FOOTBALL GAME:

Dublin v Mayo, 2006 All-Ireland semi-final

In an age when many are questioning the evolving nature of the game of Gaelic football and its entertainment value as a spectacle, it was a sheer joy – a redemption of the code – to witness the quality of the fare served up by the footballers of Mayo and Dublin in the All-Ireland semi-final at Croke Park on Sunday 3 September 2006.

The general feeling was that this was going to be a David-and-Goliath affair – red-hot favourites, unbackable Dublin, against unfancied Mayo.

Mayo in their red and green jerseys, and under the managership of Mickey Moran, were first to take the field. They immediately lay down a marker by occupying the railway goal end of the pitch for their pre-match kickabout – territory sacred to the hordes of Dublin supporters on Hill 16 behind the goal – territory, by custom, the preserve of the Dublin team where a rapturous reception always awaited them as heroes in the sky-blue jerseys.

Dublin emerged and headed for Hill 16. The railway goal was now like an artillery range with footballs flying in all directions. Well, it had to happen! Mary McNicholas, dietician to the Mayo team, was felled – out cold and taken away on a stretcher. As a further prologue to the swelling act of the impending contest, mentors from either side indulged in 'shouldering'. Happily, Mary was back for the start of the game.

> *Eventually, without any fatalities, the train hurtles out of the station and we are all left hanging on by our fingertips. We have no idea at the start of this journey that we will end up drained, stunned, and enriched. And with a blue dream dashed.*
>
> Liam Horan – *Irish Examiner*

From throw-in to final whistle the attendance of 82,148 was treated to fast and flowing, non-stop action, drama heaped on drama, delightful passing by hand and foot.

We witnessed sweeping movements up and down the pitch. We saw high fielding and catch-and-kick as in bygone days – the fare to thrill the hearts of old timers. There were wides that ought to have been points, points that might have been goals, scores that seemed to defy the laws of physics.

After four minutes Conor Mortimer pointed for Mayo. It took seventeen minutes for Dublin to open their scoring with a Conal Keaney point. In between Dublin had many misses. Mortimer had a magnificent Mayo point from a most difficult sideline ball. Alan Dillon had two points, the second a fisted overhead effort that might well have finished up in the net as Stephen Cluxton in the Dublin goal advanced. Mayo 0-4 Dublin 0-1.

A move by Dublin saw Alan Brogan's shot saved by David Clarke in the Mayo goal but the rebound was netted by Conal Keaney and Dublin were on level terms, 0-5 to 1-2. Almost immediately we were treated to a delightful solo run, all of sixty yards or more, by Shane Ryan of Dublin – a move Ray Cosgrove finished with a point.

On the half hour Jason Sherlock was most unlucky when his shot at an empty goal hit the underside of the crossbar. The ball was cleared and at the other end of the field Conor Mortimer, with an open goal, saw his shot sail over the bar. It was frenetic stuff as the ball was back at the Mayo end and an Alan Brogan goalbound shot was blocked for a 45 by the head of the diving Aidan Higgins.

Kevin O'Neill was barely a minute on the pitch when he sent over the equaliser for Mayo. Mortimer added a point. Half time score: Mayo 0-9 Dublin 1-5.

The first twelve minutes of the second half belonged to Dublin. A move involving several players led to Jason Sherlock punching the ball groundwards and into the net. They outscored Mayo by six points to one and incredibly after twelve minutes of the second half the scoreboard read Dublin 2-11 Mayo 0-10.

Mayo had gone from a first half lead of four points to being seven points down – a swing of eleven points. It looked like the end of the road. *Ach ní mar síltear bítear.*

The next twenty minutes were full of drama as Mayo clawed their way back. It started with a Ger Brady point and then Alan Dillon added his third of the day. Andy Moran was five minutes on the field when he collected a pass from Kevin O'Neill. It was like threading a needle as he edged the ball past defenders and in by the left-hand post. Mayo supporters went wild – red and green everywhere. Kevin O'Neill added a point and Alan Dillon sent over the equaliser. Mayo 1-14 Dublin 2-11. About fifteen minutes to go.

A free from an acute angle and we were treated to a Mortimer special – Mayo ahead. Shane Ryan, one of the stars of the day, departed the scene having played a superb game for Dublin. Ten minutes to go to injury time. With sixty-five minutes on the clock Mark Vaughan replaced Mossy Quinn and almost immediately Alan Brogan equalised: 1-15 to 2-12. No one had left Croke Park.

A free to Dublin. Up stepped Mark Vaughan. It looked good ... but hit the upright. Mayo were away from the rebound. A sweeping movement reached Ciarán McDonald positioned to the left of the goal not far from the sideline and close to the end line. He let fly with the left foot and gave the leather a curving path that sent over an impossible point. Time running out. Mayo 1-16 Dublin 2-12.

Back came Dublin. They won a 45, close to the sideline. Up stepped Mark Vaughan. A beauty – travelling straight on course – looked like dropping behind the black mark on the mid point of the crossbar. Up shot the hand of six-foot-plus David Clarke in the Mayo goal. He punched clear.

We were now in injury time. Jason Sherlock won a free. Dublin's fate – indeed Mayo's too – was now in the lap of the gods and the boot of Mark Vaughan. A kick that looked good drifted wide. Mark looked up at the sky and seemed to curse the gods. Soon it was all over.

Liam Horan, writing in the *Irish Examiner* the following day, captured the atmosphere of the occasion:

> *It was football in black-and-white, as our fathers knew it, and their fathers before them ... This was THE game. Like nothing you ever saw. It was as raw as a faction fight, and yet teeming with moments of sublime beauty.*

It was all that.

FOOTBALL PERSONALITIES:

Brian Dooher and Seán Cavanagh (Tyrone)

Ever since my national school days when we had a teacher called Samuel McElholm from Omagh, I have always had a soft spot for Tyrone.

I saw them defeat Derry by two points in the Ulster final of 1957 – a tense, dour, dogged affair. And if memory serves me right Jim Devlin was at full-back and his brother Eddie, a former All-Ireland minor medal winner, at centre-half-back. Legendary name on the Derry side was Jim McKeever, star midfielder and Railway Cup medal winner with Ulster.

So it was against that background that I found myself following the fortunes of the Tyrone senior footballers in recent years.

They have been immensely successful, winning the All-Ireland in 2003 v Armagh, 0-12 to 0-9; 2005 v Kerry, 1-16 to 2-10; 2008 v Kerry, 1-15 to 0-14.

Two All-Ireland final victories over the Kingdom and for good measure they also beat them in the semi-final of 2003 – 0-13 to 0-6; surely, a record sufficient for any team to merit the seal of greatness.

On a team that functioned as a well-oiled outfit, two players in particular caught my eye – Brian Dooher in the number 10 jersey at wing-forward, and Seán Cavanagh, primarily a midfielder but converted to a full-forward in the course of the 2008 All-Ireland championship. Brian and Seán were two of several players on the Tyrone team with two All-Ireland medals when they faced Kerry, the firm favourites, in the final of 2008.

Brian Dooher:

Brian, as captain, collected the Sam Maguire Cup for the second time in 2008. At thirty-three the Clann na nGael clubman has still a lot of football left in him. Weighing 12 stone 7 pounds and standing 5 feet 10 inches, his athletic frame is driven by a super engine. The man covers acres of ground, displaying in the process a seeming endless supply of energy. He moves upwards through the gears at lightning pace, advancing from defence (he drops back as necessary) to make penetrating runs upfield and goalwards. And none more impressive than his sally in the twenty-fourth minute of the 2008

All-Ireland final. Tyrone were one point behind. Having gained possession, Brian took off down the Cusack Stand sideline, avoiding a series of tackles designed to dispossess or send him over the sideline. His determination and speed heralded his intent. The move ended with a brilliant point executed from an acute angle to the right of the railway goal. It brought Tyrone level at six points each. It lifted his colleagues. A quality score that will be talked about for many a day in Tyrone.

Brian is a player of grim resolve – indefatigable, unsparing in effort, unquenchable in spirit. He has been a great captain – a team player if ever there was one. He always leads by example, whether in the gym, at training or on the field of play. His major successes to date include Ulster titles, three All-Ireland titles, three All-Stars and two National Leagues.

Seán Cavanagh:

Seán was only nineteen when he made his senior debut against Armagh in 2002. Since then, the Moy clubman has developed into one of the most accomplished footballers of the present day.

In his student days he won a McRory Cup title with St Patrick's College, Armagh, and when the final whistle blew on All-Ireland final day 2008 Seán's major successes included three All-Ireland titles, two National Leagues, two Ulster crowns and three All-Stars. The 2008 All-Star selection brought this figure to four, and on the night of the All-Star celebrations Seán received the Footballer of the Year award.

Seán's early career was at midfield. Standing 6 feet 2 inches and weighing 14 stone, he is always comfortable in possession – a skill acquired from his basketball game.

When the 2008 football championship began, Seán was at midfield for the drawn game against Down and also for the replay, which Tyrone lost. It was then that trainer Mickey Harte decided that he needed to strengthen the forward line and inject into it more power and thrust. To this end he selected Seán at full-forward for the remaining games, with liberty to roam. The move was an instant success; Seán's presence brought strength, mobility and skill to the Tyrone forward line.

By the time Tyrone reached the final, Seán was the team's leading scorer. And when not scoring himself he was making openings for colleagues. His accuracy is the product of painstaking practice

– practice that involves switching the angle of shooting until sending the ball between the posts becomes second nature.

Seán loves his football. It forms a major part of his life. As he left the pitch, following an injury in the game against Wexford, those of us watching on television saw Seán shed some tears at the thought of possibly missing the All-Ireland final.

Seán has been outstanding both as midfielder and full-forward. Interesting to note, therefore, that his two heroes of earlier years were master midfielder from Derry, Anthony Tohill and ingenious full-forward from Tyrone, Peter Canavan.

Seán's all-round footballing skills saw him chosen to play for Ireland in the International Rules in 2005, and in 2008 he was nominated to captain the Ireland team in the contests held in Australia.

His talents were spotted by those from 'down under' who seek quality players for the Australian game. Twice (2005 and 2008) he turned down attractive contract offers from Australian Football League (AFL) clubs to go and play there.

In the seven games that led to Tyrone qualifying for the All-Ireland final of 2008 the team's average score was: for 1-15; against 1-11. Incredibly, a near accurate forecast of what transpired against Kerry in an absorbing contest on final day: For 1-15; Against 0-14.

No doubt, many more glory days lie ahead for Seán.

A football selection

Pascal McConnell
(Tyrone)

Marc Ó Sé	Francie Bellew	Anthony Lynch
(Kerry)	(Armagh)	(Cork)

Tomás Ó Sé	Kieran McGeeney	Graham Canty
(Kerry)	(Armagh)	(Cork)

Darragh Ó Sé   Seán Cavanagh
(Kerry)   (Tyrone)

Stephen McDonnell	Ciarán McDonald	Brian Dooher
(Armagh)	(Mayo)	(Tyrone)

Peter Canavan	Kieran Donaghy	Colm Cooper
(Tyrone)	(Kerry)	(Kerry)

LADIES' FOOTBALL PERSONALITY:

Maeve Quinn (Leitrim)

My first memory of football was playing under-12 Boys' football with Drumreilly (Aughawillan/Drumreilly – an amalgamation) and cycling to training beside Garadice Lake, a place called Kelly's Angle, and togging out behind the bushes.

What pocket money I got was spent buying plastic footballs to practise hitting that spot on the wall. I played various underage Boys' county finals with Drumreilly but the only one we won was an under-16 title – my last year – and one I really relish.

Football is considered 'a religion' in Aughawillan and although some may have survived without it, very few have not had the call! I have been lucky to be part of a club and a community which has great pride in itself at what it can achieve, by pulling together and working hard together.

Our Ladies' club has seen great days and the work being done at underage continues to provide stars of the future. In 1997 we were the first winners of the Connacht junior club title, and it took a replay in December to decide the All-Ireland champions (oh! the joy of training with frost on the ground) with the title going to Beaufort of Kerry. We retained our Connacht junior title the following year and in 2005 won the Connacht intermediate club title, but failed to get past Abbeydorney of Kerry in the quarter-final (the eventual winners).

At home in Leitrim down through the years, we – Aughawillan Ladies – are a force to be reckoned with, and certainly have reaped the rewards of commitment, effort and hard work in good measure, contesting either League or Championship finals in nearly every year (in all but five years) since start-up in 1979. Indeed, sometimes contesting both and certainly winning our share of titles in the process – in my time of playing fifteen senior championships and eighteen senior league titles.

In 1981 I played my first All-Ireland in Mosney as captain of the Ballinamore area Community Games under-14 team, with my mother, Mary Quinn, and Pádraig Griffin as our mentors. The highlights were introducing the team and my mother to President Hillery and more especially the great reception for us at home when we returned with silver medals.

I played my first senior game for Leitrim Ladies in the Connacht Invitations League in 1982, at fourteen, in what was for me a very memorable game. I got player of the match and booked! The referee sympathised while my sister berated me for threatening to retaliate. It was twenty years later before I incurred a referee's wrath again.

Being the baby on the county team in the 1980s allowed me to just enjoy playing, without any of the pressures or responsibilities that other players had. In Leitrim the players were the backbone of the County Board. I still smile when I think of the trips to matches in Patsy Wrynne's bus with Marie McGovern blasting out 'The Boxer' and herself and Geraldine Wrynne (Creamer) rocking the Renault with 'Come on Eileen' after training in Drumshanbo.

We won five senior Connacht titles in a row from 1981 to 1985. I was fortunate to play with committed footballers who enjoyed their game while actively furthering football in their own clubs and county – not least my sisters Deirdre and Mary, who are still involved at club to national level.

A major disappointment happened in 1983 when we beat Kerry Ladies (reigning All-Ireland champions – their second of nine in a row) in the All-Ireland senior National League final. However, due to a referee's error – awarding a point scored by us to Kerry – he recorded the final result as a draw. While all and sundry acknowledged our win, a replay was set and we lost by three points.

Although a force to be reckoned with, an All-Ireland title remained elusive, losing to Kerry in the 1984 senior Championship final and the 1985 senior League final. After that, we lost a number of players to retirement and emigration and after two years we re-graded to junior in 1988.

That year – 1988 – saw us playing in Croke Park – a dream come true to play on the hallowed ground. The young guns were now the likes of Anne Marie Cox and her cousin Nicky. Anne Marie and I were again living the dream when playing in Croke Park on All-Ireland final day eighteen years later, while Helen McLoughlin was there as a selector instead of her centre-half-back position.

The memories and emotions were very different each time and I can remember in 1988 the scenes of joy; Leitrim people streaming onto the pitch and taking over Croke Park (not allowed today), and me being found by my brother Jerome in the crowd.

In 2006 there was the agony of losing, but nobody, even us, begrudged Sligo their title at the third time of asking. Although we were disappointed in the manner of our loss, Sligo certainly made up for losing the Connacht title to us that summer.

However, losing in 2006 set us up for what was, for me personally, a magical opportunity – the chance to win the Mary Quinn Cup and bring it home to Leitrim in its inaugural year. Had we won in 2006 as seniors, we could not have played in the intermediate championship.

Coming home to Leitrim with an All-Ireland cup is a very special feeling and the welcome and pride shared with you by friends and neighbours, one and all, is something you feel inside, but find hard to put into words. It is something to enjoy, remember and savour. It's indescribable – from bonfires in 1988 to walking across the county line into Leitrim as a team in 2007, the receptions held on cold rainy evenings in towns around the county, rapturous despite waiting in the cold, to visiting all the schools in the county, and the many children out to cheer – the future Leitrim players!

Maeve Quinn with her children, Eoghan and Edel, making her march of triumph.

I have been lucky to have the support of my husband, Gerry Shanley, my children, Edel and Eoghan, and to have had parents who never missed a game we played and also the support of all my sisters and brothers, especially Deirdre, who was instrumental in starting football in Aughawillan and Leitrim and remains an inspiration to me, and Mary, county chairperson in 1988 and Connacht president in 2007, who is always there for you, ready to help and advise.

My abiding memory is just the sheer enjoyment and joy of training, taking part and playing. I look forward to continuing to play club with the blue and gold of Aughawillan for many years, while cheering on the new Leitrim Ladies on their next trip to Croke Park.

Maeve Quinn, one of a family of three boys and six girls, oozes enthusiasm as she talks passionately about sport. It's an innate quality. Her mother Mary (née O'Hanlon), a Cork woman, 'played camogie and was a sports fan and a people fan'. Her father Frank 'played briefly for Leitrim' while her uncle Paddy 'played for many years'.

Mary and Frank went to every game Maeve played since her child-hood years. Family pride, parish loyalty and community spirit were engrained in them. Their presence at games fostered and nurtured Maeve's love of sport. Her mother was only sixty-four when she died in 1990, but even though she was not well at all the year she died, she still attended the matches.

Maeve played most games and was sufficiently talented to gain two Irish Ladies Soccer 'B' caps. All her siblings have been in-volved in various ways in GAA activities, most notably Jerome, who played for many years with Leitrim; Dónal, who also played with Leitrim; Deirdre, who won All-Star awards in 1981 and 1983; and Mary, also a dual All-Star winner, 1988 and 1989.

Maeve's sporting career is embellished with trophies and honours of all kinds, including: three All-Stars, 1984, 1985 and 1994; numer-ous player of the match awards at various levels; inter-provincial medals with Connacht in 1997 and 2000; four Connacht senior championships and three junior titles; Connacht intermediate title, 2005; Connacht junior club titles, 1997 and 1998; fifteen senior club county titles; eighteen senior county league titles; Leitrim Ladies player of the year 1985, 1988, 1999 and 2000; RTÉ analyst 1998 and 1999; various positions on Leitrim Ladies County Board.

Little wonder Maeve has won so much. She was only twelve when she played senior football for her club. At thirteen she was training with the Leitrim senior team and a year later was chosen to play at senior level for her county.

In a career that, so far, spans a quarter of a century – and it is not over by any means – Maeve has seen many wonderful exponents of the game. Special among them for work rate, dedication and sportsmanship were Mary Jo Curran (Kerry), Jenny Grennan (Monaghan), Juliet Murphy (Cork) and Cristina Heffernan (Mayo).

When I contacted Maeve she was training the local under-12 players – all part of a busy weekly schedule that also includes training sessions with the local club team.

Maeve first tasted All-Ireland success in 1988 when Leitrim captured the junior title with a fine win over London, 2-8 to 0-5. Her most memorable day, however, in the Leitrim jersey was Sunday 23 September 2007 when the county won the intermediate All-Ireland title in the inaugural year of the competition, beating a gallant Wexford team by 0-17 to 1-10. Maeve was in her fortieth year, playing brilliant football and making a mockery of Father Time.

The Leitrim team lined out as:

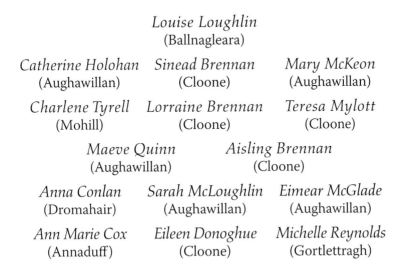

Louise Loughlin
(Ballnagleara)

Catherine Holohan   *Sinead Brennan*   *Mary McKeon*
(Aughawillan)   (Cloone)   (Aughawillan)

Charlene Tyrell   *Lorraine Brennan*   *Teresa Mylott*
(Mohill)   (Cloone)   (Cloone)

Maeve Quinn   *Aisling Brennan*
(Aughawillan)   (Cloone)

Anna Conlan   *Sarah McLoughlin*   *Eimear McGlade*
(Dromahair)   (Aughawillan)   (Aughawillan)

Ann Marie Cox   *Eileen Donoghue*   *Michelle Reynolds*
(Annaduff)   (Cloone)   (Gortlettragh)

Sub: Sinead Quinn for Lorraine Brennan

Leitrim celebrate winning 2006 Ladies Connacht Junior title.
(l-r): Sarah McLoughlin, Anne-Marie Cox, Mary McKeon, Eimear McGlade.

The trophy for the occasion was the Mary Quinn Cup – named after Maeve's mother. So it was a very special moment for Maeve when team captain Sinéad Brennan beckoned to her to come and share in the presentation ceremony. Special too was the fact that Mary Quinn's daughter (Maeve) and granddaughter (Eimear McGlade) played on the victorious team. Eimear's sisters Niamh and Gráinne play with Cavan – three daughters of Maeve's sister Eileen.

For full-forward Eileen Donoghue victory was the stuff of fairy tales. In 2006, retired and in her mid-thirties, she watched the team in action and was convinced she had something to offer: 'I am going back,' she said 'and we are going to win next year.' Sinéad, Lorraine and Aisling Brennan from Cloone club are sisters.

Sarah McLoughlin, with five points to her credit, won the player of the match award with a superb display at centre-half-forward. She just shaded it from Maeve and Ann Marie Cox, both of whom had played on the victorious junior team of 1988. Ann Marie was in inspired form, sending over frees with classical precision – seven such, and one from play.

Sinéad Quinn, who replaced the injured Lorraine Brennan just before half time, is a first cousin once removed of Maeve's.

The only 'outsider' on the team was Dublin-born Ann Conlan from Dromahair.

In the closing stages of the game Mary McKeon, staunch defender, sallied upfield from her corner-back position to score a precious point. Overall, however, it was a wonderful team effort, from goalkeeper Louise Loughlin to left-corner-forward Michelle Reynolds.

And so to the homecoming and celebrations. In the world of Gaelic games, where success is concerned, Leitrim doesn't figure prominently. Apart from victory over near neighbours Sligo in the final of the Men's senior 'B' football competition in 1990, Leitrim has no All-Ireland title of any description to its name, be it football or hurling. Indeed, it so happens that Leitrim is one of only seven counties that so far has not contested a senior All-Ireland final.

So when the lady footballers of Leitrim won the intermediate title in 2007 there was cause for great rejoicing. A county's pride was stirred. At the county bounds at Rooskey the players alighted from the bus, formed a line and triumphantly walked across it. At Mohill they sang 'Lovely Leitrim' and they finished that night in Cloone.

At one of the celebrations, an elderly man – an old timer – shook the hand of one of the players. He didn't know who she was, but simply said: 'It's an honour to shake the hand of anyone who has played in Croke Park.'

Maeve told me that her ancestors came from County Tyrone. They fled the province of Ulster at the time of the plantation in 1609. It was Tyrone's loss and Leitrim's gain.

And I haven't forgotten a quiet revolution that is taking place under our eyes. Camogie has come of age. Now it is played with teams of fifteen and on a full pitch. And Ladies' Football is rapidly becoming a salient part of our culture – the best is yet to be.

Con Houlihan

Maeve Quinn with her children, Eoghan (left) and Edel.

Picture credits

P. 11 courtesy Mary Ryan

P. 15 *A Centenary Year Publication* (The Rockies)

P. 16 courtesy of the late Jer Doheny (son)

Pp. 17, 19 (both photos), 30 (both photos) courtesy of the late Liam Lahiff, Wexford

P. 35 (top) courtesy of Marie Rochford

P. 56 from *Princes of Pigskin*, courtesy of Seamus O'Reilly

P. 58 from *Princes of Pigskin*, courtesy of *The Kerryman*

P. 67 courtesy of Eithne Neville

P. 69 courtesy of the Doyle family

Pp. 86, 179 (bottom) 180, 184, 185 and 188 courtesy Ibar Carty – P. A. Crane Collection

P. 87 courtesy of Nick Furlong

P. 97 courtesy of Michael Ahern

P. 115 courtesy of Frances Dillane

P. 122 courtesy of Dan Hogan

P. 134 (bottom left and right) courtesy of May O'Connell

P. 138 (right) courtesy of Fr Gerry Courell

P. 144 courtesy of Willie John Ring

P. 152 courtesy of the Stokes family

P. 179 (top) courtesy of Agnes Codd

P. 198 courtesy of Frankie Walsh

Pp. 203 and 204 courtesy of Tom Walsh

P. 221 courtesy of Ned Rea

P. 226 (both photos) courtesy of Denis Coughlan

P. 236 courtesy of Paddy Cullen

P. 252 courtesy of the *Irish Press*

P. 267 courtesy of Seán McMahon

P. 271 courtesy of SPORTSFILE

Pp. 296 and 303 courtesy of Brendan Moran/SPORTSFILE

P. 307 courtesy of Matt Brown/SPORTSFILE

Pp. 315 and 320 courtesy of the Leacy family

Pp. 329, 332 and 334 courtesy of James Molloy, Leitrim

All other photographs are from the author's own collection.

Index

In this index, names of places are followed by a comma and the county, and names of clubs are followed by the county in brackets. For example, 'Ardee, Co Louth' refers to the town, while 'Ardee (Louth)' refers to the club. Page numbers in italics refer to pages with photographs.